MAPS OF INDIAN RESERVES AND SETTLEMENTS
IN THE
NATIONAL MAP COLLECTION

CARTES DES RÉSERVES ET AGGLOMÉRATIONS INDIENNES
DE LA
COLLECTION NATIONALE DE CARTES ET PLANS

VOLUME II : ALBERTA
SASKATCHEWAN
MANITOBA
YUKON TERRITORY/
TERRITOIRE DU YUKON
NORTHWEST TERRITORIES/
TERRITOIRES DU NORD-OUEST

Compiled by: Linda Camponi   National Map Collection
Compilé par :   Collection nationale de cartes et plans

Assisted by: Diane Tardif-Côté   National Map Collection
Assistée de :   Collection nationale de cartes et plans

               Guy Poulin   Federal Archives Division
                                    Division des archives fédérales

NATIONAL MAP COLLECTION
COLLECTION NATIONALE DE CARTES ET PLANS

OTTAWA
1981

Public Archives   Archives publiques
Canada   Canada

Cover/Couverture: **Canada 1891**

Canadian Cataloguing in Publication Data

National Map Collection (Canada).

Maps of Indian reserves and settlements in the National Map Collection = Cartes des réserves et agglomérations indiennes de la Collection nationale de cartes et plans

Text in English and French. — Includes bibliographies.

Contents: v. 2. Alberta, Saskatchewan, Manitoba, Yukon Territory = Territoire du Yukon, Northwest Territories = Territoires du Nord-Ouest.

DSS Cat. no. SA41-1/5-2. — ISBN 0-662-51523-4 (v. 2). 1. National Map Collection—(Canada). 2. Indians of North America—Canada—Reservations—Maps—Bibliography— Catalogs. I. Camponi, Linda. II. Tardif-Côté, Diane. III. Poulin, Guy, 1949-. IV. Title. V. Title: Cartes des réserves et agglomérations indiennes de la Collection nationale de cartes et plans.

Z1209.C2N3 1980   016.912′71   C81-70102-2E

Données de catalogage avant publication (Canada)

Collection nationale de cartes et plans (Canada).

Maps of Indian reserves and settlements in the National Map Collection = Cartes des réserves et agglomérations indiennes de la Collection nationale de cartes et plans

Texte en anglais et en français.

Comprend des bibliographies.

Sommaire: v. 2. Alberta, Saskatchewan, Manitoba, Yukon Territory = Territoire du Yukon, Northwest Territories = Territoires du Nord-Ouest.

Cat. MAS n° SA41-1/5-2. — ISBN 0-662-51523-4 (v. 2). 1. Collection nationale de cartes et plans (Canada). 2. Indiens—Amérique du Nord—Canada—Réserves—Cartes—Bibliographie—Catalogues. I. Camponi, Linda. II. Tardif-Côté, Diane. III. Poulin, Guy, 1949-. IV. Titre. V. Titre: Cartes des réserves et agglomérations indiennes de la Collection nationale de cartes et plans.

Z1209.C2N3 1980   016.912′71   C81-70102-2F

Canada

Cat. No./N° de cat.: SA41-1/5-2

ISBN : 0-662-51523-4

TABLE OF CONTENTS

TABLE DES MATIÈRES

PREFACE

Since the time of initial contact between the aboriginal population and European explorers, relations between Canada's native people and the Government have been an important factor in the country's history. Today approximately 300,000 Canadian citizens are Indians registered according to the definitions of the Indian Act; many more who do not enjoy this status are of Indian descent. Representatives of these groups and other scholars concerned with this aspect of Canada's culture have initiated a growing number of research projects in the last few years.

Most registered Indians are members of some 574 separate communities or bands. Close to 2,300 reserves have been set aside for these bands; of this number, more than 300 (comprising over 3 million acres) are within the Prairie Provinces. In addition, there are over sixty officially designated Indian settlements in Alberta, the Yukon Territory and the Northwest Territories. Indian lands, including territories formerly designated for Indian use and reserves which are still in existence, are the subjects of much inquiry. While textual records are consulted frequently, other forms of documentation are sometimes overlooked. Maps and plans which form part of the archival record are often a rich source of historical information and studied in conjunction with textual material can provide a more complete picture of this aspect of Canada's past. Indeed, written documents are often unintelligible without the sketches or plans which originally accompanied them.

In 1977, at the Western Studies Conference in Calgary, Alberta, a listing of maps relating to Indian Reserves in Manitoba, Saskatchewan and Alberta was distributed by the Public Archives of Canada. Response to that listing was enthusiastic, and therefore plans to prepare a series of more complete cartobibliographies for that region and for the rest of Canada are being implemented. This is the second volume in the series. Volume I lists maps relating to the Province of British Columbia.

This catalogue lists significant cartographic documents within the holdings of the National Map Collection relating to Indian affairs in Alberta, Saskatchewan, Manitoba, the Yukon Territory and the Northwest Territories. These include maps which can be used in studies of particular reserves, as well as a selection of more general material relating to Indian matters in Canada.

The majority of the items listed form part of the records of the Central Registry System of the Indian Affairs Branch. These maps, many of which had been folded to fit into the files, require special storage conditions if their long-term preservation is to be ensured, and therefore they have been separated from the textual material they accompanied. The files themselves remain in the custody of the Federal Archives Division, Public Archives of Canada (RG 10, Black Series). A finding aid which allows access to the maps and plans according to volume and file numbers is available from the National Map Collection (RG 10M, 78903/45).

Other material listed includes Indian Lands Sales maps from the Lands and Membership Branch of the Department of Indian Affairs and Northern Development (RG 10M, 76703/9); Indian Affairs Survey Records plans (catalogued individually); maps from the Indian Claims Commission (RG 33M/115, 78903/43); and maps from other federal government departments and agencies. Finding aids for these groups exist as well, and are available to researchers in the National Map Collection. In addition, relevant material from other levels of government and from private sources has been included in this listing.

Stringent criteria have been applied in the selection of items such as general reference maps on which Indian reserves are shown. Township Plans, Sectional Maps, National Topographic System maps and provincial series maps are valuable sources. Due to the extent of these series, however, listing of individual map sheets was not possible.[1] In cases where a printed series map was used as a base on which pertinent information was added by hand, the map is included in this catalogue. These manuscript features make such items unique historical records.

Maps relating specifically to the Riel Rebellions have not been included, since this subject has been covered in depth elsewhere.[2]

Architectural material relating to Indian affairs, although a part of the National Map Collection's holdings, has not been listed in this publication.

The authors of this catalogue are indebted to their colleagues in the Public Archives of Canada for their assistance. Particular thanks are extended to William Oppen, formerly of the National Map Collection, and Jean-Pierre Lukowycz of the Federal Archives Division, for initiating this project; to Betty Kidd, Director, National Map Collection, for her support; to Dorothy Ahlgren, Chief, Government Cartographical and Architectural Records Section, for her encouragement and valuable assistance; and especially to Carmen Paul for her many hours of typing.

Users of this listing who wish to communicate comments or corrections, or acquire copies of material listed, are invited to contact the Government Cartographical and Architectural Records Section, National Map Collection, Public Archives of Canada, 395 Wellington Street, Ottawa, Canada K1A 0N3.

---

[1] Researchers are referred to unpublished finding aids in the National Map Collection and the publication *Index to Township Plans of the Canadian West/ Index de plans des cantons de l'Ouest canadien* (Ottawa: Public Archives of Canada, National Map Collection, 1974).

[2] See *The Riel Rebellions: A Cartographic History/Le récit cartographique des affaires Riel*, by William A. Oppen (University of Toronto Press in association with the Public Archives of Canada and the Canadian Government Printing Centre, 1979).

INTRODUCTION

Because the land is such an important factor in native life, its disposition has played an important role in relations between the Indian population and the Canadian government. The methods of obtaining lands desired for settlement have varied in different regions of the country according to the policies of the governing bodies of the time. The practice of the French colonial government was to set aside reserves without making treaties for the release of other lands. Britain, however, recognized Indian interest in the land and tried to obtain formal surrenders of territories wanted for development. Under British law, aboriginal title could be extinguished only by formal agreement, and only to the Crown. The Dominion government followed this course in its own dealings with native groups.

The signing of treaties was considered by the Government to be the ideal method of settling land questions with the native population. Although the Government attempted to be consistent in its dealings with Indians, it did not succeed in obtaining formal surrenders in all parts of the country. Even today approximately half of Canada's registered or "status" Indians are not governed by treaty and only about half of the land mass of the country has been formally ceded by the native people.

The first "treaty" in the west was concluded between the Hudson's Bay Company and the Indians of the Rupert's River area, where the Company established its first trading post in 1668. Rupert's Land, originally defined as the vast area comprising the lands drained by rivers flowing into Hudson's Bay, was granted to the Company in 1670. In 1688, a Royal Commission was given by King James II, authorizing the Company's representatives to make treaties on behalf of the Crown with the aboriginal population. Since the primary concern of the fur traders was not settlement,however, few of the agreements signed between the Company and the Indians involved land cession. For many years the Europeans engaged in trade with natives in western Canada without seriously disrupting their way of life.

By the mid-eighteenth century, European settlement in British North America was expanding westward with the result that conflicts were arising between settlers and the Indian population. To avoid uncontrolled encroachment of Indian territories, which could lead to hostility, provisions were included in the Royal Proclamation of 1763 (the document establishing the government of the territories recently acquired from France) to establish a tract of land "reserved" for the Indians. This territory consisted of land not already ceded or sold to the British Crown and not part of the Hudson's Bay Company territory or existing British colonies. The Proclamation forbade private purchases of Indian lands and the granting of patents for any lands in the territory not yet ceded or sold to the Crown.

In 1811, the Earl of Selkirk purchased the rights of the Hudson's Bay Company to a large tract of land in the Red River District. In 1817, Lord Selkirk negotiated a treaty with the Chippewa and Cree Indians for surrender of this land.

At the same time, colonial authorities in the east were concluding treaties with the native population. Early treaties were essentially land surrenders in return for cash grants or goods. Annuities became a standard part of most treaty terms after 1818. The allotment of reserve lands and provisions for hunting and fishing rights were not always stipulated in these early agreements.

The Robinson-Superior and Robinson-Huron Treaties, signed in 1850 in what is now northern Ontario, are considered to be the forerunners of those later negotiated in Western Canada. These were the first treaties to include what were to become standard provisions: once-for-all expenditures, annuities, reserve lands and hunting and fishing rights for the Indians.

The British North America Act of 1867 designated "Indians, and Lands reserved for the Indians" as a federal matter. Therefore, as each territory was added to the Dominion, jurisdiction of its Indian affairs fell to the federal government.

In 1869, the Hudson's Bay Company ceded its territorial rights to the Crown in return for a cash settlement and certain other benefits. Rupert's Land and the "North Western Territory" were combined to form the North-West Territories of Canada. Some of the inhabitants of the Red River Settlement, including Indians, Métis and a few whites, set up their own "provisional government" in opposition to the new territorial administration. This group, led by Louis Riel, attempted to prevent the new governor of the Territories, William McDougall, from assuming his duties. The uprising was suppressed without bloodshed. Partly because of these disturbances, the Government was prompted to create a separate province, Manitoba, of the Red River Settlement in 1870.

By 1871, with the pressures of westward expansion of European development and the diminishing supply of game, the survival of the Plains Indians was threatened and some of them saw the dominance of the white settlers over their territory as inevitable. Many were eager to enter into peace agreements with the newcomers, hoping in this way to secure the right to continue unmolested in their own way of life. Almost all of Western Canada is now included in the series of treaties numbered 1 through 11, signed between 1871 and 1921. The exceptions are most of British Columbia and the Yukon Territory, and the areas of the present Northwest Territories occupied by the Inuit. These treaties were patterned on earlier agreements signed in Ontario and on treaties concluded in the United States after the Revolution.

The first such agreement was signed on August 3, 1871 at Stone Fort or Lower Fort Garry in southern Manitoba, with the Chippewas and Swampy Crees. Six more treaties, similar to the first, were concluded in the 1870s in the present-day Prairie Provinces. Terms of these included the relinquishment of territorial rights from Lake Superior to the Rocky Mountains, permission to hunt and fish on Crown lands, gifts and annuities, agricultural assistance and educational facilities. Reserve lands were allocated on the basis of 160 acres per family of five for Treaties 1, 2 and 5, and 640 acres per family of five for Treaties 3, 4, 6 and 7. These lands were not to be sold or alienated without the consent of the Indians concerned.

Reserves were also granted in the 1870s to a number of Sioux Indians who came north from the United States to avoid conflicts with the American government.

In 1885, dissatisfaction on the part of the Métis population and some Indians, led by Louis Riel, resulted in the North-West Rebellion. Indians not yet settled on reserves and those of the Duck Lake District of Saskatchewan took part in the uprising, which was put down by force. The government later offered land scrip (certificates which could be exchanged for land) to those Indians and half-breeds not eligible or not wishing to be included under treaty.

In 1899, Treaty 8 was signed with the Indians of what is now northern Alberta and Saskatchewan. In 1900, the treaty area was expanded to include parts of British Columbia and the present-day Northwest Territories. In 1905, Treaty 9 was made with Indians in northern Ontario, and in 1906, Indians of northern Saskatchewan signed Treaty 10. According to the terms of these three agreements, reserves of up to 640 acres per family of five were to be allotted. Other terms were similar to those of previous treaties.

Treaty 5 was extended to cover northern Manitoba in 1908, and in 1921, when oil was discovered at Norman Wells, Treaty 11 was signed with Indians of the western Northwest Territories. Again reserves of 640 acres per family of five were stipulated; however, no reserves have yet been established under Treaties 8 and 11 in the Northwest Territories.

Responsibility for Indian affairs has been accorded varying degrees of importance by the Canadian government since 1867, and administrative changes reflect this shift of emphasis. At Confederation, Indian matters were placed under the control of the Department of Secretary of State for the Provinces, the Secretary of State being named the Superintendent General of Indian Affairs. In 1873, the Indians and Indian Lands Branch was created within the new Department of the Interior. At that time two superintendencies were created to administer the western treaty areas: the Manitoba Superintendency (including areas governed by Treaties 1, 2, 3 and 4) and the North-West Territories Superintendency (including areas under Treaties 5, 6 and 7). Under each superintendent were Indian agents who were responsible for Indian bands in their agencies.

The first Indian Act (39 Vic. c. 18), which established a registry of natives eligible for certain privileges, while at the same time delineating the boundaries of activities allowed to these individuals, was passed in 1876. Eskimos (Inuit) and those taking half-breed scrip were specifically excluded from the provisions of this legislation. In 1880, the Department of Indian Affairs was created to represent the Dominion government in all native matters.

By 1898, several administrative divisions called inspectorates had been established in the West, including three in Manitoba and three in the Northwest Territories. In 1911 the Fort Smith Indian Agency was set up for the administration of the Treaty 8 area, and the Fort Simpson Agency for non-treaty Indians of the Mackenzie Basin and other areas. In 1926 another agency was established at Fort Resolution.

The Department of Indian Affairs continued to operate until 1936, when Indian Affairs became a branch of the Department of Mines and Resources. In 1949 the Branch was transferred to the Department of Citizenship and Immigration. A revised Indian Act (15 Geo. VI c. 29) came into effect in 1951. In 1965 the Indian Affairs Branch was moved to the Department of Northern Affairs and National Resources. Since 1966 Indian and Inuit affairs have been among the responsibilities of the Department of Indian Affairs and Northern Development, also referred to as the Department of Indian and Northern Affairs. Today the Department operates through regional and district offices.

Historical evidence of relations between native groups and the Government of Canada is found in the records of every administrative body assigned the responsibility for native affairs. A great many cartographical items have been created by these departments and others in the course of their dealings with native people.

These range from printed maps and atlases produced for public distribution to sketches hastily made to accompany letters from individuals to Indian agents. Rough drafts, official surveys and maps made for Royal Commissions are all part of the federal archival record, and all such documents have been included in this listing.

It must be stressed that this catalogue is not definitive. Provincial archives and other institutions hold material valuable for research. Many archival maps relating to Indian affairs remain with other records of federal government departments, either in the departments' current records systems, or with material held by the Federal Archives Division of the Public Archives of Canada. The transfer of cartographical items of historical value to the National Map Collection will take place over the years, and it is hoped that this listing can be revised periodically to include these new acquisitions.

We trust that this volume will be useful to scholars of native history and to native people seeking a more complete understanding of their heritage.

BIBLIOGRAPHY

Canada, Department of Citizenship and Immigration, Indian Affairs Branch. *Indians of the Prairie Provinces (An Historical Review)*. Ottawa : n.p., 1960.

Canada, Department of Indian Affairs and Northern Development. *The Canadian Indian: A Brief Outline/Les Indiens du Canada: un bref exposé*. Ottawa: Information Canada, 1973.

Canada, Department of Indian Affairs and Northern Development. *The Canadian Indian: Yukon and Northwest Territories/Les Indiens du Canada: Yukon et Territoires du Nord-Ouest*. Ottawa: Information Canada, 1973.

Canada, Department of Indian Affairs and Northern Development. *Schedule of Indian Reserves and Settlements*. Ottawa: Information Canada, 1972.

Canada, Indian Claims Commission, Research Resource Centre. *Indian Claims in Canada: An Introductory Essay and Selected List of Library Holdings/Revendications des Indiens au Canada: un exposé préliminaire et une sélection d'ouvrages disponibles en bibliothèque*. Ottawa: Information Canada, 1975.

Canada, Public Archives of Canada, Public Records Division. *Records Relating to Indian Affairs (RG 10)/Archives ayant trait aux affaires indiennes (RG 10)*. General Inventory Series, No. 1. Ottawa: Information Canada, 1975.

Cumming, Peter A. and Mickenberg, Neil H., et al., eds. *Native Rights in Canada*. Second edition. Toronto: The Indian-Eskimo Association of Canada in association with General Publishing Co. Ltd., 1972.

FORMAT

General Organization

Current provincial and territorial boundaries have been respected in the arrangement of the entries, regardless of what province or district the reserves were in at the time of map production. Maps have been listed by reserve name whenever possible, even when several reserves are shown on one map. Where this was not possible, maps have been listed by agency name. Since agency names and boundaries have changed over the years, researchers are advised to consult entries under other agency names. Entries are arranged alphabetically, then by date.

Reserve Names and Numbers

The authority used for reserve names and numbers is the *Schedule of Indian Reserves and Settlements* (Ottawa: Department of Indian Affairs and Northern Development, 1972). For reserves which are not listed in this schedule, such as reserves which no longer exist, schedules published in departmental annual reports have been used as a guide whenever possible. For areas never officially confirmed as Indian reserves, the names which were in use when the maps were created have been used.

Map Titles

Titles have been transcribed as they appear on the maps. Additions to original titles have also been recorded. Punctuation has been changed when necessary. Information which does not appear on the maps is inserted in brackets. Usually information in brackets has been obtained from related documentation.

Dates

Entries are arranged chronologically by date of map production. If the date does not appear on the map, it has been supplied in brackets, thus: [1885]. Dates stamped on the map or dates of related documentation have been used. The date of additions to a map is recorded after this first date. When more than one addition appears, the latest has been used. If the later date appears on the map, it is listed thus: 1885 (1898). If it has been determined from other sources, it is given in brackets, thus: 1885 [1898]. In cases where the date could not be ascertained, the letters "N.D./S.D." (i.e. no date) have been used. Undated entries are placed before dated entries.

Multiple Copies

Duplicates or other versions of a map have been referred to as copies. Researchers are advised that all copies of a map should be consulted.

Cross-References

Alternate names and alternate spellings of names have been listed with a "Refer to/Consulter" reference to the name under which entries for that reserve or agency appear. For example, "**Ahtahkakoop No. 104** - Refer to/Consulter: **Atakakup No. 104**" indicates that entries for that reserve are found under the name **Atakakup No. 104.** Often, several reserves or agencies are shown on one map. In these cases, the complete title has been listed under one reserve or agency name. Under the names of other reserves or agencies shown, "See/Voir" references are given for the appropriate date. For example, "**Keeseekoose No. 66A** - 1910 - See/Voir: **Keeseekoose No. 66**" indicates that a 1910 map listed under **Keeseekoose No. 66** also shows Keeseekoose Reserve No. 66A.

Illustrations

Those entries marked with an asterisk (*) are seen illustrated in this volume.

PRÉFACE

Depuis l'époque où les premiers contacts se sont établis entre la population aborigène et les explorateurs européens, les relations entre les autochtones du Canada et les gouvernements ont joué un rôle important dans l'histoire du pays. Aujourd'hui, environ 300 000 citoyens canadiens sont des Indiens inscrits conformément aux définitions de la Loi sur les Indiens; des citoyens beaucoup plus nombreux, qui ne jouissent pas de ce statut, sont d'ascendance indienne. Depuis quelques années, des représentants de ces groupes et des spécialistes de cet aspect de la culture canadienne ont mis sur pied un nombre grandissant de projets de recherche.

La plupart des Indiens inscrits sont membres de quelque 574 communautés séparées ou bandes. Près de 2 300 réserves, dont 300 (plus de 3 millions d'acres) dans les Prairies, ont été mises à la disposition de ces bandes. D'autre part, il y a plus de soixante agglomérations indiennes, officiellement désignées, en Alberta, dans le Territoire du Yukon et dans les Territoires du Nord-Ouest. Les terres indiennes, y compris les territoires autrefois réservés à l'usage des Indiens et les réserves encore existantes, font l'objet d'un grand nombre de demandes d'information. On consulte fréquemment les textes, mais parfois on néglige d'autres formes de documentation. Les cartes et les plans conservés dans des archives constituent souvent des sources abondantes d'information historique et, si on les étudie conjointement avec les textes, ils peuvent offrir une image plus complète de cet aspect du passé au Canada. En fait, les documents écrits sont souvent inintelligibles si on ne consulte pas en plus les dessins ou les plans qui les accompagnaient à l'origine.

En 1977, à la *Western Studies Conference*, à Calgary, en Alberta, les Archives publiques du Canada ont distribué une liste de cartes sur les réserves indiennes du Manitoba, de la Saskatchewan et de l'Alberta. Cette liste a connu un tel succès que, par la suite, on a décidé de préparer des cartobibliographies plus complètes pour cette région et pour le reste du Canada. Voici le second volume de cette série. Le premier volume présentait la liste des cartes de la Colombie-Britannique.

Ce catalogue donne la liste des cartes importantes se rapportant aux affaires indiennes de l'Alberta, de la Saskatchewan, du Manitoba, du Territoire du Yukon et des Territoires du Nord-Ouest, conservées par la Collection nationale de cartes et plans. On y trouve des cartes destinées à l'étude de certaines réserves en particulier, ainsi qu'un choix de documents d'intérêt plus général touchant les affaires indiennes du Canada.

La majorité des documents énumérés font partie des Archives centrales de la Direction des affaires indiennes. Ces cartes, dont un grand nombre avaient dû être pliées pour être rangées dans les classeurs, exigent des conditions particulières d'entreposage si l'on veut assurer leur conservation à long terme et, par conséquent, elles ont été séparées des documents qui les accompagnaient. Les dossiers eux-mêmes restent confiés aux soins de la Division des archives fédérales, Archives publiques du Canada (RG 10, série noire). À la Collection nationale de cartes et plans, on peut consulter un instrument de recherche qui permet de repérer les cartes et les plans d'après le numéro du volume et le numéro du dossier (RG 10M, 78903/45).

Parmi les autres documents énumérés, citons les cartes relatives aux ventes de terrains indiens qui proviennent de la Direction de la gestion foncière et de l'effectif des bandes du ministère des Affaires indiennes et du Nord canadien (RG 10M, 76703/9); les plans *Indian Affairs Survey Records* (catalogués individuellement); les cartes de la Commission d'étude des revendications des Indiens (RG 33M/115, 78903/43); et les cartes provenant d'autres ministères et agences du gouvernement fédéral. Des instruments de recherche existent également pour ces groupes et sont mis à la disposition des chercheurs à la Collection nationale de cartes et plans. De plus, dans cette liste, on a inclus des documents pertinents provenant d'autres niveaux de gouvernement et de sources privées.

Des critères rigoureux nous ont guidés pour établir une sélection des documents comme cela s'est fait dans le cas des cartes générales sur lesquelles figurent les réserves indiennes. Les plans de cantons, les cartes *Sectional*, les cartes du Système national de référence cartographique et les cartes des séries provinciales constituent des ressources précieuses. Cependant, à cause de l'ampleur de ces séries, on n'a pu faire une liste de toutes les cartes qui les composent.[1] Toutefois, lorsqu'une carte de série a été utilisée comme un document de travail auquel on a ajouté à la main des renseignements utiles, ce document apparaît dans le catalogue. Ces indications manuscrites font de ces cartes des documents historiques uniques en leur genre.

Les cartes se rapportant spécifiquement aux rébellions de Louis Riel ne sont également pas incluses, ce sujet ayant déjà été traité en profondeur.[2] Les documents architecturaux relatifs aux affaires indiennes, bien que faisant partie des fonds de la Collection nationale de cartes et plans, ne figurent pas dans cette publication.

Les auteurs de ce catalogue remercient ici leurs collègues des Archives publiques du Canada qui les ont aidés dans leur tâche. Ils remercient spécialement William Oppen, autrefois de la Collection nationale de cartes et plans, et Jean-Pierre Lukowycz, de la Division des archives fédérales, qui sont à l'origine de ce projet; Betty Kidd, directrice de la Collection nationale de cartes et plans, pour son aide; Dorothy Ahlgren, chef de la Section des documents cartographiques et architecturaux du gouvernement, pour ses encouragements et sa précieuse collaboration; et en particulier, ils adressent leurs remerciements à Carmen Paul pour les nombreuses heures de dactylographie qu'elle a fournies.

Nous invitons les utilisateurs de cette liste qui souhaitent faire part de leurs commentaires, suggérer des corrections ou encore qui désirent acquérir des copies des documents cités, à communiquer avec la Section des documents cartographiques et architecturaux du gouvernement, Collection nationale de cartes et plans, Archives publiques du Canada, 395, rue Wellington, Ottawa, Canada K1A 0N3.

---

(1) Les chercheurs peuvent se référer aux instruments de recherche non publiés de la Collection nationale de cartes et plans, et à la publication *Index de plans des cantons de l'Ouest canadien/Index to Township Plans of the Canadian West* (Collection nationale de cartes et plans, Archives publiques du Canada, Ottawa, 1974).

(2) Voir: *Le récit cartographique des affaires Riel/The Riel Rebellions: A Cartographic History*, de William A. Oppen (University of Toronto Press avec la collaboration des Archives publiques du Canada et du Centre d'édition du gouvernement du Canada, 1979).

INTRODUCTION

Le territoire étant un élément primordial de la vie des autochtones, il n'est pas étonnant que sa répartition ait joué un rôle important dans les relations entre les populations indiennes et le gouvernement canadien. Les méthodes utilisées pour obtenir les terres convoitées par les autorités gouvernementales en vue de la colonisation ont varié selon les régions ou la politique en cours à l'époque. Ainsi le gouvernement colonial français avait pour pratique d'établir des réserves sans signer de traités pour la cession d'autres territoires. Toutefois la Grande-Bretagne reconnaissant le droit des Indiens au territoire, tenta d'obtenir des cessions officielles pour les terres destinées à être exploitées. Selon la loi britannique, les droits de propriété des autochtones ne pouvaient être abolis que par entente officielle et en faveur seulement de la Couronne. Le gouvernement du Dominion observa cette pratique dans ses transactions avec les groupes autochtones.

Le gouvernement estimait que la meilleure façon de régler les questions territoriales avec la population autochtone était de signer des traités. Cependant, bien qu'il eût tenté des négociations uniformes avec les Indiens, il ne réussit jamais à obtenir des renonciations officielles dans chaque partie du pays. Encore aujourd'hui, près de la moitié des Indiens inscrits du Canada n'est pas visée par les traités et les autochtones n'ont cédé officiellement que la moitié tout au plus du territoire du pays.

Le premier traité conclu dans l'Ouest liait la Compagnie de la baie d'Hudson et les Indiens de la région de la rivière de Rupert, région où la compagnie avait établi son premier poste de traite en 1668. La terre de Rupert, qui englobait à l'origine le vaste territoire arrosé par les rivières se jetant dans la baie d'Hudson, fut octroyée à la compagnie en 1670. En 1688, cette même compagnie se vit accorder par le roi Jacques II une commission royale autorisant ses représentants à conclure des traités avec la population autochtone au nom de la Couronne. Mais comme les commerçants de fourrures ne s'intéressaient pas particulièrement à la colonisation, les ententes signées entre la compagnie et les Indiens faisaient rarement état de cessions de territoires. Pendant de nombreuses années, les Européens firent ainsi du commerce avec les autochtones de l'Ouest du Canada sans que leur mode de vie en soit véritablement modifié.

Au milieu du XVIIIᵉ siècle, la colonisation de l'Amérique du Nord britannique s'étendit vers l'Ouest engendrant des conflits entre les colons européens et les peuples indiens. Pour éviter que les Blancs n'empiètent exagérément sur les territoires des Indiens, ce qui aurait pu amener des conflagrations, on inclut certaines clauses dans la proclamation royale de 1763, (document établissant la souveraineté britannique sur les territoires récemment acquis de la France). En effet, des dispositions y prévoyaient que les terres n'ayant pas été cédées ou vendues à la Couronne britannique, de même que celles n'appartenant ni à la Compagnie de la baie d'Hudson ni aux colonies britanniques existantes, seraient réservées aux Indiens. La proclamation défendait aux particuliers l'achat de toutes terres indiennes et interdisait l'octroi de lettres patentes pour toutes terres de la région non encore cédées ou vendues à la Couronne.

En 1811, le comte de Selkirk acheta les droits de la Compagnie de la baie d'Hudson sur une large bande de terre, dans le district de la rivière Rouge, négociant par la suite en 1817, un traité de renonciation avec les Indiens Chippewas et Cris.

À la même époque, les autorités coloniales concluaient dans l'est du pays des traités avec la population autochtone. Les premières ententes consistaient essentiellement en renonciations de territoires en échange d'argent comptant ou de marchandises. Après 1818, on ajouta à la plupart des traités des dispositions sur le versement de rentes annuelles, bien que l'octroi de terres réservées et les droits de chasse et de pêche n'y étaient pas toujours stipulés.

Les traités *Robinson-Superior* et *Robinson-Huron*, signés en 1850 dans la région qui constitue maintenant le nord de l'Ontario, laissaient présager les conditions des ententes négociées plus tard dans l'Ouest. Il s'agit en effet des premiers traités à inclure des clauses qui allaient s'appliquer partout: versements forfaitaires, rentes annuelles, terres de réserve, droits de chasse et de pêche pour les Indiens.

L'Acte de l'Amérique du Nord britannique de 1867 accordait juridiction au gouvernement fédéral sur les questions relatives aux « Indiens et terres réservées aux Indiens ». L'admission de tout nouveau territoire au Dominion relevait donc du gouvernement fédéral, de même que toutes les questions relatives aux Indiens qui occupaient ces terres.

En 1869, la Compagnie de la baie d'Hudson céda ses droits territoriaux à la Couronne en échange d'un règlement monétaire et de certains autres avantages. La terre de Rupert et le « Territoire du Nord-Ouest » furent donc réunis pour former les Territoires du Nord-Ouest du Canada. Sous la conduite de Louis Riel, un groupe d'habitants de la colonie de la rivière Rouge, composé d'Indiens, de Métis et de quelques Blancs, établit alors son propre gouvernement provisoire en vue de s'opposer à la nouvelle administration territoriale et d'empêcher le nouveau gouverneur des Territoires, William McDougall, de remplir ses fonctions. Ce soulèvement fut maîtrisé sans effusion de sang, mais ce fut l'un des facteurs qui, en 1870, poussèrent le gouvernement à faire de la colonie de la rivière Rouge une province distincte appelée Manitoba.

En 1871, en raison des pressions causées par la poussée continue des Européens vers l'Ouest et la diminution des réserves de gibier, les Indiens des Prairies voyaient leur survie menacée, alors que certains considéraient comme inévitable la domination des colons blancs sur leurs territoires. Nombre d'entre eux désiraient donc conclure des ententes pacifiques avec les nouveaux venus, espérant ainsi obtenir le droit de conserver sans problèmes leur façon de vivre. Presque tout l'Ouest du Canada est maintenant visé par une série de traités numérotés de un à onze et signés entre 1871 et 1921; le Yukon et la majeure partie de la Colombie-Britannique font exception, de même que les terres occupées par les Inuit dans les Territoires du Nord-Ouest actuels. Ces traités s'inspiraient de ceux signés auparavant en Ontario et de ceux conclus aux États-Unis après l'Indépendance.

Le premier de ces traités fut signé le 3 août 1871 au fort Stone ou Petit fort Garry, entre les Chippewas et les Moskégons du sud du Manitoba. Six autres traités semblables furent conclus au cours des années 1870, sur le territoire occupé actuellement par les provinces des Prairies. Par ces traités, les Indiens abandonnaient leurs droits territoriaux depuis le lac Supérieur jusqu'aux montagnes Rocheuses, mais obtenaient en contrepartie les droits de chasse et de pêche sur les terres de la Couronne, des dons, des rentes annuelles, une aide agricole et des installations scolaires. On leur alloua également des terres de réserve à raison de 160 acres par famille de cinq personnes pour les traités 1, 2 et 5, et de 640 acres par famille de cinq personnes pour les taités 3, 4, 6 et 7. On ne vendrait ou aliénerait ces terres sans le consentement des Indiens concernés.

En plus, on octroya dans les années 1870 des réserves à un certain nombre de Sioux originaires des États-Unis, montés vers le nord pour éviter les conflits avec le gouvernement américain.

En 1885 l'insatisfaction des Métis et de certains Indiens, sous la conduite de Louis Riel, entraîna la rébellion du Nord-Ouest. Les Indiens du district de Duck Lake en Saskatchewan, et ceux qui n'étaient pas encore établis sur des réserves, prirent part à ce soulèvement qui fut maté par la force. Le gouvernement offrit plus tard des certificats de concession de terres aux Indiens et aux Métis qui ne pouvaient pas ou ne voulaient pas être inclus dans les traités.

En 1899, le traité nº 8 fut signé avec les Indiens de la région qui constitue maintenant le nord de l'Alberta et de la Saskatchewan. La zone visée par le traité fut étendue en 1900 à certaines régions de la Colombie-Britannique et aux Territoires du Nord-Ouest actuels. En 1905, les Indiens du nord de l'Ontario signèrent le traité nº 9, et en 1906, ceux du nord de la Saskatchewan, le traité nº 10. Selon les termes de ces trois ententes, les Indiens devaient disposer de réserves allant jusqu'à 640 acres par famille de cinq; les autres conditions étaient semblables à celles des traités précédents.

Le traité nº 5 fut étendu au nord du Manitoba en 1908, et le traité nº 11 fut signé avec les Indiens du secteur ouest des Territoires du Nord-Ouest en 1921, lorsqu'on découvrit du pétrole à Norman Wells. Ces traités prévoyaient eux aussi des réserves d'un maximum de 640 acres par famille de cinq, mais aucune réserve n'a encore été établie dans les Territoires du Nord-Ouest en vertu des traités nos 8 et 11.

Depuis 1867, l'importance accordée par le gouvernement canadien aux affaires indiennes a varié selon les époques et les changements administratifs reflètent ces fluctuations. Lors de la Confédération, les affaires indiennes furent placées sous l'autorité du Secrétariat d'État pour les provinces, alors que le secrétaire d'État fut nommé surintendant général pour les Affaires indiennes. En 1873, la Direction des Indiens et des terres indiennes fut créée au sein du nouveau ministère de l'Intérieur. À la même époque, deux surintendances furent établies pour l'administration des régions visées par les traités de l'Ouest : celle du Manitoba, chargée des régions auxquelles s'appliquaient les traités nos 1, 2, 3 et 4; celle du Nord-Ouest, chargée des territoires régis par les traités nos 5, 6 et 7. Chaque surintendant avait sous ses ordres des agents indiens responsables des bandes relevant de leur agence.

Le premier *Acte des Sauvages* (39 Vic., c. 18) fut adopté en 1876 afin de déterminer quels autochtones étaient admissibles à certains privilèges, tout en délimitant les activités qui leur étaient permises. Les Inuit étaient expressément exclus des dispositions de cette loi, de même que ceux qui avaient reçu des certificats de concession de terres. En 1880, le ministère des Affaires indiennes fut créé pour représenter le gouvernement du *Dominion* dans tous les domaines touchant les autochtones.

En 1898, plusieurs divisions administratives, appelées «inspectorats», avaient été créées dans l'Ouest, dont trois au Manitoba et trois dans les Territoires du Nord-Ouest. En 1911, l'agence indienne de Fort Smith fut établie pour assurer l'administration du territoire régi par le traité nº 8, et l'agence de Fort Simpson, pour s'occuper des Indiens du bassin du Mackenzie et d'autres régions qui n'étaient pas visées par des traités. En 1926, une agence fut ouverte à Fort Resolution.

Le ministère des Affaires indiennes poursuivit son activité jusqu'en 1936, date à laquelle ses responsabilités furent confiées à une direction du ministère des Mines et Ressources. En 1949, cette direction fut transférée au ministère de la Citoyenneté et de l'Immigration. Une nouvelle loi sur les Indiens (15 Geo. VI, c. 29) fut promulguée en 1951. En 1965, la Direction des affaires indiennes fut confiée au ministère du Nord canadien et des Ressources nationales. Depuis 1966, les affaires indiennes et inuit relèvent du ministère des Affaires indiennes et du Nord canadien, qui œuvre aujourd'hui par l'entremise de bureaux régionaux et de bureaux de districts.

Les dossiers de tous les organismes administratifs chargés des affaires indiennes contiennent de la documentation historique sur les relations entre les groupes autochtones et le gouvernement du Canada. Ces ministères et ces autres organismes ont notamment créé de nombreux documents cartographiques dans le cadre de leur travail avec les peuples autochtones. Ainsi, on y retrouve des cartes et des atlas imprimés produits pour la diffusion publique et des croquis dessinés à la hâte pour accompagner les lettres envoyées par des particuliers à des agents indiens. Qu'il s'agisse de brouillons sommaires, de relevés officiels, ou de cartes réalisées à l'intention de commissions royales d'enquête, tous ces documents d'archives du gouvernement fédéral sont inclus dans le présent répertoire.

Il convient de souligner cependant que ce catalogue n'est pas définitif. Les dépôts d'archives provinciaux et divers autres établissements possèdent eux aussi des documents utiles à la recherche. Par ailleurs, de nombreuses cartes d'archives portant sur les affaires indiennes sont encore conservées avec d'autres documents des ministères fédéraux. On peut les retracer dans les dossiers actifs des ministères en cause ou dans les documents conservés à la Division des Archives fédérales, aux Archives publiques du Canada. Les documents cartographiques d'intérêt historique seront transférés graduellement à la Collection nationale de cartes et plans et il faut espérer que la présente liste pourra être révisée périodiquement pour y inclure ces nouvelles acquisitions.

Ce volume devrait cependant être très utile aux chercheurs qui étudient l'histoire des premiers habitants de notre pays, ainsi qu'aux autochtones désireux de mieux comprendre le patrimoine de leur peuple.

BIBLIOGRAPHIE

Canada, Archives publiques du Canada, Division des archives fédérales. *Archives ayant trait aux affaires indiennes (RG 10)/Records Relating to Indian Affairs (RG 10)*. Collection de l'inventaire général, n° 1. Ottawa, Information Canada, 1975.

Canada, Commission d'étude des revendications des Indiens, Centre de documentation et d'aide à la recherche. *Revendications des Indiens au Canada: un exposé préliminaire et une sélection d'ouvrages disponibles en bibliothèque/Indian Claims in Canada: An Introductory Essay and Selected List of Library Holdings*. Ottawa, Information Canada, 1975.

Canada, ministère de la Citoyenneté et de l'Immigration, Direction des Affaires indiennes. *Indians of the Prairie Provinces (An Historical Review)*. Ottawa, n.p., 1960.

Canada, ministère des Affaires indiennes et du Nord canadien. *Les Indiens du Canada: un bref exposé/The Canadian Indian: A Brief Outline*. Ottawa, Information Canada, 1973.

Canada, ministère des Affaires indiennes et du Nord canadien. *Les Indiens du Canada: Yukon et Territoires du Nord-Ouest/The Canadian Indian: Yukon and Northwest Territories*. Ottawa, Information Canada, 1973.

Canada, ministère des Affaires indiennes et du Nord canadien. *Schedule of Indian Reserves and Settlements*. Ottawa, Information Canada, 1972.

Cumming, Peter A. et Mickenberg, Neil H., et al., eds. *Native Rights in Canada*. Deuxième édition. Toronto: The Indian-Eskimo Association of Canada in association with General Publishing Co. Ltd., 1972.

PRÉSENTATION

Organisation générale

Dans la rédaction des notices, on a respecté les frontières provinciales et territoriales actuelles sans tenir compte de la province ou du district où se trouvaient les réserves au moment où la carte a été dressée. Les cartes sont classées par noms de réserves chaque fois que c'est possible, même si plusieurs réserves figurent sur la même carte. Lorsque ce n'est pas possible, les cartes sont classées par noms d'agences. Comme les noms d'agences et les frontières ont changé au cours des années, on conseille aux chercheurs de consulter les notices sous d'autres noms d'agences. Les notices sont disposées par ordre alphabétique, puis chronologique.

Noms et numéros de réserves

On s'est basé sur *Schedule of Indian Reserves and Settlements* (ministère des Affaires indiennes et du Nord canadien, Ottawa, 1972) pour déterminer les noms et les numéros de réserves. Dans le cas des réserves qui ne figurent pas sur cette liste, par exemples celles qui n'existent plus, on s'est fondé chaque fois que c'était possible sur les listes publiées dans les rapports annuels du ministère. Pour les régions qui n'ont jamais été officiellement confirmées comme réserves indiennes, on a utilisé les noms en usage au moment où les cartes ont été établies.

Titres des cartes

On a transcrit les titres tels qu'ils apparaissent sur les cartes. On a aussi noté les additions aux titres originaux. On a changé la ponctuation lorsque c'était nécessaire. Les renseignements qui ne figurent pas sur les cartes sont mis entre crochets. Ces renseignements proviennent généralement de documents connexes.

Dates

Les notices sont disposées par ordre chronologique suivant la date d'établissement de la carte. Si la date ne figure pas sur la carte mais peut être déterminée à l'aide des dates tamponnées sur la carte ou des dates des documents connexes, elle est indiquée entre crochets comme ceci : [1885]. La date des additions à la carte est notée après la date initiale. Lorsqu'il y a plus d'une addition, c'est la dernière qui a été retenue. Si la dernière date apparaît sur la carte, on l'écrit ainsi : 1885 (1898). Lorsqu'elle a été déterminée au moyen d'autres sources, on l'écrit ainsi : 1885 [1898]. Au cas où la date n'a pu être déterminée avec certitude, on emploie les lettres N.D./S.D. (c'est-à-dire sans date). Les notices sans date sont placées avant les notices datées.

Exemplaires multiples

Les duplicata ou les versions successives d'une carte ont été désignés comme « copies ». Les chercheurs devraient consulter tous les exemplaires d'une carte.

Renvois

Les autres noms et les noms orthographiés d'une façon différente ont été classés avec la référence « Refer to/Consulter » ajoutée au nom sous lequel les notices pour cette réserve ou cette agence apparaissent. Par exemple, « **Ahtahkakoop n° 104** - Refer to/Consulter: **Atakakup n° 104** » indique que les notices pour cette réserve se trouvent sous le nom **Atakakup n° 104**. Souvent, plusieurs réserves ou plusieurs agences figurent sur une seule carte. En ce cas, le titre complet a été inscrit sous une seule réserve ou un seul nom d'agence. Sous les noms des autres réserves ou des autres agences qui figurent sur la carte, on donne les références « See/Voir » pour la date appropriée. Par exemple, « **Keeseekoose n° 66A**-1910-See/Voir : **Keeseekoose n° 66** » indique qu'une carte de 1910 classée sous **Keeseekoose n° 66** montre aussi la réserve Keeseekoose n° 66A.

Illustrations

Les notices explicatives dont une illustration se trouve dans le présent ouvrage ont été signalées par un astérisque[*].

CANADA — GENERAL MAPS/CANADA — CARTES GÉNÉRALES

[1775]   A map of the north west parts of America [showing locations of Indian tribes/indiquant le territoire des tribus indiennes] . . . by . . . Alexr. Henry. [Original in Library of Congress/L'original se trouve à la Bibliothèque du Congrès.]

1801   A map of America, between latitudes 40 and 70 north, and longitudes 45 and 180 west, exhibiting Mackenzie's track from Montreal to Fort Chipewyan & from thence to the North Sea in 1789 & to the West Pacific Ocean in 1793. London. Published 15 Oct., 1801 by Alexander Mackenzie. . . . [2 copies]

[1817]   Plan of the Indian territories comprehended between the 46th and 53rd degrees of north latitude, and the 90th and 101st degrees of west longitude from Greenwich. By Jos. Bouchette, Sur. Genl. &c. &c.

1857   Aboriginal map of North America, denoting the boundaries and the locations of various Indian tribes. John Arrowsmith, Litho. . . . 31st July & 11th August, 1857. [3 copies]

1857   Map of the north west part of Canada, Indian territories & Hudson's Bay. Compiled and drawn by Thos. Devine, Provincial Land Surveyor & Draftsman . . . Crown Lands Department, Toronto, March 1857. . . . [9 copies]

1872   Province of Manitoba and portions of North West Territories [showing areas of Treaties No. 1 and 2/indiquant les régions visées par les traités n°s 1 et 2]. Copy of map accompanying Treaty No. 2, executed August 1871. . . . Indian Office, Ottawa, May 1872.

1875   Map of part of the North West Territory including the Province of Manitoba, exhibiting the several tracts of country ceded by the Indian Treaties 1, 2, 3 and 4. To accompany report of the . . . Minister of the Interior dated 20th January, 1875. . . . J. Johnston, Chief Draftsman . . . . [3 copies]

[1875]   [Map of Canada showing distribution of Indian and Inuit tribes/Carte du Canada indiquant la répartition des tribus indiennes et inuit.] Photo. Lith. by the Burland-Desbarats Lith. Co.

1877   Map of part of the North West Territory, including the Province of Manitoba. Exhibiting the several tracts of country ceded by the Indian Treaties 1, 2, 3, 4, 5 and 6. To accompany report of the . . . Minister of the Interior, January 1877. Compiled and drawn by J. Johnston, Chief Draftsman. Printed & published . . . [in the/au] Domn. Lands Office . . . Ottawa, 1st March, 1877. . . . Preliminary edition.

1877   Map of part of the North West Territory, including the Province of Manitoba. Exhibiting the several tracts of country ceded by the Indian Treaties 1, 2, 3, 4, 5, 6 and 7. To accompany report of the . . . Minister of the Interior, January 1877. Compiled and drawn by J. Johnston, Chief Draftsman. Domn. Lands Office. Preliminary edition . . . .

CANADA

1877 [1966]   The Indian Treaties, N.W.Ts., 1871-1877. [C.C.J. Bond, 1966.]

1878   Map of part of the North West Territory, including the Province of Manitoba. Exhibiting the several tracts of country ceded by the Indian Treaties 1, 2, 3, 4, 5, 6 and 7. To accompany report of the . . . Minister of the Interior. Compiled and drawn by J. Johnston, Chief Draftsman. Dominion Lands Office, Ottawa, 1st March, 1878. . . . Preliminary edition.

[1880]   Telegraph lines [and Indian reserves/et les réserves indiennes] of Manitoba & North-West Territories. Public Works Canada . . . . Drawn by Gust.-Smith.

1882   Map of country extending from Lake Superior to Fort Pelly shewing Indian reservations. Department of Indian Affairs, Ottawa, 1882. Compiled and drawn by W.A. Austin, C.E., D.L.S., Indian Reserve Surveys . . . .

1883 (1899)*   Dominion of Canada. General map of part of the North-West Territories including the Province of Manitoba, shewing Dominion Land Surveys [and treaty areas/et les régions visées par les traités] . . . . Dominion Lands Office, Department of the Interior, Ottawa . . . 15th March, 1883. [Additions to 1899/Additions jusqu'en 1899.]

1884   Map of the country between Lakes Superior and Winnipeg, from latest surveys and explorations. Compiled and drawn by J. Johnston, Chief Draftsman. Published by authority of the . . . Minister of the Interior . . . Ottawa, 1st Sept., 1884. [3 copies]

1886   Public Works Canada — North West Territory — Canadian Pacific Railway — Telegraph lines, trails and Indian reserves . . . March 1886. . . . Based on Capt. Deville's map, 31st Dec., 1884, Mr. Gisborne's map, 1885, and maps of Indian Department, 1883-84, 85. Drawn by E.A. Mara. Ottawa, 1st March, 1886 . . . .

1886   Dominion of Canada. Map shewing Mounted Police stations & patrols [and Indian reserves/et les réserves indiennes] throughout the North-West Territories, during the year 1886. . . . Compiled, drawn and published under the superintendence of J. Johnston, Chief Draftsman, Department of the Interior. . . . [2 copies]

1888 [1973]   Dominion of Canada. Map shewing Mounted Police stations & patrols throughout the North-West Territories, during the year 1888. Also boundaries of Indian treaties and location of Indian reserves . . . . Reproduced, from original (1888), by the Surveys and Mapping Branch, Department of Energy, Mines and Resources. . . . [2 copies]

1889   Dominion of Canada. Map shewing Mounted Police stations & patrols throughout the North-West Territories, during the year 1888. Also boundaries of Indian treaties and location of Indian reserves . . . . North-West Mounted Police stations are corrected to February, 1889. Compiled, drawn and published under the superintendence of J. Johnston, Chief Draftsman, Department of the Interior. . . . [2 copies]

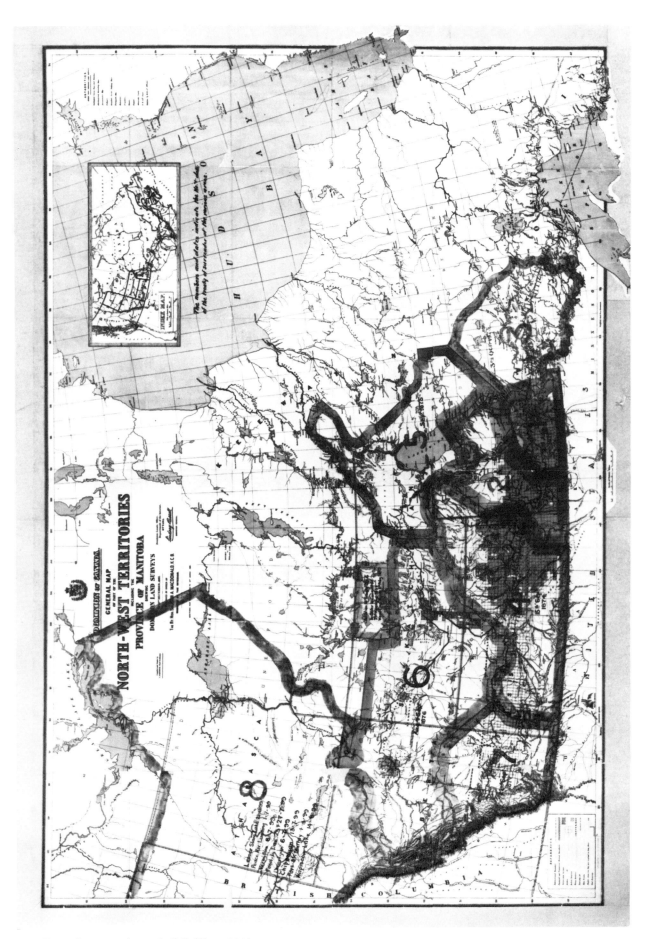

Canada 1883 (1899) (NMC 11690).

CANADA

1890   Dominion of Canada. Map showing Mounted Police stations & patrols throughout the North-West Territories, during the year 1889. Also boundaries of Indian treaties and location of Indian reserves. . . . North-West Mounted Police stations are corrected to 1st January, 1890. Compiled, drawn and published under the superintendence of J. Johnston, Chief Draughtsman, Department of the Interior. . . .

[1890]   [Map showing the Athabasca District and its boundary as a proposed province/Carte du district de l'Athabaska et des limites qu'on se propose de lui donner pour qu'il constitue une province.] (Sgd.) W. Scott Simpson. . . .

[1890]   [Diagrams No. 1 to 3 showing proposed road allowance systems for the North West Territories/Schémas nos 1 à 3 indiquant les modèles de concession pour les réseaux routiers qu'on se propose de donner aux Territoires du Nord-Ouest.] To accompany letter of Indian Commissioner re road allowances.

[1890]   [Figures No. 1 to 6 showing proposed road allowance system for the North West Territories/Schémas nos 1 à 6 indiquant les modèles de concession pour les réseaux routiers qu'on se propose de donner aux Territoires du Nord-Ouest.] W.A. Austin.

1891   Dominion of Canada. Map showing Mounted Police stations & patrols throughout the North-West Territories, during the year 1890. Also boundaries of Indian treaties and location of Indian reserves. . . . North-West Mounted Police stations corrected to 1st January, 1891. Compiled, drawn and published under the superintendence of J. Johnston, Chief Draughtsman, Department of the Interior. . . .

1891   Map of the Dominion of Canada showing Indian reserves. To accompany Annual Report of 1891. . . . Department of Indian Affairs. W.A. Austin, C.E., D.L.S., A.G., Surveyor & Chf. Draughtsman. [3 copies]

1891   [Map showing part of Mackenzie and Peace Rivers in the North West Territories, Canada/Carte indiquant une partie du Mackenzie et de la rivière de la Paix dans les Territoires du Nord-Ouest du Canada.] Privy Council, Canada, 52, O.C. 26 Jan./91.

1892   Indian Treaties 1, 2, 3, 4. This plan is a copy of the original plan by Ross . . . in the Dept. of Interior no. 669. . . . F.C., Ottawa, 3rd February, 1892. [2 copies]

1892   Dominion of Canada. Map showing Mounted Police stations & patrols [and Indian reserves/et les réserves indiennes] throughout the North West Territories, during the year 1891. . . . North-West Mounted Police stations are corrected to 1st January, 1892. . . . [3 copies]

1893   Dominion of Canada. Map showing Mounted Police stations & patrols [and Indian reserves/et les réserves indiennes] during the year 1892. . . . North-West Mounted Police stations are corrected to 1st January, 1893. . . . [3 copies]

1900   Map showing the territory ceded under Treaty No. 8, and the Indian tribes therein.

1904   Dominion of Canada. Map showing Mounted Police stations [and Indian reserves/et les réserves indiennes] in the North West Territories, 1904. . . . James White, F.R.G.S., Geographer, Dept. of the Interior.

[1906]   . . . No. 29. Aborigines of Canada, Alaska and Greenland. . . . [Department of the Interior, *Atlas of Canada*, 1906].

1908   Map of the Dominion of Canada [showing boundaries of Indian treaties], 1908 . . . from latest information furnished by James White, F.R.G.S., Geographer, Department of the Interior, Canada. . . .

1912   Indian treaties, 1850-1912. Compiled under the direction of James White, F.R.G.S. Base map from plate of Map of Dominion of Canada, Dept. of Interior. [2 copies]

[1912]   Aborigines of Canada, Alaska and Greenland. Geographic Board, Canada. Compiled by James White, F.R.G.S. [2 copies]

[1915]   Aborigines of Canada, Alaska and Greenland. [Department of the Interior, *Atlas of Canada*, 1915.]

1932   Map 270A. Aborigines of Canada. Linguistic families and tribal locations . . . about 1525 A.D. [and/et] . . . about 1725 A.D. Canada Department of Mines . . . Geological Survey and National Museum. . . . Issued 1932. Ethnology by D. Jenness, 1929. . . .

1939   Map 1a. Native tribes of North America. Kroeber: Cultural and natural areas of native North America. Copyright, 1939, by the Regents of the University of California. To accompany Univ. Calif. Publ. Am. Arch. and Ethn., Vol. 38.

1939   Map 1b. Native tribes of North America. Kroeber: Cultural and natural areas of native North America. Univ. Calif. Publ. Am. Arch. and Ethn., Vol. 38, 1939.

1939   Map 6. Native cultural areas of North America. . . . Kroeber: Cultural and natural areas of native North America. Univ. Calif. Publ. Am. Arch. and Ethn., Vol. 38, 1939.

1949   Dominion of Canada 1924, showing Indian reserves indicated in red (revised Sept. '49). Department of the Interior, Canada . . . Natural Resources Intelligence Service. . . .

[1957]   Aboriginal population. . . . Compiled from information supplied by the National Museum of Canada and the Dominion Bureau of Statistics. [Department of mines and Technical Surveys, *Atlas of Canada*, 1957.]

CANADA

[1957]   Population indigène . . . Établi d'après les données du Musée national du Canada et du Bureau fédéral de la Statistique. [Ministère des Mines et des Relevés techniques, *Atlas du Canada,*1957.]

1959   Canada, 1959. Indian treaties. Produced and printed by the Surveys and Mapping Branch . . . Department of Mines and Technical Surveys. . . .

1961   Canada, 1961. Indian treaties. Produced and printed by the Surveys and Mapping Branch . . . Department of Mines and Technical Surveys, Ottawa. . . .

1965   Canada, showing location of Indian bands with linguistic affiliations, 1965. Information compiled by the Indian Affairs Branch, Department of Citizenship and Immigration. Produced and printed by the Surveys and Mapping Branch, Department of Mines and Technical Surveys, Ottawa.

1966   Canada, 1966. Indian treaties. Department of Energy, Mines and Resources, Surveys and Mapping Branch. . . . 1961. . . . Minor revisions 1966.

1967   Map [of Canada/du Canada] showing centres of activity. Canada Department of Indian Affairs and Northern Development. 1967. Printed by the Surveys and Mapping Branch, Department of Energy, Mines and Resources.

1968   Canada, showing location of Indian bands with linguistic affiliations, 1968. Information compiled by the Indian Affairs Branch, Department of Indian Affairs and Northern Development. Produced and printed by the Surveys and Mapping Branch, Department of Energy, Mines and Resources Ottawa.

1969   Canada, showing location of Indian bands & Eskimo groups, 1969. Information compiled by the Indian Affairs Branch, Department of Indian Affairs and Northern Development. Produced and printed by the Surveys and Mapping Branch, Department of Energy, Mines and Resources, Ottawa.

1971   Canada . . . Indian treaties. Revised map, April 1971. Produced and printed by the Surveys and mapping Branch . . . Department of Energy, Mines and Resources . . . [for/pour le compte du] Department of Indian Affairs and Northern Development.

1971   Les peuples du Nord-Est. Auteurs : Jean-Pierre Arbour, Francine Belliveau, André Lavallée. . . . Production : Pédagogie Nouvelle Inc. ©1971 Amerix Productions ltée/Ltd., Montréal. Carte n° 3. *Le Canada et son histoire.*

1971   *Atlas of Indian Reserves & Settlements of Canada, 1971.* Department of Indian Affairs and Northern Development. [20 maps/20 cartes]

[1971]   Indian lands and languages. . . . [Department of Energy, Mines and Resources, *The National Atlas of Canada*, 1971.]

[1971]   Terres et langues indiennes . . . . [Ministère de l'Énergie, des Mines et des Ressources, *L'Atlas national du Canada,*1971.]

[1971]   Indian and Eskimo population, 1961. . . . [Department of Energy, Mines and Resources, *The National Atlas of Canada*, 1971.]

[1971]   Population indienne et esquimaude, 1961 . . . [Ministère de l'Énergie, des Mines et des Ressources, *L'Atlas national du Canada,* 1971.]

[1974]   Indian lands and languages. . . . [Department of Energy, Mines and Resources, *The National Atlas of Canada*, 1974.]

[1974]   Terres et langues indiennes. . . . [Ministère de l'Énergie, des Mines et des Ressources, *L'Atlas national du Canada,* 1974.]

[1974]   Indian and Eskimo population, 1961. . . . [Department of Energy, Mines and Resources, *The National Atlas of Canada*, 1974.]

[1974]   Population indienne et esquimaude, 1961. . . . [Ministère de l'Énergie, des Mines et des Ressources, *L'Atlas national du Canada,* 1974.]

1977*   Canada, 1970. . . . Indian treaties. Revised map, October 1977. Produced and printed by the Surveys and Mapping Branch . . . Department of Energy, Mines and Resources . . . [for Department of/pour le compte du ministère des] Indian and Northern Affairs.

1977   Canada, 1970. . . . Traités conclus avec les Indiens. Carte révisée en octobre 1977. Établie et imprimée par la Direction des levés et de la cartographie . . . Ministère de l'Énergie, des Mines et des Ressources . . . [pour le ministère des/for Department of] Affaires indiennes et du Nord.

1977   *Special ARDA in relation to the future direction of native socio-economic development/L'entente spéciale ARDA et l'orientation future du développement socio-économique des autochtones.* . . . Discussion paper/Document de travail. February 10, 1977/le 10 février, 1977. [Department of] Regional Economic Expansion/ [Ministère de l'] Expansion économique régionale. [5 maps (English); 5 maps (French)/5 cartes (anglaises); 5 cartes (françaises)]

1980   Canada. Indian and Inuit communities and languages. Produced by the Surveys and Mapping Branch, Department of Energy, Mines and Resources, Ottawa, Canada. Printed 1980. The National Atlas of Canada, 5th edition.

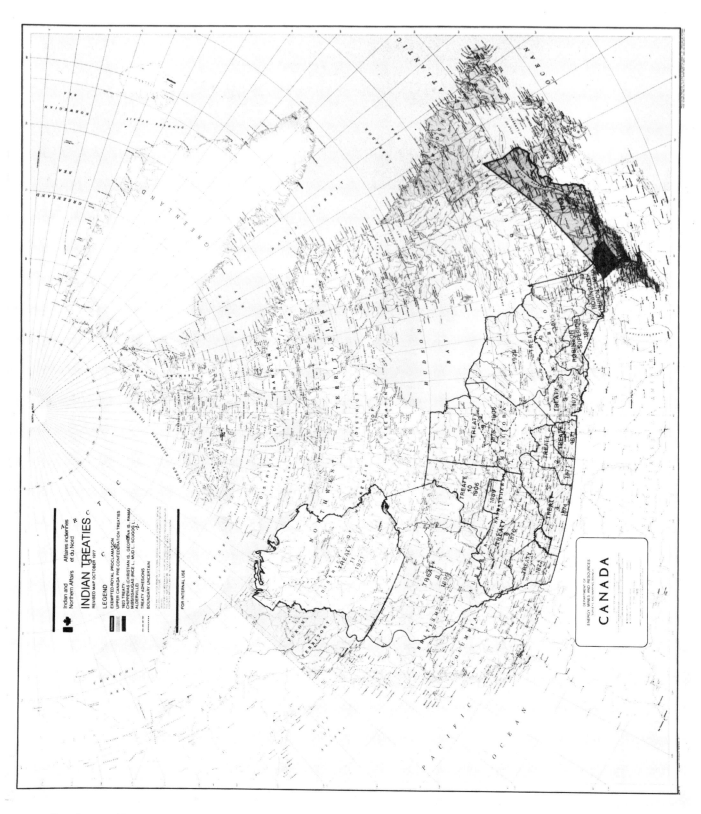

Canada 1977 (C 14555).

N.B. This map is an aide-memoire for normal research and merely attempts to show as accurately as possible the geographical boundaries of areas affected by the treaties . . . A detailed rationale may be obtained from the Research Division (INA).

Canada 1977 (C 14555).

N.B. Cette carte constitue un aide-mémoire pouvant être utile au cours de simples recherches et indique aussi exactement que possible les limites géographiques des régions touchées par les traités . . . On peut se procurer l'analyse détaillée des traités à la Division de la Recherche (MAIN).

1980   Canada. Agglomérations et langues indiennes et inuit. Établie par la Direction des levés et de la cartographie, Ministère de l'Énergie, des Mines et des Ressources, Ottawa, Canada. Imprimée en 1980. L'Atlas national du Canada, 5ᵉ édition.

1980   Occupation de la région Athabasca-Mackenzie par les groupes autochtones, selon Émile Petitot/Land occupancy of the Athabasca-Mackenzie Region by the native groups, according to Émile Petitot. Carte réalisée au Laboratoire de cartographie, Département de géographie, Université Laval, Québec, 1980. Par Raymond Fortin.

1980   Toponymie autochtone de la région Athabasca-Mackenzie (classification linguistique)/Indigenous toponymy of the Athabasca-Mackenzie Region (linguistic classification). Carte réalisée au Laboratoire de cartographie, Département de géographie, Université Laval, Québec, 1980. Par Raymond Fortin.

[1980]   Indian tribes of North America. Copyright Prairie Crafts. Printed in Canada.

ALBERTA - GENERAL MAPS/ALBERTA - CARTES GÉNÉRALES

1883   Map showing the distribution of the Indian tribes of British Columbia [and part of Alberta/et une partie de l'Alberta.] By W.F. Tolmie and G.M. Dawson. Geological and Natural History Survey of Canada. . . 1883. . . .

1912   Map of British Columbia and part of western Canada, showing the lines of Canadian Pacific Railway. Corrected to January 1st, 1912.

ALBERTA - AGENCIES/ALBERTA - AGENCES

Stony

[1909]   [Map showing lands proposed to be reserved for the Stony Indians, in the vicinity of the Red Deer River/Carte indiquant les terrains qu'on se propose de constituer en réserve pour les Assiniboines, à proximité de la rivière Red Deer.] [2 copies]

ALBERTA - RESERVES AND SETTLEMENTS/
ALBERTA - RÉSERVES ET AGGLOMÉRATIONS

Alexander No. 134

1906   Tr. 6. Plan of the subdivision of part of . . . Alexander's [corrected to/corrigé pour] Alexander Reserve No. 134 in Townships 55 and 56, Range 27, West of 4th M. and Township 56, Range 1, West of 5th M., Alta. Surveyed by J.K. McLean, D.L.S., 1906. . . . [2 copies]

Alexis No. 133

1905   Treaty No. 6, N.W.T. Plan of re-survey of Indian Reserve, Lake St. Ann, Alberta. Alexis No. 133. Re-surveyed by J. Lestock Reid, D.L.S., 1905. . . .

Alinckwoonay No. 151D

1905 (1928)   See/Voir: **Peace River Crossing No. 151**

1916 (1929)   See/Voir **Taviah Moosewah No. 151C**

Assineau River No. 150F

1912 (1922)   Tr. 8. Plan of Assineau Indian Reserve No. 150F in Tp. 74, Range 8, W. of 5th Meridian, Lesser Slave Lake, Alta. . . . 5th November, 1912. Certified correct, J.K. McLean, D.L.S. [Additions 1922/ Additions en 1922.]

Battle River

Refer to/Consulter: **Samson No. 137A**

Bear Lake No. 151H

Refer to/Consulter: **Louison Cardinal No. 151H**

Bear's Ears No. 126

1886   Treaty No. 6, N.W.T. Survey of Indian Reserve No. 126 for the band of Chief Muskegwatic at Washatanow or Hollow Hill Creek. . . . Surveyed in Sept. & Octo. 1886 by John C. Nelson, D.L.S. in charge Indian Res. Surveys. . . .

Bear's Paw No. 142

Refer to/Consulter: **Stony No. 142, 143 & 144**

Beaver No. 152

1905 (1928)   Plan of Reserve No. 152 for band of Beaver Indians near Dunvegan. Treaty No. 8. Surveyed by J. Lestock Reid, D.L.S., 1905. . . . [Additions 1928/Additions en 1928.]

1929   Plan of subdivision of Beaver Indian Reserve No. 152 in Tps. 81 &
            82, Rgs. 3 & 4, W. 6th Mer., Alberta. Surveyed by W.E. Zinkan,
            D.L.S., 1929. . . . Traced by G.B.R. . . .

Beaver Lake No. 131

1908 (1911) Plan, Beaver Lake Indian Reserve No. 153 [corrected to/corrigé pour]
             131. Treaty No. 6 Alberta. . . . J. Lestock Reid, D.L.S., March 1908.
             [Additions 1911/Additions en 1911.]

Beaver Lake No. 153

            Refer to/Consulter: **Beaver Lake No. 131**

Beaver Ranch No. 163

1912 (1919) Plan of Beaver Ranch Indian Reserve No. 163 for part of Tall Crees
             band in Tps. 108 & 109, R. 11, W. 5 M., Peace River, Alta. Fort
             Vermilion, Alta., 13th July, 1912. Certified correct, J.K. McLean,
             D.L.S. [Additions to 1919/Additions jusqu'en 1919.]

Big Horn No. 144A

1910   See/Voir: **Kootenay Plains**

[1910]   See/Voir: **Kootenay Plains**

Bigstone No. 166

            Refer to/Consulter: **Wabasca No. 166**

Bigstone No. 166A

            Refer to/Consulter: **Wabasca No. 166A**

Bigstone No. 166B

            Refer to/Consulter: **Wabasca No. 166B**

Blackfoot No. 146

1886 (1940) Treaty No. 7. Survey of the boundaries of the Blackfoot Indian
             Reserve on Bow River, Nor' West Territories, as settled by amended
             treaty June 20th, 1883. Surveyed by J.C. Nelson, D.L.S. Drawn
             by A.W. Ponton, D.L.S., June and July 1883 . . . Regina, N.W.T.,
             May 14th, 1886. . . . [Additions to 1940/Additions jusqu'en 1940.]

[1888]   Sketch showing part of Blackfoot Reserve, Township 23, Range 24,
            West 4th I. M. [relative to a strip of land situated between the
            northern boundary of the Reserve and the Canadian Pacific Railway
            track/concernant une bande de terre située ente l'extrémité nord
            de la réserve et la voie ferrée du Canadien Pacifique].

ALBERTA

1889   [Sketch of a proposed timber limit for the Blackfoot Indians, consisting of a part of Township No. 26, Range 7, West of the 5th Meridian, excepting Sections 1, 12 and 13/Croquis d'une concession forestière qu'on se propose de donner aux Pieds-noirs et comprenant une partie du canton N° 26, rang 7, à l'ouest du 5ᵉ méridien, à l'exception des sections 1, 12 et 13.] Traced, W.A. Austin, 12-6-89.

1889 (1904)   Treaty No. 7, N.W.T. Indian Reserve (Blackfoot) No. 146 on Bow River. As settled by amended treaty, June 20th, 1883. Surveyed by J.C. Nelson, D.L.S., June & July 1883. Approved . . . 27th Feb., 1889. [Additions 1904/Additions en 1904.]

1891   Sketch for Indian Commr. [showing proposed timber limit for Blackfoot Indians/indiquant la concession forestière proposée pour les Pieds-noirs]. J.C.U., 6/8/91.

1893 (1894)   Gleichen. Plan shewing parcels of land required for enlarging station grounds. S.E. 1/4 Sec 13, Tp. 22, R. 23, W. of 4th P.M. . . . [Surveyed by/Relevé par.] (Sd.) Ths. Turnbull, D.L.S. . . . 30 . . . January, 1893. . . . Traced . . . 8-3-94.

1896   General plan showing irrigation canal constructed on the Blackfoot Indian Reserve. A.W. Ponton, D.L.S., 25/8/96. [2 copies]

1897   [Map showing area required for C.P.R. ballast pit on Blackfoot Indian Reserve No. 146/Carte indiquant les terrains situés sur la réserve indienne Blackfoot N° 146 dont le Canadien Pacifique a besoin pour y installer une carrière destinée à l'extraction de ballasts.] . . . Geo. A. Bayne . . . May 22, 1897.

[1898]   Blackfoot Reserve. . . . [Plan showing/Plan indiquant] original boundaries of irrigation ditch . . . changes effected . . . [and/et] further changes proposed.

[1901]   [Map showing location of schools under the auspices of the English Church on the Blackfoot Reserve/Carte indiquant l'emplacement des écoles de la réserve Blackfoot placées sous les auspices de l'Église anglicane.]

[1902]   [Two sketches showing site of old school and proposed sites for new school on Blackfoot Reserve/Deux croquis indiquant l'emplacement de l'ancienne école et les emplacements proposés pour la nouvelle école de la réserve Blackfoot.]

[1903]   [Map showing a piece of land on the Blackfoot Reserve, east of the Horse-Shoe bend on Bow River, covering seven or eight sections, West of Township 20/Carte indiquant une partie de la réserve Blackfoot, située à l'est du coude Horse-Shoe, sur la rivière Bow, et couvrant sept ou huit sections, à l'ouest du canton 20.] Blackfoot Indian Agency, Gleichen, Alta. [Taken from Mr. McKenna's report/Tirée du rapport de M. McKenna.]

[1904]   [Rough sketch showing the portion of the Blackfoot Reserve to be covered by the lease and to be fenced by the Circle Ranch Company. Drawn by Mr. Markle/Croquis préliminaire montrant la partie de la réserve Blackfoot définie dans le bail et qui devra être clôturée par la *Circle Ranch Company*. Dessiné par M. Markle.]

[1904]   [Plan of the Blackfoot Reserve, showing the portion south of the Bow River covered by application of the Circle Ranch Company for grazing privileges/Plan de la réserve Blackfoot indiquant la partie située au sud de la rivière Bow et qui fait l'objet de la demande présentée par la *Circle Ranch Company* pour y profiter de droits de pâturage.]

1907   Portion of Blackfoot Reserve, Bow River. R.M. Ogilvie, Archt., March 07.

1907   Plan showing proposed school site, Blackfoot Boarding School, Gleichen, Alta. R.M. Ogilvie, Archt., March 07.

1909   See/Voir: **Stony No. 142, 143 & 144**

1910   Plan of part of Township 20, Ranges 19, 20 and 21, W. 4th M., being surrendered portion of the Blackfoot Indian Reserve No. 146, Alberta, Surveyed by William H. Waddell, D.L.S. 1910. . . . R.G. Orr.

1910 (1926)   Tr. 7. Plan of south 1/2 of Township 20, Range 20, West of 4th Meridian in Blackfoot Indian Reserve, Alberta, No. 146. Surveyed under instructions from the Department of Indian Affairs. Dated August 24, 1910. William H. Waddell, D.L.S. . . . [Additions 1926/Additions en 1926.]

1910 (1926)   Tr. 7. Plan of part of Township 21 and Township 20, Range 23, West of 4th Meridian in Blackfoot Indian Reserve, Alberta, No. 146. Surveyed under instructions from the Department of Indian Affairs. Dated August 24, 1910. William H. Waddell, D.L.S. . . . [Additions to 1926/Additions jusqu'en 1926.]

1910 (1949)   Tr. 7. Plan of Township 20, Range 24, West of 4th Meridian in Blackfoot Indian Reserve No. 146, Alberta. Surveyed under instructions from the Department of Indian Affairs. Dated August 24, 1910. William H. Waddell, D.L.S. . . . [Additions to 1949/Additions jusqu'en 1949.]

1910 (1958)   Tr. 7. Plan of part of Township 20, Range 19, West of 4th Meridian, in Blackfoot Indian Reserve, Alberta. Surveyed under instructions from the Department of Indian Affairs. Dated August 24, 1910. William H. Waddell, D.L.S. . . . [Additions to 1958/Additions jusqu'en 1958.]

ALBERTA

1910 (1958)   Tr. 7. Plan of south 1/2 of Township 20, Range 21, West of 4th Meridian, in Blackfoot Indian Reserve, Alberta. Surveyed under instructions from the Department of Indian Affairs. Dated August 24, 1910. William H. Waddell, D.L.S. . . . [Additions to 1958/Additions jusqu'en 1958.]

1910 (1958)*   Tr. 7. Plan of parts of Townships 21 and 20, Range 22, West of 4th Meridian, in Blackfoot Indian Reserve, Alberta. Surveyed under instructions from the Department of Indian Affairs. Dated August 24, 1910. William H. Waddell, D.L.S. . . . [Additions to 1958/Additions jusqu'en 1958.]

1910 (1958)   Tr. 7. Plan of parts of Township 22 and Township 21, Range 24, West of 4th Meridian, in Blackfoot Indian Reserve, Alberta. Surveyed under instructions from the Department of Indian Affairs. Dated August 24, 1910. William H. Waddell, D.L.S. . . . [Additions to 1958/Additions jusqu'en 1958.]

1911   Plan of part of Tp. 20, R. 22; Tp. 20 and part of Tp. 21, R. 23; Tp. 20 and part of Tp. 21 and 22, R. 24, W. 4th M., being surrendered portion of the Blackfoot Indian Reserve No. 146, Alberta. Surveyed by William H. Waddell, D.L.S., 1910. . . . R.G. Orr, 1911.

1915   Canadian Pacific Railway Co., Department of Natural Resources. Plan shewing right of way, main canal "B", Horseshoe Bend Dam and flooded area above dam, Blackfoot Indian Reserve, Alberta. . . . [Surveyed by/Relevé par] C.M. Hoar. . . . 1st . . . Feby., 1915. . . .

1918   Plan of parts of Tps. 20 & 21, Rgs. 19 & 20, W. 4 M., Blackfoot I.R., Alberta. Surrendered for lease 1918. Surveyed by W.R. White, D.L.S., May 1918. . . .

1923   Treaty 7. Plan of part of Township 22, Range 24, West of Fourth Meridian, in Blackfoot Indian Reserve No. 146, Alberta. Subdivided for Indian purposes. 12th October, 1922, Donald Robertson, D.L.S. G.P., 30th April, 1923.

[1926]   Proposed site for memorial perpetuating signing Blackfoot Treaty, 1887.

Blackfoot Timber Limit No. 146C

1892   Timber Limit "C" on the Canadian Pacific Railway at Castle Mountain, Alberta, reserved for the Blackfoot Indians. Surveyed by A.W. Ponton, D.L.S. in Aug., Sept. & Oct. 1892.

Blood No. 148

1883   Survey of the boundaries of the Blood Indian Reserve between Belly & St. Mary's Rivers, as settled by amended treaty, July 2, 1883. By J.C. Nelson, D.L.S.

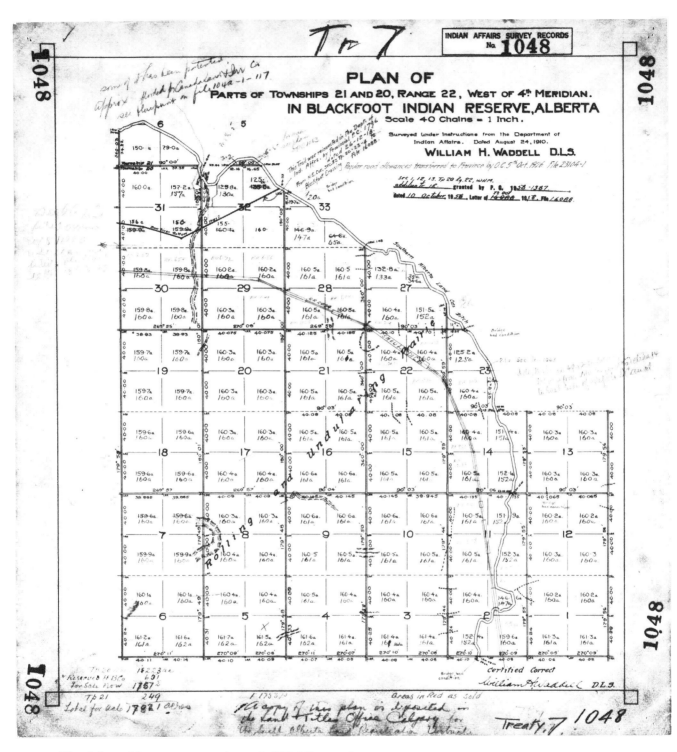

Blackfoot No. 146 1910 (1958) (NMC 5638).

ALBERTA

[1883]   [Plan showing location of proposed buildings on the Blood Reserve for the new Agency/Plan indiquant l'emplacement de la nouvelle agence qu'on se propose d'édifier sur la réserve Blood.]

1886   [Two plans showing/Deux plans indiquant]the farm instructor's house and the employees' house, Blood Reserve. Indian Commissioner's Office, N.W.T., 1886.

1887   Copy. Field & gardens for teacher. Boarding house. Boys & missionary. Proposed plan of Methodist mission, Lower Blood Agency. December 22nd, 1887. (Signed) John McLean.

1888 (1930)   Treaty No. 7, North West Territories. Survey of the part of the North West 1/4 Sec. 3, Tp. 8, Rg. 22, W. of 4th I.M., lying between the Belly & St. Mary's River at "Whoop-up" and not included in the Blood Indian Reserve. Surveyed in 1888 by John C. Nelson, D.L.S. in charge of Indian Reserve Survey. [Additions to 1930/Additions jusqu'en 1930.]

1891   Plot shewing the left bank of part of St. Mary's River near Lees Creek [and the spot where the trespass was committed by Mr. Hiram Hansen/et l'endroit où la violation de propriété a été commise par M. Hiram Hansen]. Sd., J.C. Nelson, March 11th, 1891.

1897   Canadian Pacific Railway. Crows Nest Pass section. Plan shewing line from Lethbridge through the Blood Indian Reserve and the Peigan Indian Reserve. Montreal, 5th July, 1897. . . . [2 copies]

[1899]   C.P.R. Crow's Nest Branch. Sketch showing pipe line for water supply at Belly River.

1915   Tr. 7. Blood Indian Reserve. Plan of part of Tp. 4, R. 26, West of 4th M. J.F. Hamilton, D.L.S. & A.L.S., Lethbridge, Alta., July 7th, 1915.

1963   Blood Indian Reserve, Alberta. Topographic map. Information provided by the Indian Affairs Branch, Department of Citizenship and Immigration, Ottawa, 1962. Produced and printed by the Surveys and Mapping Branch, Department of Mines and Technical Surveys, Ottawa, 1963.

Blood No. 148A

1883 (1888)   Treaty No. 7, N.W.T. Plan of Timber Limit A on Belly River, reserved for the Blood Indians. . . . Reserved in August 1883. . . . John C. Nelson, D.L.S. in charge of I.R. Surveys. [Additions to 1888/ Additions jusqu'en 1888.]

[1963]   Blood Indian Reserve timber limit, Alberta. Surficial geology.

Blood Timber Limit

Refer to/Consulter: **Blood No. 148A**

Blue Quill No. 123

        Refer to/Consulter: **Kehiwin No. 123**

Blue Quill No. 125

        Refer to/Consulter: **Saddle Lake No. 125**

Bobtail No. 139

1885 (1887)   See/Voir: **Montana No. 139**

1887   See/Voir: **Samson No. 137A**

1909   See/Voir: **Montana No. 139**

1909 (1947)   See/Voir: **Montana No. 139**

Boyer No. 164

1912   Tr. 8. Plan of Boyer River Indian Reserve No. 164 for the Fort Vermilion band of Beaver Indians in Tp. 109, Range 14, W. 5 M., Peace River, Alta. Fort Vermilion, Alta., August 1st, 1912. Certified correct, J.K. McLean, D.L.S.

Castle Mountain No. 146C

        Refer to/Consulter: **Blackfoot Timber Limit No. 146C**

Chiniquay No. 144

        Refer to/Consulter: **Stony No. 142, 143 & 144**

Clearwater No. 175

1915 (1917)   Treaty 8. Plan of Clearwater River Indian Reserve No. 175 for the Indians of the Cree band, situate in Township 88, Range 7, West of the 4th Mer. Surveyed by R.H. Knight, D.L.S., 1915 and Donald F. Robertson, D.L.S., 1915 . . . [Additions 1917/Additions en 1917.]

Cold Lake No. 149

1903 (1911)   Plan of Cold Lake Indian Reserve No. 149. Treaty No. 6, N.W.T. J. Lestock Reid, D.L.S., December 1903 . . . [Additions to 1911/Additions jusqu'en 1911.]

1908   Plan of R.C. mission property, Cold Lake Indian Reserve No. 149. Treaty No. 6, Sask. Surveyed by J. Lestock Reid, D.L.S., August 1907. . . . January 28th, 1908.

ALBERTA

Cold Lake No. 149A

1908   Treaty 6. Plan of Fishing Station No. 149A for the Cold Lake Indians, Cold Lake, Alta. . . . Surveyed by J. Lestock Reid, D.L.S., August 1907. . . . January 28th, 1908.

Cold Lake No. 149B

1915   Treaty 6. Plan of Cold Lake Indian Reserve No. 149B, Alberta, for the Indians of the Chipewyan band. Compiled from surveys made by M.W. Hopkins, D.L.S., 1909 and Donald F. Robertson, D.L.S., 1915. . . .

David Tustawits No. 151F

1905 (1928)   See/Voir: **Peace River Crossing No. 151**

1906   See/Voir: **Duncan Tustawits No. 151E**

Drift Pile River No. 150

1901   Treaty No. 8, N.W.T. Plan of Drift Pile River Reserve No. 150, situated on the south shore of Lesser Slave Lake, surveyed for Chief Kinoosayo and a portion of his band. . . . Surveyed in August 1901 by A.W. Ponton, D.L.S. . . .

1912 (1919)   Tr. 8. Plan showing additions made by J.K. McLean, D.L.S. in 1912 to Driftpile River Indian Reserve No. 150, Township 73, Ranges 11 to 13, W. 5th M., Lesser Slave Lake, Alta. . . . [Additions to 1919/ Additions jusqu'en 1919.]

Duncan Tustawits No. 151E

1905 (1928)   See/Voir: **Peace River Crossing No. 151**

1906   Plan of Shaftesbury Settlement [and Reserves No. 151E, 151F and 151G], Province of Alberta. Surveyed by H.W. Selby, D.L.S., 3rd May, 1905. . . . Department of the Interior, Ottawa, 23rd May, 1906. . . . [2 copies]

1916 (1929)   See/Voir: **Taviah Moosewah No. 151C**

Eagle Tail No. 147

Refer to/Consulter: **Peigan No. 147**

Enoch Le Potac No. 135

Refer to/Consulter: **Stony Plain No. 135**

20

Ermineskin No. 137

> Refer to/Consulter: **Ermineskin No. 138**

Ermineskin No. 138

1885 (1886)   See/Voir: **Samson No. 137**

1887 (1926)   Plan accompanying appendix to field-notes of the survey of Indian Reserves Nos. 138 & 137, at Bear's Hill, N.W.T. for the bands of Chiefs Sampson & Ermine-Skin, showing the dividing line between them. Surveyed in November 1887 John C. Nelson, D.L.S. in charge Indian Reserve Surveys. . . . [Additions to 1926/Additions jusqu'en 1926.]

1889   Treaty No. 6, N.W.T. Indian Reserve No. 138, Chief "Ermine-Skin". Surveyed by John C. Nelson, D.L.S., Aug. & Sept. 1885. Approved . . . 23rd Jan., 1889.

1909   Plan of Indian Reserve No. 138, Province of Alberta, showing the subdivision between the bands of Chiefs Ermineskin and Louis Bull. Ponoka, Alta., July 30th, 1909. . . . J.K. McLean, D.L.S.

[1918]   [Plan showing Ermineskin Reserve No. 138, Louis Bull Reserve No. 138B and the land owned by Janse Brothers Limited/Plan indiquant la réserve Ermineskin N° 138, la réserve Louis Bull N° 138B et le terrain appartenant à *Janse Brothers Limited*.]

Fishing No. 138A

> Refer to/Consulter: **Pigeon Lake No. 138A**

Fishing Station No. 121A

1907   Treaty 6. Plan of Fishing Station I.R. No. 121A for Frog Lake Indians, Sask. I.R. 121A received in exchange for an equal area surrendered at the south east corner of Indian Reserve No. 121. Surveyed by J. Lestock Reid, D.L.S., summer season, 1907.

Fishing Station No. 138A

> Refer to/Consulter: **Pigeon Lake No. 138A**

Fishing Station No. 149A

> Refer to/Consulter: **Cold Lake No. 149A**

Fitzgerald No. 196

[1914]   Proposed reserve for wood bison, fur-bearers, etc. . . .

ALBERTA

Fort McKay No. 174

1915 (1917)   Treaty 8. Plan of Fort McKay I.R. No. 174 for the Indians of the Chipewyan band situate in Township 94, Range II, West 4 Mer. Surveyed by Donald F. Robertson, D.L.S., 1915. . . . [Additions 1917/Additions en 1917.]

Fort Vermilion

[1890]   [Sketch showing homes and other buildings in the vicinity of Vermilion/Croquis indiquant les maisons et autres bâtiments situés dans le voisinage de Vermilion.]

Fox Lake No. 162

1912 (1914)   Plan of the Fox Lake Indian Reserve No. 162 for the Little Red River Cree band in Tps. 109 and 110, Rgs. 3 and 4, W. of 5th M., Alta. Fort Vermilion, Alta., 13th July, 1912. Certified correct, J.K. McLean, D.L.S. [Additions 1914/Additions en 1914.]

Freeman No. 150B

1901 (1905)   Treaty No. 8. Plan of Indian Reserve No. 150B, Freeman I.R., in the south part of Lesser Slave Lake Settlement, N.W.T. Surveyed for the Freeman family (No. 19), members of the band of Chief Kinoosayo No. 150, under instructions dated April 22nd, 1901 from the Sup't Gen'l of Indian Affairs. Certified correct, A.W. Ponton, D.L.S. [Additions 1905/Additions en 1905.]

Frog Lake No. 121

Refer to/Consulter: **Unipouheos No. 121**

Frog Lake No. 122

Refer to/Consulter: **Puskiakiwenin No. 122**

Gillian Bell No. 151G

1905 (1928)   See/Voir: **Peace River Crossing No. 151**

1906   See/Voir: **Duncan Tustawits No. 151E**

Good Fish Lake No. 128

Refer to/Consulter: **White Fish Lake No. 128**

Gregoire Lake No. 176

1915 (1916)   Treaty 8. Plan of Gregoire Lake Indian Reserves No. 176, 176A and 176B for the Indians of the Cree band situate in Townships 85 and 86, Range 8, W. 4 M. Surveyed by Donald F. Robertson, D.L.S., 1915. . . . [Additions 1916/Additions en 1916.]

Gregoire Lake No. 176A

1915 (1916)   See/Voir: **Gregoire Lake No. 176**

Gregoire Lake No. 176B

1915 (1916)   See/Voir: **Gregoire Lake No. 176**

Halcro No. 150C

1901 (1905)   Treaty No. 8, N.W.T. Plan of Indian Reserve No. 150C surveyed for (No. 40) Thomas Halcro, member of the band of Chief Kinoosayo No. 150, under instructions dated April 22nd, 1901 from the Sup't Gen'l of Indian Affairs. Surveyed by A.W. Ponton, D.L.S., in 1901. . . . [Additions 1905/Additions en 1905.]

Hay Lands No. 120A

1897 (1903)   Treaty No. 6, N.W.T. Plan of hay lands near Moose Lake in the Onion Lake Agency, set apart for the Department of Indian Affairs. . . . Surveyed in October 1897 by A.W. Ponton, D.L.S. [Additions to 1903/Additions jusqu'en 1903.]

High River

[1883]   Two sketches showing the proposed site for the construction of school buildings at High River/Deux croquis indiquant le site proposé pour la construction de l'école à High River.]

Horse Lakes No. 152B

1914 (1949)   Tr. 8. Plan of Horse Lakes Indian Reserve No. 152B, situate in Tp. 73, Rgs. 11 & 12, W. of 6 M. Compiled from surveys by W.G. McFarlane, D.L.S. and D.F. Robertson, D.L.S., 1914. . . . [Additions to 1949/Additions jusqu'en 1949.]

Jacob No. 143

Refer to/Consulter: **Stony No. 142, 143 & 144**

James Seenum No. 128

Refer to/Consulter: **White Fish Lake No. 128**

Janvier No. 194

1922 (1952)   Plan of Janvier Indian Reserve No. 194 in Tp. 80, Rge. 5, W. 4th Mer., Alberta. Surveyed by J.L. Coté, D.L.S., 1922. . . . Drawn by G.P. . . . [Additions to 1952/Additions jusqu'en 1952.]

ALBERTA

John Felix Tustawits No. 151B

1950 (1928)   See/Voir: **Peace River Crossing No. 151**

1910 (1929)   Alberta. Plan of Township 81, Range 4, West of the Fifth Meridian [showing John Felix Tustawits Reserve No. 151B, surrendered/ indiquant la réserve John Felix Tustawits n° 151B qui a été cédée]. Department of the Interior, Ottawa, 25th April, 1910. . . . [Additions 1929/Additions en 1929.]

Kehiwin No. 123

1885   Treaty No. 6, N.W.T. Plan for Indian Reserve, Chief Kee Heewin. . . . Surveyed in October 1884 by A.W. Ponton, D.L.S. . . . Indian Office, Regina, Assa., March 19th, 1885.

1904   Sketch of Keheewin Indian Reserve No. 123 as adjusted, 1904.

[1904]   [Plan showing the approximate position of the Kehiwin Reserve and other reserves in the area/Plan indiquant l'emplacement approximatif de la réserve Kehiwin et des autres réserves dans cette région.]

1905   Treaty No. 6. Plan of Keheewin [corrected to/corrigé pour] Kehiwin Indian Reserve No. 123 as adjusted 1904. J. Lestock Reid, D.L.S., January 11th, 1905.

Kinoosayoo's No. 150

Refer to/Consulter: **Drift Pile River No. 150**

Kinoosayoo's No. 150A

Refer to/Consulter: **Sucker Creek No. 150A**

Kinoosayoo's No. 150B

Refer to/Consulter: **Freeman No. 150B**

Kinoosayoo's No. 150C

Refer to/Consulter: **Halcro No. 150C**

Kinoosayoo's No. 150D

Refer to/Consulter: **Pakashan No. 150D**

Kinoosayoo's No. 150E

Refer to/Consulter: **Swan River No. 150E**

Kinoosayoo's No. 150F

        Refer to/Consulter: **Assineau River No. 150F**

Kinoosayoo's No. 150G

        Refer to/Consulter: **Sawridge No. 150G**

Kinoosayoo's No. 150H

        Refer to/Consulter: **Sawridge No. 150H**

Kinuso No. 150E

        Refer to/Consulter: **Swan River No. 150E**

Kootenay Plains

1910   [Map showing land within the Rocky Mountains Forest Reserve applied for by the Indian Department, within which to select 26,040 acres/Carte indiquant les terres de la réserve forestière Rocky Mountains pour lesquelles le ministère des Affaires indiennes a présenté une demande et dont il doit choisir 26 040 acres.] Copied . . . 18/8/10.

[1910]   [Rough sketch showing the position of the land asked for by the Stony Indians near the head waters of the Saskatchewan, including the Kootenay Plains on both sides of the river/Croquis préliminaire indiquant l'emplacement des terrains demandés par les Assiniboines, près du cours supérieur de la Saskatchewan, y compris les plaines Kootenay sur les deux rives de la rivière.]

[1910]   Plan showing Kootenay Plains, Northern Alberta [showing Indian houses and those built by white men/indiquant les habitations indiennes et celles construites par les Blancs].

[1910]   See/Voir: **Stony No. 142, 143 & 144**

Little Hunter No. 125

        Refer to/Consulter: **Saddle Lake No. 125**

Louis Bull No. 138B

1909   Tr. 6. Plan of Louis Bull Indian Reserve No. 138 B, part of Tp. 45, Rge. 25, W. 4th M., Province of Alberta, showing part surrendered for sale shaded. Hobbema, Alta., 6th Oct., 1909. Certified correct, J.K. McLean, D.L.S. (2 copies)

1909   See/Voir: **Ermineskin No. 138**

[1918]   See/Voir: **Ermineskin No. 138**

ALBERTA

Louison Cardinal No. 151H

1905 (1928)*   Plan of Indian Reserve Bear Lake No. 151 H. Treaty No. 8. Allotted to Louison Cardinal No. 23 of the Peace River Crossing band about 20 miles N.W. of the Peace River Crossing. Surveyed by J. Lestock Reid, D.L.S., 1905 . . . [Additions to 1928/Additions jusqu'en 1928.]

1913 (1929)   Alberta. Plan of Township 84, Range 23, West of the Fifth Meridian [showing Louison Cardinal Reserve No. 151H, surrendered/indiquant la réserve Louison Cardinal n° 151H, cédée]. Department of the Interior, Ottawa. 10th November, 1913. . . . [Additions 1929/Additions en 1929.]

Makaoo No. 120

1904 (1927)   . . . Plan of resurvey of Seekaskootch & Makaoo Indian Reserves No. 119 & 120. Treaty No. 6, N.W.T. J. Lestock Reid, D.L.S., February 1904. [Additions to 1927/Additions jusqu'en 1927.]

[1904]   See/Voir: **Kehiwin No. 123**

1915   Tr. No. 6. Plan of proposed lands for Roman Catholic and English missions in Indian Reserve No. 120, Sask. Surveyed by D.F. Robertson, D.L.S., 1915.

Ma-me-o Beach No. 138A

Refer to/Consulter: **Pigeon Lake No. 138A**

Michel No. 132

1892 (1911)   Treaty No. 6, North West Territories. Plan showing survey of J.L. Hirondelle's claim in Indian Reserve No. 132. Band of Chief "Michel Calahoo". . . . John C. Nelson, D.L.S., 21/4/1892. [Additions to 1911/Additions jusqu'en 1911.]

1904   Tr. 6. Plan of subdivision of a portion of Indian Reserve No. 132, comprising parts of Townships 53, 54 and 55, Range 27, West of 4th Meridian. Surveyed by R.W. Lendrum, D.L.S., Novr. 1903. . . . Strathcona, Alberta, N.W.T., Feby. 12th, 1904. [2 copies.]

[1905]   Edmonton Indian Agency. This map shows the location of the 1/4 Sec. of land claimed by the L'Hirondelle Estate - N.E. 1/4 of 24-53-27 [Michel Reserve No. 132/Réserve Michel n° 132].

1906   Tr. 6. Plan of subdivision of part of Michel Calahoo [corrected to/corrigé pour] Michel Indian Reserve No. 132 in Townships 53 and 54, Range 26, W. of 4th M., Alberta. White Whale Lake, Alta., 5th Sept., 1906. Certified correct, J.K. McLean, D.L.S.

PLAN OF

INDIAN RESERVE BEAR LAKE
Nº 151 H

TREATY Nº 8

Allotted to Louison Cardinal Nº 28
of the Peace River Crossing Band about
20 miles N W of the Peace River Crossing

Bear Lake

Surrendered for sale
20ᵗʰ Sept 1928

160ᵃᶜ

Scale 20 chs - 1 inch

Surveyed by J Lestock Reid D.L.S

1905

Confirmed by O.C. 23ʳᵈ June 1925. File 27/131-8   Su plan 849-A.
Area 160. ac ±

J. 194555

Tr 8.

Louison Cardinal No. 151H 1905 (1928) (NMC 5721).

ALBERTA

[1909]   [Sketch of Michel Reserve No. 132 showing the land which J. L'Hirondelle leased while he was living, and the house and stable outside of the Reserve/Croquis de la réserve Michel n° 132 indiquant les terres louées par J. L'Hirondelle de son vivant, ainsi que la maison et l'écurie situées en dehors de la réserve.]

1912 (1918)   Plan of subdivision of the Michel Indian Reserve No. 132, Alberta. Surveyed by J.K. McLean, D.L.S., 1912. . . . R.G. Orr, 1912. [Additions to 1918/ Additions jusqu'en 1918.]

[1912]   Plan showing survey of J.L. Hirondelle's claim in Indian Reserve No. 132, band of Chief Michel Calahoo.

Michel Calahoo No. 132

Refer to/Consulter: **Michel No. 132**

Montana No. 139

1885 (1887)   Treaty No. 6, N.W.T. Indian Reserve No. 139 on Battle River. Chief "Bobtail". . . . Surveyed in Aug. & Sept. 1885 by . . . John C. Nelson, D.L.S. . . . [Additions 1887/Additions en 1887.]

1887   See/Voir: **Samson No. 137A**

1909   Plan of Bobtail Indian Reserve No. 139, showing part surrendered for sale in Townships XLIII & XLIV, Ranges XXIII & XXIV [corrected to/corrigé pour] 24 & 25, W. 4th M., Province of Alberta. Hobbema, Alta., 5th Aug., 1909. Certified correct, J.K. McLean, D.L.S. [2 copies]

1909 (1947)   Tr. 6. Plan of Bobtail Indian Reserve No. 139, showing part surrendered for sale, part retained by Montana band and part added to Samson I.R. in Townships XLIII & XLIV, Ranges XXIII & XXIV [corrected to/corrigé pour] XXIV & XXV, W. 4th M., Province of Alberta. Hobbema, Alta., 5th August, 1909. Certified correct, J.K. McLean, D.L.S. [Additions to 1947/Additions jusqu'en 1947.]

Morley

Refer to/Consulter : **Stony No. 142, 143 & 144**

Namur Lake No. 174B

1915 (1925)   Tr. 8. Plan of Namur Lake Indian Reserve No. 174-B in Tps. 97 & 98, Ranges 16 & 17, W. of 4th Mer. for the Fort McKay band of Chipewyan Indians. Surveyed by Donald F. Robertson, D.L.S., 1915. . . . [Additions 1925/Additions en 1925.]

Namur River No. 174A

1915 (1930)   Tr. 8. Plan of Namur River Indian Reserve No. 174-A in Townships 97 & 98, Range 16, W. 4th. Mer. for the Fort McKay band of Chipewyan Indians. Surveyed by Donald F. Robertson, D.L.S., 1915. . . . [Additions 1930/Additions en 1930.]

Neepee Chief No. 152A

1905 (1932)   Plan of No. 152A Indian Reserve, Green Island Flat, for Beaver Indians, Dunvegan (Neepee Chief). Treaty No. 8. Surrendered. Surveyed by J. Lestock Reid, D.L.S., 1905. . . . [Additions to 1932/Additions jusqu'en 1932.]

1910 (1929)   Alberta. Plan of Townships 80, Range 3, West of the Sixth Meridian [showing Neepee Chief Reserve No. 152A, surrendered/indiquant la réserve Neepee Chief n° 152A, cédée]. Department of the Interior, Ottawa, 16th March, 1910. . . . [Additions 1929/Additions en 1929.]

Onion Lake Haylands No. 120A

Refer to/Consulter: **Hay Lands No. 120A**

Ooneepowohayoos No. 121

Refer to/Consulter: **Unipouheos No. 121**

Pakan No. 125

Refer to/Consulter: **Saddle Lake No. 125**

Pakan No. 128

Refer to/Consulter: **White Fish Lake No. 128**

Pakashan No. 150D

1901 (1925)   Treaty No. 8, N.W.T. Plan of Indian Reserve No. 150D, Pakashan . . . surveyed for (No. 74) John Pakashan and five children, members of the band of Chief Kinoosayo No. 150, under instructions dated April 22nd, 1901, from the Department of Indian Affairs. Surveyed by A.W. Ponton, D.L.S., 1901. . . . [Additions 1925/Additions en 1925.]

Papaschase No. 136

1884 (1892)   Treaty No. 6, N.W.T. Plan of Indian Reserve No. 136. Chief Papaschase (Wood Pecker). Surveyed in September 1884 by J.C. Nelson, D.L.S. . . . in charge I.R. Surveys. [Additions to 1892/Additions jusqu'en 1892.]

ALBERTA

[1885]   Treaty No. 6, N.W.T. Sketch showing the survey of the boundaries of an Indian Reserve for the band of Chief "Papaschase" (Woodpecker). John C. Nelson, Domn. Land Surveyor.

1890   Treaty No. 6, North West Territories. Sketch of the subdivision into sections of the lands reserved for the band of Chief "Papaschase", heretofore known as Indian Reserve No. 136. Surveyed in Octo. 1890 by John C. Nelson, D.L.S. in charge Indian Reserve Surveys.

1890   Treaty No. 6, North West Territories. Plan of the subdivision into sections of the lands reserved for the band of Chief "Papaschase", heretofore known as Indian Reserve No. 136, at the Two Hills near Edmonton. Resurveyed in Oct. 1890 by John C. Nelson, D.L.S. in charge of Indian Reserve Surveys. . . . [7 copies]

Peace River Crossing No. 151

1905 (1928)   Plan of Indian Reserves No. 151, 151A, 151B, 151C, 151D, 151E, 151F and 151G for Peace River Landing band. Treaty No. 8. Surveyed by J. Lestock Reid, D.L.S., 1905. [Additions to 1928/Additions jusqu'en 1928.]

1916 (1929)   See/Voir: **Taviah Moosewah No. 151C**

1929   Plan of subdivision of Peace River Crossing I.R. No. 151, in Tp. 82, Rge. 24, W. 5th. Mer., Alberta, 1929. Surveyed by W.E. Zinkan, D.L.S. . . . [2 copies]

Peace River Crossing 151A

1905 (1928)   See/Voir: **Peace River Crossing No. 151**

Peigan No. 147

1882 (1936)   Treaty No. 7. Survey of the boundaries of the Peigan Indian Reserve on Crow Lodge Creek, North West Territories. Chief Eagle Tail. No. 147. . . . Surveyed in Sept. 1882 by John C. Nelson, D.L.S. . . . [Additions to 1936/Additions jusqu'en 1936.]

1887   Plan of North-West Mounted Police Reserve north of the Peigan Indian Reserve, Tp. 9, Rge. 27, West of 4th I.M. Surveyed by C.F. Miles, D.L.S., August 4th & 5th, 1887.

[1889]   Plan showing [Peigan Reserve and/réserve Peigan et] a proposed fence of the Walrond Cattle Co.

1897   Plan of a road diversion from the Macleod-Pincher Creek Trail across the Canadian Pacific Railway - Crows Nest Pass Branch through West 1/2 of Sec. 30, Township 8, Range 27, West 4th M. and the Peigan Indian Reserve No. 147. [Surveyed by/relevé par] Richard Jermy Jephson, D.L.S. . . . 1897.

1897	Plan of a road diversion from the Macleod-Pincher Creek Trail around the Canadian Pacific Railway - Crows Nest Pass Branch through the Peigan Indian Reserve No. 147 at Scott's Coulée. [Surveyed by/relevé par] Richard Jermy Jephson, D.L.S. . . . 1897. . . .
1897	See/Voir: **Blood No. 148**
[1903]	[Plan of a proposed road from the settlements on the north fork of the Oldman River, Township 9, Range 1, West of the Fifth Meridian, to the Mcleod-Pincher Creek Trail/Tracé d'une route qu'on se propose de construire depuis les installations à la fourche nord de la rivière Oldman, canton 9, rang 1, à l'ouest du cinquième méridien, jusqu'à la piste McLeod-Pincher Creek.]
1904	C.P.R., Western Division. Brocket, Alberta [Peigan reserve No. 147/réserve Peigan n° 147.] Drawn by C.M., Calgary, 26th March, 1904. . . .
1904	General plan of pipe line and works connected therewith constructed by the Canadian Pacific Railway Company at Brocket [Peigan Reserve No. 147/réserve Peigan n° 147]. . . . Office of the Supt. of Irrigation, Calgary, September 14th, 1904. . . .
1906	Brocket. [Plan showing/Plan indiquant] extra land required for water supply [for railway purposes/pour l'usage du chemin de fer]. Division Engineer's Office, Calgary, June 13th, 06. . . .
1908	Canadian Pacific Railway, Crows Nest Branch. Plan shewing land required for water supply of Brocket in the Peigan Indian Reserve. . . . [Surveyed by/Relevé par] George McPhillips. . . 23rd. . . May, 1908. . . .
1909	Tr. 7. Plan of part of Peigan Indian Reserve No. 147 in Townships 7 and 8, Range 28, West of 4th M., Province of Alberta. Surrendered for sale August 1909. Brocket, Alta., 15th September, 1909. Certified correct, J.K. McLean, D.L.S. [4 copies]
1909 (1936)	Plan of subdivision of part of Peigan Indian Reserve No. 147, Province of Alberta, for Indian purposes. Brocket, Alta., 15th Sept. 1909. Certified correct, J.K. McLean, D.L.S. [Additions 1936/Additions en 1936.]
[1909]	Plan showing different proposals for surrender at Brocket, Peigan Indian Reserve.
[1920]	Plan of Lots A, B, and C at Brocket, Peigan Indian Reserve - No. 147. Surveyed by J.E. Woods, A. & D.L.S. . . .
1940	Plan of additional right of way for main canal through Peigan Indian Reserve, Province of Alberta, Lethbridge Northern Irrigation District. . . . [Surveyed by/Relevé par] P.M. Sauder, Dominion Land Surveyor . . . 9th Jan., 1940. . . .

ALBERTA

Peigan (Timber Limit) No. 147B

1888   Treaty No. 7, N.W.T. Plan of Timber Limit B showing sections reserved for the Peigan Indians. Surveyed in 1883 & 1888 by John C. Nelson, D.L.S.

1897   See/Voir: **Blood No. 148**

Pigeon Lake No. 138A

1893 (1952)   Treaty No. 6. Survey of Indian Reserve No. 138a, fishing station at Pigeon Lake for Indians of Hobbema Agency. . . . Surveyed in August 1893 by A.W. Ponton, D.L.S. . . . [Additions to 1952/ Additions jusqu'en 1952.]

1923   Plan of Ma-me-o Beach, subdivision of part of Indian Reserve No. 138A, Tp. 46, R. 28, W. 4. . . . [Surveyed by/Relevé par] J.L. Coté, A.L.S. . . . 19th. . . May. . . 1923. . . . [2 copies]

Puskiakiwenin No. 122

[1904]   See/Voir: **Kehiwin No. 123**

1905   Plan of resurvey of Indian Reserve No. 122. Treaty No. 6. J. Lestock Reid, D.L.S., January 11th, 1905.

Rabbit Lake No. 142B

Refer to/Consulter: **Stony No. 142B**

Red Deer Industrial School

1884   Plan of Township No. 38, Range 27, West of Fourth Meridian [relating to the site for the Red Deer Industrial School/relatif au site de l'école industrielle Red Deer]. . . . Dominion Lands Office, Ottawa, 5th August, 1884. . . .

1887   Township No. 36, Range 1, West of Fifth Meridian [relating to the site for the Red Deer Industrial School/relatif au site de l'école industrielle Red Deer]. . . . Dominion Lands Office, Ottawa, 18th January, 1887. . . .

1889   . . . Plan of Township No. 38, Range 28, West of Fourth Meridian [relating to the site for the Red Deer Industrial School/relatif au site de l'école industrielle Red Deer]. . . . Dominion Lands Office, Ottawa, 10th December, 1889. . . .

[1890]   Sketch showing proposed site for the Methodist Industrial School at the Red Deer River, Alberta.

[1898]   Rough plan of road to Swan Lake District going across property owned by Red Deer Industrial School.

1899   Plan showing survey of road allowance diversion through Sections 14-15 a portion of the S.W. 1/4 of 13 in Tp. 38, Rge 28, W. of 4th Meridian [relating to Red Deer Industrial School/relatif au site de l'école industrielle de Red Deer]. By A. McFee, D.L.S., 1898 . . . 16th . . . January, 1899. . . .

[1899]   Red Deer Industrial School. Rough sketch of Sect. 14, 3/4 of which is owned by the school.

[1907]   Plan of Section 14, Township 38, Range 28, West of 4th Meridian, showing the lands held by the Red Deer Indian Industrial School.

Saddle Lake No. 125

1886 (1925)   Treaty No. 6, N.W.T. Survey of Indian Reserve No. 125 at Saddle Lake for the band of Chiefs Pakan, Thos. Hunter & Blue Quill. . . . Surveyed in Octo. & Novr. 1886 by John C. Nelson, D.L.S. in charge Indian Reserve Surveys. . . . [Additions to 1925/Additions jusqu'en 1925.]

1897   Treaty No. 6, N.W.T. Plan of addition to Indian Reserve No. 125 in lieu of Indian Reserve No. 126 surrendered. . . . Surveyed in September 1897 by A.W. Ponton, D.L.S.

[1897] (1926)   . . . Plan of Saddle Lake Indian Reserve No. 125. Compiled from townships plans and field notes of J.C. Nelson, D.L.S., 1886 and A.W. Ponton, D.L.S., 1897. Treaty 6. Drawn by H.W.F. . . . [Additions to 1926/Additions jusqu'en 1926.]

[1904]   See/Voir: **Kehiwin No. 123**

1926   Plan of subdivision of surrendered portion of Saddle Lake I.R. No. 125, Townships 57, 58, Ranges 10, 11, W. 4th Meridian, Alberta. Surveyed by W. Christie, D.L.S., 1926. . . . [2 copies]

St. Albert Industrial School

1917   Farm of Robert Hume, Esq. Sept. 25th, 1917. Julian Garrett, Appraiser.

St. Joseph Industrial School

[1889]   [Map showing school land and hay land applied for, for St. Joseph Industrial School/Carte indiquant le terrain de l'école et le terrain à foin demandés pour l'école industrielle Saint-Joseph.]

1903   St. Joseph's Industrial School, Dunbow, Alta. Sent with report, 22 June, 1903. (Sgd.) A. Mc Gibbon, Insp. . . .

ALBERTA

Samson No. 137

1885 (1886)	Treaty No. 6, N.W.T. Survey of Indian Reserves Nos. 138 [corrected to/corrigé pour] 137, 137 [corrected to/corrigé pour] 138 at Bear's Hill for the bands of Chiefs Sampson & Ermine Skin. . . . Surveyed in Septr. & Octo. 1885 by John C. Nelson, D.L.S. in charge Indian Reserve Surveys. . . . [Additions 1886/Additions en 1886.]
1887	See/Voir: **Samson No. 137A**
1887 (1926)	See/Voir: **Ermineskin No. 138**
1909	Plan of that part of Samson Indian Reserve No. 137 surrendered for sale, being part of Township XLIV, Ranges XXIV & XXV, W. 4th M., Province of Alberta. Hobbema, Alta., 2nd August, 1909, certified correct, J.K. McLean, D.L.S. [2 copies]
1909	See/Voir: **Montana No. 139**
1909 (1947)	See/Voir: **Montana No. 139**

Samson No. 137A

1885 (1887)	See/Voir: **Montana No. 139**
1887	Treaty No. 6, North West Territories. Plan of Methodist mission claim on Battle River. . . . Surveyed in October 1887 by John C. Nelson, D.L.S. in charge Indian Res. Survey. . . .
1887	[Plan showing the portion of land claimed by the Methodist Missionary Society for Indian mission purposes on the Battle River Reserve/Plan indiquant la partie du terrain réclamée par la *Methodist Missionary Society* pour établir une mission dans la réserve Battle River.] John C. Nelson, D.L.S., Regina, May 4th, 1887.
1909	See/Voir: **Montana No. 139**
1909 (1947)	See/Voir: **Montana No. 139**

Samson No. 138

Refer to/Consulter: **Samson No. 137**

Sarcee No. 145

1883 (1908)	Treaty No. 7, N.W.T. Survey of Indian Reservation for the Sarcees (Chief Bull's Head) at Fish Creek. John C. Nelson, D.L.S., Ottawa, Nov. 2nd, 1883. [Additions to 1908/Additions jusqu'en 1908.]
[1889]*	Plan of Roche Manes camp, showing site of proposed school [and location of Indian houses nearby, Sarcee Reserve/et l'emplacement des habitations indiennes voisines, réserve Sarcee].

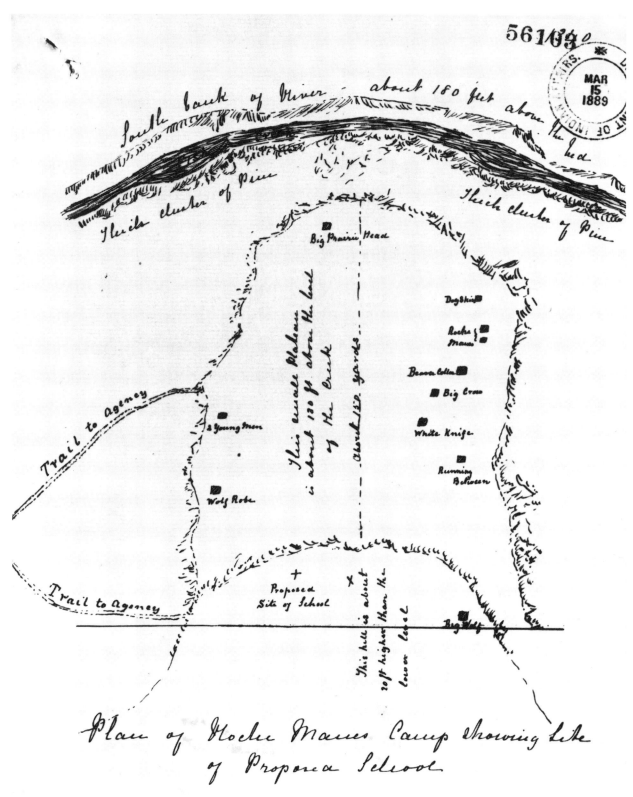

South bank of River ... about 180 feet above the bed

Their cluster of Pine

Their cluster of Pine

Big Prairie Head

Dog Skin

Rocky Maur

Beaver Collar

Big Crow

White Knife

Running Between

Trail to Agency

2 Young Men

Wolf Robe

This whole Plateau is about 120 ft above the bed of the Creek

About 150 yards

Trail to Agency

+
Proposed
Site of School

×
This hill is about 20 ft higher than the lower level

Big Wolf

Plan of Hockn Maus Camp showing site of Proposed School

Sarcee No. 145 [1889] (NMC 12339).

ALBERTA

1909   See/Voir: **Stony No. 142, 143 & 144**

[1910]   Calgary Sheet, West of Fifth Meridian. Sectional map. Special edition shewing lands disposed of . . . [and Sarcee and Stony Reserves/et les réserves Sarcee et Stony]. Department of the Interior, Ottawa. . . .

1913   Plan of subdivision of a portion of Sarcee Indian Reserve No. 145, surrendered Feb. 28th, 1913. I.J. Steele, Dominion Land Surveyor, Calgary, June 1913. [2 copies]

[1913] [1915]   See/Voir: **Stony No. 142, 143 & 144**

[1915]   Location of wells in the Sarcee Indian Reserve, Alberta. Compiled in the office of the Supervisory Mining Engineer, Department of the Interior, Ottawa.

[1918]   General plan of manoevre area [in relation to lots on the Sarcee Reserve to be purchased for the erection of a military hospital/ se rapportant aux lots de la réserve Sarcee qui devront être achetés pour y construire un hôpital militaire]. M.D. 13, Calgary, Alberta. Department of Militia and Defence.

Sawridge No. 150G

1912 (1914)   Tr. 8. Plan of Sawridge Indian Reserve No. 150G in Tps. 72 and 73, R. 5, W. of 5th M. and Tp. 73, R. 4, W. of 5th M., Lesser Slave Lake, Alta. Sawridge, Alta., 16th September, 1912. Certified correct, J.K. McLean, D.L.S. . . . [Additions 1914/Additions en 1914.]

1912 (1914)   See/Voir: **Sawridge No. 150H**

Sawridge No. 150H

1912 (1914)   Tr. 8. Plan of Sawridge Indian Reserve No. 150H in Tp. 73, Range 6, W. of 5th Meridian, Lesser Slave Lake, Alta. Surveyed by J.K. McLean, D.L.S., September 1912. . . . [Additions to 1914/Additions jusqu'en 1914.]

Sharphead No. 141

1885   Treaty No. 6, N.W.T. Plan of Indian Reserve No. 141, Battle River, Chief Sharp-Head. . . . Surveyed in October 1885 by J.C. Nelson, D.L.S. . . .

[1887]   Plan of Township No. 42, Range 26, West of Fourth Meridian [showing the portion of land on the Sharphead Reserve granted to the Methodist Church/indiquant la partie du terrain de la réserve Sharphead donnée à l'église méthodiste].

1898   Treaty No. 6, N.W.T. Plan of subdivision survey of Indian Reserve No. 141 in Township 42 & 43, Ranges 25 & 26, West of 4th Meridian. Surveyed by A.W. Ponton, D.L.S., June & July 1898. [2 copies]

[pre 1911]   Plan of the sub-division of Sec. 6, Township 43, Range 26, W. 4th M. Wood lot, Sharphead. J. Lestock Reid, D.L.S.

Stony No. 133A

Refer to/Consulter: **Wabamun No. 133A**

Stony No. 133B

Refer to/Consulter: **Wabamun No. 133B**

Stony No. 142, 143 & 144

1887 (1926)   Treaty No. 7, N.W.T. Plan of Methodist mission claim at Morleyville. Surveyed in Nov. 1887 by John C. Nelson, D.L.S. in charge Indn. Res. Surveys. [Additions to 1926/Additions jusqu'en 1926.]

1889   Treaty No. 7, N.W.T. Indian Reserves (Stony) Nos. 143, 142 & 144, at Morleyville. Chiefs "Jacob" "Bears Paw" & "Chiniquy". Resurveyed by John C. Nelson, D.L.S., Oct. & Nov. 1888. Approved . . . 23rd Jan., 1889. [3 copies]

1891   Plan of the Stony Indian Reserves Nos. 142, 143, 144, on Bow River at Morley, Alberta. Chiefs Bear's Paw, Jacob & Chiniquay. Surveyed by J.C. Nelson, D.L.S., 1891. . . .

1891   Treaty No. 7, N.W.T. Re-survey of Indian Reserves 142, 143, 144 for the Stony Indians on Bow River, at Morley. Chiefs "Bear's Paw", "Jacob" & "Chinniky". Chas. P. Aylen, D.L.S., Regina, Novr. 20th, 1890. Certified correct, John C. Nelson, D.L.S. in charge I.R. Surveys, Feby. 3d., 1891. [2 copies]

[1891]   [Plot of triangulation of part of Bow River in Stony Indian Reserve at Morleyville/Relevé par triangulation d'une partie de la rivière Bow dans la réserve indienne Stony, à Morleyville.]

1894   Plan showing land required for ballast pit in the Stony Indian Reserve, Township 25, Range 6, W. 5th P.M. Sd. Thos. Turnbull, D.L.S., July 20th, 1894, Winnipeg.

1902   Plan shewing survey of old trail from Canmore to Morley in Tps.: 24 & 25, Rgs.: 7, 8, 9, 10, W. of 5 M. (Stony I.R.), by A.P. Patrick, D.L.S., 1901. . . . 13th . . . December, 1902. . . .

1905 (1926)   Tr. 7. Plan showing the portions of the Stony Indian Res. No. 143 to be exchanged for a portion of the Morley Methodist mission property. Surveyed in Aug. 1905 by J. Lestock Reid, D.L.S. [Additions 1926/ Additions en 1926.]

ALBERTA

1906	[Plan showing the position of the Kananaskis Falls on the Bow River, at the mouth of the Kananaskis River./Plan indiquant l'emplacement des chutes Kananaskis sur la rivière Bow, à l'embouchure de la rivière Kananaskis.]
[1906]	[Sketch showing the Horse Shoe Falls on the Bow River in the Stony Indian Reserve./Croquis indiquant l'emplacement des chutes Horse Shoe, sur la rivière Bow, dans la réserve indienne Stony.]
[1906]	[Rough sketch showing part of the Stony Reserve situated between the Canadian Pacific Railway and the Bow River, and the portion of the reserve on the north side of the Bow River./Croquis préliminaire indiquant la partie de la réserve Stony située entre la voie ferrée du Canadian Pacifique et la rivière Bow, ainsi que la partie de la réserve située sur la rive Nord de la rivière Bow.]
1907	Topographical map showing Bow River [and Stony Indian Reserve/et la réserve indienne Stony]. Calgary Power & Transmission Co. C.H. Mitchell, C.E., Chief Engineer, Toronto, Sept. 1907.
1907	Map of Bow River in vicinity of Horse Shoe Falls, Stoney Indian Reserve, showing portion of lands required by Calgary Power & Transmission Co. . . . Toronto, April 16th, 1907. . . .
1908	Plan of 1000 acres desired by Calgary Power and Transmission Co., Stony Indian Reserve, Alberta. C.H. Mitchell, Engineer. . . Mar. 12- 1908.
1909	Calgary Land District. [Map showing the location of Stony Reserve No. 142, 143 & 144 and other reserves in the area./Carte indiquant l'emplacement de la réserve Stony nos 142, 143 & 144 et des autres réserves de la région.] Department of the Interior. . . 1909. . . .
[1909]	[Map showing disposition of land around the Stony Reserve./Carte indiquant l'utilisation des terrains situés autour de la réserve indienne Stony.]
1910	Morley Sheet, West of Fifth Meridian. Sectional map. Special edition shewing lands disposed of . . . to June 15th 1910 [and Stony Reserve No. 142, 143 and 144/et la réserve Stony nos 142, 143 et 144]. Department of the Interior, Ottawa. . . .
[1910]	[Sketch showing the location of the Stony Indian Reserve on the Bow River./Croquis indiquant l'emplacement de la réserve indienne Stony sur la rivière Bow.]
[1910]	[Map showing strip of land between the Kananaskis and Bow Rivers, north of the Canadian Pacific Railway, belonging to the Stony Indians of the Morley Reserve./Carte indiquant la bande de terre située entre les rivières Kananaskis et Bow, au nord de la voie ferrée du Canadien Pacifique, appartenant aux Indiens Assiniboines de la réserve Morley.]

[1910]   [Portion of map showing lands proposed to be set aside for Stony Indians, near the reserve at Morley, and at Kootenay Plains/Partie de carte indiquant les terrains qu'on se propose de donner aux Indiens Assiniboines, près de la réserve à Morley et sur les plaines Kootenay.]

[1910]   See/Voir: **Sarcee No. 145**

1911   Preliminary plan of Township 26, Range 7, West of the 5th Meridian [showing part of Stony Reserve and other Indian lands/indiquant une partie de la réserve Stony et d'autres terres indiennes]. To 15th September, 1911. Department of the Interior, Ottawa.

1911   Preliminary plan of Township 27, Range 7, West of the 5th Meridian [showing vacant lands near Stony Reserve/indiquant les terrains inoccupés proches de la réserve Stony]. To 15 September, 1911. Department of the Interior, Ottawa.

1912   Compiled plan of Morley Station grounds showing leases, trails, etc. Stoney I.R. R.G. Orr, 1912.

1913 [1915]   Bow River and storage surveys. . . Topographic sheet[s] . . . [showing flooded lands/indiquant les terres inondées]. Jan 1913. Department of the Interior, Canada . . . Water Power Branch. . . . [7 maps/3 copies; 7 cartes/3 copies]

[1913] [1915]   Key map of Bow River Basin above Calgary . . . shewing topographical sheets . . . illustrating lands in I.R. affected. . . . To accompany report on Power and Storage Investigations by M.C. Hendry, B.A. Sc. . . . [5 copies]

[1915]   Location of wells in the Stoney Indian Reserve.

1916   Canadian Pacific Railway, Laggan subdivision. Plan shewing land in Stoney Indian Reserve, Tp. 25, R. 7, W. 5 M., Alberta, required for ballast pit. . . . [Surveyed by/Relevé par] C.D. Brown, A.L.S. . . . 1916.

1930   Ghost-Radnor developm[ent]. . . . Plan showing land required for "reservoir site" near Morley, Alta., being portions of the Morleyville Settlement and Stony Indian Reserve . . . 1928. J.T. Carthew, D.L.S. . . . Calgary Power Company Limited . . . March 8th, 1930.

Stony No. 142B

1905   Alberta. Plan of Township 28, Range 5, west of the Fifth Meridian [showing disposition of lands near the Stony Reserve/indiquant l'utilisation des terrains proches de la réserve Stony]. . . . Department of the Interior, Ottawa, 5th July, 1905. . . .

ALBERTA

1905	Alberta. Plan of Township 29, Range 5, West of the Fifth Meridian [showing disposition of lands near the Stony Reserve/indiquant l'utilisation des terrains proches de la réserve Stony]. . . . Department of the Interior, Ottawa, 27th July, 1905. . . .
1905	Alberta. Plan of Township 27, Range 6, West of the Fifth Meridian. . . . Department of the Interior, Ottawa, 2nd August, 1905. . . . [3 copies]
1905	Alberta. Plan of Township 28, Range 6, West of the Fifth Meridian [showing disposition of lands near the Stony Reserve/indiquant l'utilisation des terrains proches de la réserve Stony]. . . . Department of the Interior, Ottawa, 8th June, 1905. . . .
1905	Alberta. Plan of Township 29, Range 6, West of the Fifth Meridian [showing disposition of lands near the Stony Reserve/indiquant l'utilisation des terrains proches de la réserve Stony]. . . . Department of the Interior, Ottawa, 28th March, 1905. . . .
1906	Alberta. Plan of Township 30, Range 6, West of the Fifth Meridian [showing disposition of lands near the Stony Reserve/indiquant l'utilisation des terrains proches de la réserve Stony]. . . . Department of the Interior, Ottawa, 15th February, 1906. . . .
1911	See/Voir: **Stony No. 142, 143 & 144**
[1914]	[Map showing land required in Township 27, Range 6, West of 5th Meridian, for the Stony Indian Reserve No. 142B/Carte indiquant les terrains nécessaires à la réserve indienne Stony n° 142B dans le canton 27, rang 6, à l'ouest du cinquième méridien.] [2 copies]
[1915]	See/Voir: **Stony No. 142, 143 & 144**

Stony No. 143

Refer to/Consulter: **Stony No. 142, 143 & 144**

Stony No. 144

Refer to/Consulter: **Stony No. 142, 143 & 144**

Stony Plain No. 135

1884	Treaty No. 6, N.W.T. Sketch showing the survey of the boundaries of an Indian Reserve for the band of Chief Tommy Le Potac. Surveyed by John C. Nelson, Dominion Land Surveyor, September 1884.
1884 (1911)	Stony Plain. Treaty No. 6, N.W.T. Plan of Indian Reserve No. 135, Chief Tommy La Potac. Surveyed in Sept. 1884 by J.C. Nelson, D.L.S. . . . in charge I.R. Surveys. [Additions 1911/Additions en 1911.]

1902   Treaty No. 6, North West Territories. Plan showing subdivision survey of the north part of the Stony Plain Indian Reserve No. 135, for which a surrender was taken from Chief Enoch's band on 20th January, 1902, comprising Sections 29, 30, 31, 32, Township 52, Range 25, and Sections 25, 26, 27, 28, 29, 32, 33, 34, 35, & 36, Township 52, Range 26, West of Fourth Meridian. Surveyed under instructions from the Superintendent General of Indian Affairs, dated Ottawa, 7th May, 1902, by A.W. Ponton, D.L.S. . . . [2 copies]

1908 (1925)   Alberta. Plan of Stony Plain Indian Reserve No. 135 in Township 52, R's. 25 and 26, W. of the 4th, showing surrendered portion. Surveyed by A.W. Ponton, D.L.S., 1902 and J.L. Reid, D.L.S., 1908. . . . [Additions 1925/Additions en 1925.]

1908 (1925)   Treaty No. 6, N.W.T. Plan of subdivision survey of part of Stony Plain Indian Reserve No. 135 in Township No. 52, Range 25, West of 4th Meridian. Surveyed by . . . J. Lestock Reid, D.L.S., 1908. Department of Indian Affairs. . . . [Additions 1925/Additions en 1925.]

1912 (1931)   Plan of subdivision for Indian purposes of unsurrendered portion of Stony Plain Indian Reserve No. 135 in Tp. 52, R. 26, W. 4th M. Treaty 6, Alberta. Certified correct, J.K. McLean, D.L.S., Ottawa, 9th February, 1912. [Additions to 1931/Additions jusqu'en 1931.]

Sturgeon Lake No. 154

1909   Plan of Sturgeon Lake Indian Reserve No. 154 and of Reserves 154A & 154B. Treaty No. 8, Alberta. J. Lestock Reid, D.L.S., March 1909.

Sturgeon Lake No. 154A

1909   See/Voir: **Sturgeon Lake No. 154.**

Sturgeon Lake No. 154B

1909   See/Voir: **Sturgeon Lake No. 154**

Sucker Creek No. 150A

1901*   Treaty No. 8, N.W.T. Plan of Sucker Creek Reserve No. 150A, situated on the south shore of Lesser Slave Lake. Surveyed for Councillor Moostoos and a portion of Chief Kinoosayos band. . . . Surveyed in September 1901 by A.W. Ponton, D.L.S.

1912 (1918)   Tr. 8. Plan showing additions made to Sucker Creek Indian Reserve No. 150A, by J.K. McLean, D.L.S. in 1912, in Tp. 74, Rgs. 14 & 15, W. 5 M., Lesser Slave Lake, Alta. . . . [Additions to 1918/Additions jusqu'en 1918.]

225388

Treaty No.8

N.W.T

PLAN of SUCKER CREEK RESERVE No. 150A

Situated on the South shore of Lesser Slave Lake

surveyed for

Councillor Moostoos and a portion of

Chief Kinoosayos band

Area 18.68 Sq. Miles

Surveyed in September
1901
by A.W.Ponton D.L.S.

BUFFALO LAKE

St. Peter's Mission

H.B. Company

Latitude 55°33'
Longitude 116°08'

LESSER SLAVE LAKE SETTLEMENT

Hay and willow

Poplar bush

Spruce and tamarac
level country.

Poplar bush

Open country along the Creek
undulating surface, rich
loam soil.

SUCKER CREEK

Poplar bush, undulating surface.
clay loam soil

Poplar, undulating, soil clay loam. Spruce and Tamarac, low level country.

LESSER SLAVE LAKE

a to b	N. 26° 33' E.	32.89
a - c	S. 20° 16' W.	137.09
c - d	N. 76° 16' W.	64.89
d - e	S. 15° 44' W.	65.00
e - f	N. 69° 52' W.	128.00
f - g	North	592.83

This Reserve has been laid out for the following
Indians, members of Chief Kinoosayos band.

Paid Annuity under Number and Names		Number in family
2	Councillor Moostoos	2
7	Okimow	7
8	Felix Estatchekoon	4
9	Alex Young	5
10	Michel Misinicunape	7
11	Bazil do	3
12	Edward do	3
21	Benjamin do	6
30	SeeKuchees	6
33	Joseph Matuskies	1
35	Alexander Moostoos	5
38	Mary Spoon	1
39	Marie Seeasapcuncchus	2
43	Joseph Keesaynees	1
46	Francois Keesaynees	1
57	Baptiste Moosoos Keesaynees	2
64	Squaxis	1
67	Mardineau	6
69	Angele Tranquille	1
70	Mary Beaver	1
72	Casimere Cardinal	5

The hay and willow swamp along
the Lake shore has been included
in the Reserve but three thousand
acres has been deducted from the
total area on account of water and
waste land.

Scale 40 Chains = 1 inch

Sucker Creek No. 150A 1901 (C 107330).

Swan River No. 150E

1912	Treaty 8. Plan of Swan River Indian Reserve No. 150E in Tps. 73 & 74, Rgs. 9 & 10, W. 5 M., showing original reserve and addition by J.K. McLean, D.L.S. in 1912, Lesser Slave Lake, Alta. . . .
1918	Edmonton, Dunvegan & B.C. Railway. Sketch showing land required for townsite purposes in Kinoosayo Indian Reserve No. 150E, Alta. Office of Chief Engineer, Edmonton, Alta., Dec. 27th, 1918.
1945	Plan showing addition to Kinuso, being part of Indian Reserve No. 150E in Tp. 73, R. 10, W. 5th M. C.B. Atkins, A.L.S., 1945. . . .
1953 (1954)	Plan of parcels 1, 2, 3, 4, 5, 6, 7, 8, 9 and 10 in Sections 15, 14, 22 and 23, Tp. 73, R. 10, W. of 5th M. in Swan River I.R. No. 150E, Alberta. Compiled from official surveys by G. Palsen, D. & A.L.S., 9th October, 1951. . . . 18th March, 1953. Drawn by S.K. [Additions 1954/Additions en 1954.]

Tall Cree No. 173

1915 (1924)	Treaty 8. Plan of Tall Cree Indian Reserves No. 173 and 173A situate in Tps. 102-103, R. 9, and 104, R. 10, W. 5 Mer., Province of Alberta, 1915. . . . Surveyed by P.M.H. LeBlanc, D.L.S. . . . [Additions 1924/Additions en 1924.]

Tall Cree No. 173A

1915 (1924)	See/Voir: **Tall Cree No. 173**

Taviah Moosewah 151C

1905 (1928)	See/Voir: **Peace River Crossing No. 151**
1916 (1929)	Alberta. Plan of Township 82, Range 24, West of the Fifth Meridian [showing surrendered Reserves No. 151C and 151D and other reserves in the area/indiquant les réserves cédées nos 151C et 151D et les autres réserves de la région]. Department of the Interior, Ottawa, 23rd May, 1916. . . . [Additions 1929/Additions en 1929.]

Timber Limit A

Refer to/Consulter: **Blood No. 148A**

Timber Limit B

Refer to/Consulter: **Peigan (Timber Limit) No. 147B**

Timber Limit C

Refer to/Consulter: **Blackfoot Timber Limit No. 146C**

ALBERTA

Tommy LePotac No. 135

      Refer to/Consulter: **Stony Plain No. 135**

Unipouheos No. 121

1885	Plan, Indian Reserve. . . No. 121, Treaty No. 6, North Saskatchewan River, Chief Oo nee pow o hay oo, shewing allerations [sic] in boundaries, 1884. Certified correct, A.W. Ponton, Dominion Land Surveyor, Indian Office, Regina, Assa., March 19th, 1885. Revised 14-8-85. . . .
[1904]	See/Voir: **Kehiwin No. 123**
1905	Plan of resurvey of Indian Reserve No. 121. Treaty No. 6. J. Lestock Reid, D.L.S., January 11th, 1905.
1907	Treaty 6. Plan showing surrendered portion of Frog Lake Indian Reserve No. 121 in exchange for the Fishing Station I.R. No. 121A on the south shore of Frog Lake and adjacent to said I.R. No. 121, Sask. Surveyed . . . summer season 1907, J. Lestock Reid, D.L.S.
1922	Sketch showing position of cemetery containing graves of men killed in Frog Lake massacre, 1885, and the position of buildings burned by the Indians, 1885. N.E. 1/4 Sec. 10, Tp. 56, Rg. 3, W. 4th Mer. S.L. Evans, D.L.S., 1922. . . .

Unipouheos No. 121A

      Refer to/Consulter: **Fishing Station No. 121A**

Utikoomak Lake No. 155

1909 (1910)	Plan of Utikuma Indian Reserve No. 155. Treaty No. 8, Alberta. J. Lestock Reid, D.L.S., March 1909. [Additions 1910/Additions en 1910.]

Utikoomak Lake No. 155A

1909	Plan of Utikuma Indian Reserve No. 155A. Treaty No. 8, Alberta. J. Lestock Reid, D.L.S., March 1909.

Utikoomak Lake No. 155B

1909	Plan of Utikuma Lake Indian Reserve No. 155B. Treaty No. 8, Alberta. J. Lestock Reid, D.L.S., March 1909.

Wabamun No. 133

      Refer to/Consulter: **Alexis No. 133**

Wabamun No. 133A

1891 (1892)	Treaty No. 6, North-West Territories. Survey of the boundaries of Indian Reserves (Stony) Nos. 133a & 133b at White Whale or Mirror (Wabamun) Lake for the band of Chief "Alexis". . . . Surveyed in Nov. & Dec. 1891 by John C. Nelson, D.L.S. in charge of Indian Reserve Surveys. [Additions 1892/Additions en 1892.]
1906 (1936)	Treaty No. 6, N.W.T. Survey of the boundaries of Indian Reserve (Stony) No. 133a at White Whale or Wabamun Lake. Resurveyed by J.K. McLean, D.L.S., 1906. W.R.W., Dec. 22nd, 1906. . . . [Additions to 1936/Additions jusqu'en 1936.]
1909	Plan of Methodist mission claim in Indian Reserve No. 133A at Whitewhale Lake, Province of Alberta. Certified correct, J.K. McLean, D.L.S., November 13th, 1909.
1911	Plan of townplot of Duffield, Wabamun Indian Reserve No. 133A. Surveyed by J.K. McLean, D.L.S., 1911. . . . [2 copies]
1911	Tr. No. 6. Plan of portion of Wabamun Indian Reserve No. 133A surrendered for sale. Surveyed by J.K. McLean, D.L.S., 1911. . . . [3 copies]
1911	Plan of the townplot of Duffield in Secs. 26, 27, 34 & 35, Tp. 52, Rge. 3 W. 5 M., Wabamun Indian Reserve No. 133A, Alberta. Surveyed by J.K. McLean, D.L.S., 1911. . . . Traced, F.T.S. . . . [2 copies]

Wabamun No. 133B

1891 (1892)	See/Voir: **Wabamun No. 133A**
1906 (1936)	See/Voir: **Wabamun No. 133A**
1906 (1953)	Treaty 6. Plan of the townplot of Wabamun on Indian Reserve No. 133B at the east end of Wabamun (White Whale) Lake, Alberta. Surveyed by J.K. McLean, D.L.S., 1906. W.R. White, Nov. 1906. . . . [Additions to 1953/Additions jusqu'en 1953.]
1912	Plan of the townplot of Wabamun on Indian Reserve No. 133B at the east end of Wabamun "(White Whale)" Lake, Alberta. Surveyed in 1906 by J.K. McLean, D.L.S. . . . R.G. Orr, 1912. [2 copies]

Wabasca No. 166

1913 (1925)	Treaty 8. Plan of Indian Reserves No. 166, 166A and 166B for the Lake Wabiskaw band of Cree Indians in Tps. 79 and 80, Ranges 22, 23, 24, 25 and 26, West of 4th M., Alberta, as surveyed by I.J. Steele, D.L.S., 1913. I.J. Steele, September 16th, 1913. [Additions to 1925/Additions jusqu'en 1925.]

ALBERTA

Wabasca No. 166A

1913 (1925)   See/Voir: **Wabasca No. 166**

Wabasca No. 166B

1913 (1925)   See/Voir: **Wabasca No. 166**

Wabasca No. 166C

1913 (1930)   Treaty 8. Plan of Indian Reserve No. 166C for a part of the band of Cree Indians at Lake Wabiskaw, Alberta. I.J. Steele, Sept. 10th, 1913. [Additions 1930/Additions en 1930.]

Wahsatenow No. 126

Refer to/Consulter: **Bear's Ears No. 126**

White Fish Lake No. 128

1886   Plan of Wesleyan mission on White-Fish I.R. No. 128, Alberta. Surveyed by J.C. Nelson, D.L.S., 1886. (Tr.6.)

1886 (1945)   Treaty No. 6, N.W.T. Survey of Indian Reserve No. 128 at Whitefish Lake for the band of Chief Pakan. . . . Surveyed in August & September 1886 by John C. Nelson, D.L.S. in charge Indn. Res. Surveys. . . . [Additions to 1945/Additions jusqu'en 1945.]

[1887]   Plan of Township No. 62, Range 13, West of Fourth Meridian [showing the portion of land on the White Fish Lake Reserve granted to the Wesleyan mission, Methodist Church/indiquant la partie des terrains de la réserve White Fish Lake donnée à la mission wesleyenne de l'Église méthodiste.]

White Fish Lake No. 155

Refer to/Consulter: **Utikoomak Lake No. 155**

White Fish Lake No. 155A

Refer to/Consulter: **Utikoomak Lake No. 155A**

White Fish Lake No. 155B

Refer to/Consulter: **Utikoomak Lake No. 155B**

White Whale Lake No. 133A

Refer to/Consulter: **Wabamun No. 133A**

White Whale Lake No. 133B

Refer to/Consulter: **Wabamun No. 133B**

William McKenzie No. 151K

1905 (1928)   Plan of Indian Reserve at Little Prairie, No. 151K, for William McKenzie, No. 11, Peace River Landing band. Treaty No. 8. Surveyed by J. Lestock Reid, D.L.S., 1905. [Additions to 1928/Additions jusqu'en 1928.]

1929   Plan of subdivision of William McKenzie I.R No. 151K in Tp. 81, Rge. 19, W. 5th Mer., Alberta, 1929. Surveyed by W. Zinkan, D.L.S. . . . [2 copies]

SASKATCHEWAN — GENERAL MAPS/
SASKATCHEWAN — CARTES GÉNÉRALES

[1884]   [Plan showing the allotment of land to the Manitoba and North
              Western Railway/Plan indiquant les terrains donnés à la *Manitoba
              and North Western Railway*.]

1929   Saskatchewan, 1929 [showing Indian reserves and lands admin-
              istered by Indian Affairs/indiquant les réserves indiennes et les
              terrains gérés par le ministère des Affaires indiennes.] Department of
              the Interior, Canada . . . Natural Resources Intelligence Service.
              . . . Compiled & engraved at the Chief Geographer's Office.

SASKATCHEWAN — AGENCIES/
SASKATCHEWAN — AGENCES

Battleford

1909   Battleford Land District. [Map showing location of Reserve No. 112A,
              held in common by the Thunderchild and Moosomin bands, and other
              reserves in the area/Carte indiquant l'emplacement de la réserve n°
              112A, appartenant en commun aux bandes Thunderchild et
              Moosomin, ainsi que celui d'autres réserves de la région.] Department
              of the Interior . . . 1909.

[1909]   [Map showing location of proposed new reserve for the Moosomin
              band, at Murray Lake, and other reserves in the area/Carte indiquant
              l'emplacement de la nouvelle réserve qu'on se propose de donner à la
              bande Moosomin, à Murray Lake, et celui d'autres réserves de la
              région.]

1910   Battleford Land District. [Map showing present and proposed timber
              lands for Thunderchild's band, and other reserves in the area/Carte
              indiquant les concessions forestières appartenant présentement à la
              bande Thunderchild et celles qu'on se propose de lui donner ainsi que
              d'autres réserves de la région.] Department of the Interior . . .
              1910. . . .

1911   Battleford Land District. [Map showing timber lands for Thunder-
              child's band, and other reserves in the area/Carte indiquant les
              concessions forestières de la bande Thunderchild et d'autres réserves
              de la région.] Department of the Interior . . . 1911. . . .

1912 [1915]   Saskatchewan. Battleford Sheet, West of Third Meridian. Sectional
              map [showing lands required for Thunderchild and Moosomin bands,
              and other reserves in the area/indiquant les terrains demandés pour
              les bandes Thunderchild et Moosomin, ainsi que d'autres réserves de
              la région]. Revised to the 29th August, 1912. . . .

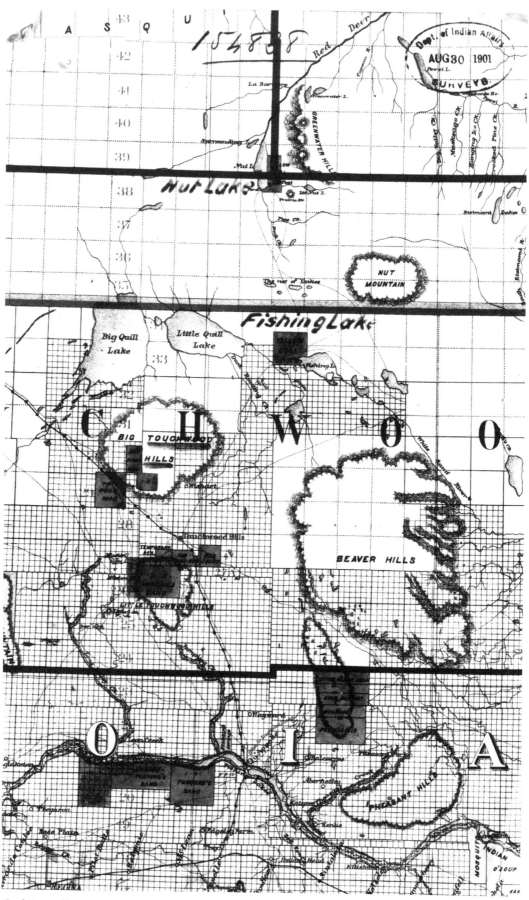

Qu'Appelle [1901] (NMC 12469).

Qu'Appelle

1884 Sectional Map No. 1 of Manitoba and Northwestern Railway of Canada. Land grants [showing the location of Piapot Reserve and other reserves in the area/indiquant l'emplacement de la réserve Piapot et d'autres réserves de la région]. . . . Map accompanying . . . letter of 19th Sept., 1884.

1884 Sectional map No. 2 of Canadian Pacific Railway lands, from Second to Third Initial Meridian. Map . . . showing position of Piapots old Reserve, [new Reserve and other reserves in the area/de la nouvelle réserve et des autres réserves de la région], accompanying letter of 20th Oct., 1884. W.K. Jandowski, Draughtsman. . . .

[1901]* [Plan showing the location of Indian reserves in the Qu'Appelle Agency/Plan indiquant l'emplacement des réserves indiennes dans l'agence Qu'Appelle.]

SASKATCHEWAN - RESERVES AND SETTLEMENTS/
SASKATCHEWAN - RÉSERVES ET AGGLOMÉRATIONS

Ahtahkakoop No. 104

Refer to/Consulter: **Atakakup No. 104**

Amisk Lake No. 184

1919 (1930)   Treaty 6. Plan of Amisk Lake Indian Reserve No. 184 for Pelican
                 Narrows band. Surveyed by W.R. White, O. & D.L.S., July 1919.
                 [Additions 1930/Additions en 1930.]

Assiniboine No. 76

1883   Treaty No. 4, N.W.T. Indian Head Reserve . . . John C. Nelson, D.L.S.,
                 Ottawa, Nov. 2nd, 1883.

1884   See/Voir: **Piapot No. 75**

1885   Treaty No. 4, N.W.T. Indian Reserve No. 76 at Indian-Head. Chief
                 "The Man Who Took The Goat". . . . Surveyed in June 1885 by . . .
                 John C. Nelson, D.L.S. . . .

1889   Treaty No. 4, N.W.T. Indian Reserve No. 76, Chief "The Man Who
                 Took The Goat", Indian-Head-Hills. Surveyed by John C. Nelson,
                 D.L.S., June 1885. Approved . . . 23rd Jan., 1889.

1890   Treaty No. 4, North West Territories. Subdivision survey of part of
                 Indian Reserve No. 76 at Indian Head. Band of Chief "The-Man-Who-
                 Took-The-Goat". Surveyed in Sept. & Oct. 1890 by John C. Nelson,
                 D.L.S. in charge of Indian Reserve Surveys.

1901 (1952)   Plan of Assiniboine Indian Reserve No. 76. Treaty No. 4. Township 15
                 & 16, Range 11 & 12, West 2nd M. J. Lestock Reid, D.L.S., August-Sept.
                 1901. [Additions to 1952/Additions jusqu'en 1952.]

[1904]   . . . Rough sketch of [Assiniboine] Reserve [showing sections pro-
                 posed to be sold/indiquant les sections qu'on se propose de vendre].

1905   Plan of subdivision of part of Assiniboine Indian Reserve No. 76 in
                 Township 15, Ranges 11 and 12, W. 2nd M. Surveyed by J.K. McLean,
                 D.L.S., Aug. and Sept. 1905. . . . [2 copies]

1906   Indian Reserve (Assiniboine) No. 76. Sketch showing survey of road
                 diversions in Sections 2, 12, 13, 23, 24 & 25, Tp. 15, R. 11, -2 & in
                 Section 19, Tp. 15, R. 10, -2. Survey . . . 06.

1914 (1925)   Plan of subdivision of the surrendered portion of Assinaboine [sic]
                 Indian Reserve No. 76, Saskatchewan. Surveyed by J.K. McLean,
                 D.L.S., 1905 . . . A.C. Garner, D.L.S., 1907 . . . W.T. Thompson,
                 D.T.S., 1902 . . . E.W. Murray, S. & D.L.S., 1914. G.P. 12th May, 1925.

Atakakup No. 104

1891   Treaty No. 6, N.W.T. Subdivision survey of part of Indian Reserve No. 104 into 40 acre lots. Chief Ahtahkakoop. Surveyed in Sept. & Octo. 1891 by A.W. Ponton, D.L.S. . . .

1906   Treaty No. 6. Plan of re-survey of Indian Reserve No. 104, "Ahtahkahkoop" of "Sandy Lake". Boundaries re run summer season 1906 by J. Lestock Reid, D.L.S.

Battleford Industrial School

1911   Grand Trunk Pacific Branch Lines Company, Battleford Branch. Located line through Battleford Indian Industrial School Reserve . . . District of West Saskatchewan, Province of Saskatchewan. Office of Chief Engineer . . . 1911. . . . [5 copies]

1911   Grand Truck Pacific Branch Lines Co., Battleford Branch. Right of way required through Battleford Indian Industrial School Reserve, N.W. 1/4 Sec. 17, T. 43, R. 16, W. 3rd Mer., District of West Saskatchewan, Province of Saskatchewan. Office of Chief Engineer, 21st April, 1911, J.A. McC. . . . [2 copies]

[1911]   [Plan showing where the right of way is required through Battleford Industrial School Reserve by the Grand Trunk Pacific Branch Lines Co./Plan indiquant où la *Grand Trunk Pacific Branch Lines Co.* demande un droit de passage sur les terrains de la réserve de l'école industrielle Battleford.

Beardy No. 97 & Okemasis No. 96

1887 (1934)   Treaty No. 6, N.W.T. Survey of Indian Reserve No. 97—should be 96 and 97—at Duck Lake for the bands of Chiefs Beardy & Ogemasis. . . . Surveyed in August 1887 by John C. Nelson, D.L.S. in charge Indian Res. Surveys. [Additions 1934/Additions en 1934.]

1889   Treaty No. 6, N.W.T. Subdivision survey of part of Indian Reserves Nos. 96 & 97, Chiefs Okemasis & Beardy, at Duck Lake. Surveyed in August 1889 by A.W. Ponton, D.L.S. . . .

[1909]   Plan of resurvey of the Okemasis and Beardy Indian Reserve No. 96 & 97. Treaty No. 6. J. Lestock Reid, D.L.S.

1916   Boundaries of the first system of survey in the vicinity of Prince Albert, Province of Saskatchewan, R.L.S., 28-6-16. . . .

1923 (1940)   Treaty 6. Plan of Duck Lake battlefield in Okemasis and Beardy Indian Reserves 96 and 97, Saskachewan. Surveyed 1922. Donald F. Robertson, Chief Surveyor, Dept. of Indian Affairs. G.P., 17th Feb., 1923. [Additions 1940/Additions en 1940.]

SASKATCHEWAN

Big Head No. 124

1915 (1919)   Treaty 6. Plan of Big Head Indian Reserve No. 124 situate at Lac des Iles for the Indians of the Cree band. Surveyed by I.J. Steele, D.L.S., 1912 and Donald F. Robertson, D.L.S., 1915. . . . [Additions to 1919/ Additions jusqu'en 1919.]

Big River No. 118

1899 (1908)   Treaty No. 6, N.W.T. Plan of Indian Reserve No. 118 on Big River and Whitefish Lake for Indians of Big River, Whitefish, Stony and Pelican Lakes. Surveyed in July and Augt. 1898 by T.D. Green, D.L.S. Department of Indian Affairs, Ottawa, Ont. 4th May, 1899. . . . [Additions 1908/Additions en 1908.]

1908   Plan, surrendered portion of Big River Indian Reserve No. 118. Treaty No. 6, Saskatchewan. J. Lestock Reid, D.L.S., February 1908.

Big River No. 118A

1908 (1939)   . . . Plan, Indian Reserve No. 118A. Addition for Big River Indians of Reserve No. 118. Treaty 6, Saskatehewan [sic]. Surveyed by J. Lestock Reid, D.L.S., February 3rd, 1908. [Additions to 1939/ Additions jusqu'en 1939.]

1919   Sketch plan of Carlton to Green Lake trail through I.R. 118A, Tp. 52-8-3. Surveyed by J. Bourgeois, D.L.S., 1888. D.H.C. 16-7-19, J.P.M.

[1919]   Big River I.R. 118A, Saskatchewan. Plan of Township 52, Range 8, Range 7, West of the Third. . . . Department of the Interior, Ottawa, 17th December, 191[9]. . . .

Birch Portage No. 184A

1919 (1930)   Treaty 6. Plan of Birch Portage Indian Reserve No. 184-A for Pelican Narrows band, Sask. Surveyed by W.R. White, July 1919. [Additions 1930/Additions en 1930.]

Birch River No. 27

1883 (1918)   Plan of Birch River Indian Reserve south of the Great Saskatchewan River. . . . Treaty 5, 1882. W.A. Austin, C.E., D.L. Surveyor. Glo'ster, March 1883. [Additions 1918/Additions en 1918.]

Broadview No. 72

Refer to/Consulter: **Kahkewistahaw No. 72**

Budd's Point No. 20D

1926 (1930)   Treaty 5. Plan of Budds Point I.R. No. 20D at Cumberland Lake, Sask. Surveyed by G.H. Herriot, D.L.S., 1926. [Additions 1930/Additions en 1930.]

Canoe Lake No. 165

1912 (1930)   Tr. 10. Plan of part of Canoe Lake Indian Reserve No. 165, Province of Saskatchewan. Surveyed by Donald F. Robertson, D.L.S., 15th Aug., 1912. [Additions 1930/Additions en 1930.]

Canoe Lake No. 165A

1912 (1930)   Tr. 10. Plan of part of Canoe Lake Indian Reserve No. 165A . . . S.W. shore Canoe Lake. Surveyed by: — Donald F. Robertson, D.L.S., 15th Aug., 1912. [Additions 1930/Additions en 1930.]

Canoe Lake No. 165B

1912 (1930)   Plan of part of Canoe Lake Indian Reserve No. 165 . . . B. Try. 10. Surveyed by Donald F. Robertson, D.L.S., 15th Aug., 1912. [Additions 1930/Additions en 1930.]

Carrot River No. 27A

1884 (1895)   See/Voir: **Pas Mountain No. 30**

1912 (1951)   Tr. 5. Plan of Indian Reserve No. 27A adjoining the 2nd Meridian and the Carrot River; being part of the land given The Pas band in exchange for the Birch River Reserve No. 27, surrendered. Surveyed and certified by H.B. Proudfoot, January 1912, D.L. Surveyor. . . . [Additions 1951/Additions en 1951.]

Carrot River No. 28

Refer to/Consulter: **Shoal Lake No. 28**

Carrot River No. 28A

Refer to/Consulter: **Shoal Lake No. 28A**

Carrot River No. 29A

1894 (1908)   Treaty No. 5, Saskatchewan. Red Earth [corrected to/corrigé pour] Carrot River Indian Reserve No. 29A, situated on the Carrot River about ten miles west from Shoal Lake and about sixty miles west from "The Pas". Surveyed for the Red Earth band of Indians, a branch of The Pas Mountain band. This reserve is substituted for the abandoned reserve at Flute River. Surveyed by S. Bray, C.E., D.L.S., Asst. Chief Surveyor, Dept. of Indian Affairs, Dec. 8th, 1894. [Additions 1908/Additions en 1908.]

1911   See/Voir: **Red Earth No. 29**

Carrot River No. 100A

Refer to/Consulter: **Cumberland No. 100A**

SASKATCHEWAN

Carry the Kettle No. 76

      Refer to/Consulter: **Assiniboine No. 76**

Chacachas No. 71

      Refer to/Consulter: **Ochapowace No. 71**

Chacastapasin No. 98

1892   [Plan showing northeastern corner of Chacastapasin Reserve No. 98/Plan indiquant l'extrémité nord-est de la réserve Chacastapasin n° 98.] J.C.U., 16/4/92.

1898   Treaty No. 6, N.W.T. Plan of the subdivision survey of the Chacastapasin Indian Reserve No. 98 situated in Townships 46A and 47A, Ranges 25 and 26, W. of 2nd I.M. Ottawa, Ont., 26th Oct., 1898. Certified correct, T.D. Green, D.L.S. . . . [2 copies]

1908   [Map showing Chacastapasin Reserve No. 98 in the vicinity of Sugar and Birch Islands in the South Saskatchewan River/Carte indiquant l'emplacement de la réserve Chacastapasin n° 98 dans le voisinage des îles Sugar et Birch, sur la rivière South Saskatchewan.] Copy . . . 5/11/08.

Churchill Lake No. 193A

1923 (1930)   Treaty 10. Plan of Churchill Lake I.R. No. 193A for the Chipewyan Indians of the Peter Pond Lake band, Sask. Surveyed by W.A.A. McMaster, D.L.S., 1923. [Additions 1930/Additions en 1930.]

Cote No. 64

1889   Treaty No. 4, N.W.T. Indian Reserve No. 64, Chief "Gabriel Cote". Surveyed by William Wagner, D.L.S., January 1877. Approved . . . Jany. 23rd, 1889.

1893   Sketch shewing parcel of land surveyed for Crow Stand Presbyterian Boarding School, Reserve of Chief Coté. Surveyed in October 1893 by John C. Nelson, D.L.S. in charge Indian Reserve Surveys. . . . Treaty 4.

1897 (1902)   Map of Indian Reserves Nos. 64-66, Swan River Agency, Treaty No. 4, as surveyed for the bands of Chiefs Coté and Kesickonse [corrected to /corrigé pour] Keeseekoose. . . . Certified correct, A.W. Ponton, D.L.S. in charge of Indian Reserve Surveys, Man. & N.W.T. Regina, 19th February, 1897. [Additions to 1902/Additions jusqu'en 1902.]

1904   Kamsack, a subdivision of part of Gabriel Coté Indian Reserve No. 64, Assiniboia. . . . R.M.O., Nov. 16/04. [2 copies]

1906   Plan of the subdivision of the surrendered portion of the Coté Indian Reserve No. 64, Saskatchewan. Surveyed by J. Lestock Reid, D.L.S., 1906. . . . [4 copies]

1907 (1933)   Plan of subdivision of Coté Indian Reserve No. 64 and showing surrendered portion in red. Treaty No. 4. Surveyed 1906. J. Lestock Reid, D.L.S., December 1907. [Additions to 1933/Additions jusqu'en 1933.]

1908   Addition to Kamsack, a subdivision of part of Gabriel Cote Indian Reserve No. 64, Saskatchewan. [Surveyed by/Relevé par] George Bartlett Bemister, Dominion Land Surveyor . . . 1908. . . .

[1908]   [Three plans of parts of Township 30, Range 32, West of First Meridian, in surrendered portion of Gabriel Cote Indian Reserve/ Trois plans des parties du canton n° 30, rang n° 32, à l'ouest du premier méridien, dans le secteur cédé de la réserve indienne Gabriel Coté.]

[1908]   Sketch of part of Coté Indian Reserve, Saskatchewan [near Kamsack/ près de Kamsack].

[1909]   Gabriel Cote Indian Reserve [showing lands to be added to McAuley's homestead and lands to be transferred to the Indian Department/indi-quant les terrains à ajouter à l'exploitation agricole McAuley et les terrains à transférer au ministère des Affaires indiennes].

[1910]   [Three plans showing survey of north boundary of Kamsack, Cote Indian Reserve No. 64./Trois plans indiquant le levé de l'extrémité nord de Kamsack, dans la réserve indienne Coté n° 64.]

[1910]   [Rough sketch showing a fraction of Section 29, Township 30, Range 34, West of 1st Meridian, lying north of the Assiniboine River, belonging to the Cote Reserve/Croquis préliminaire indiquant une partie de la section n° 29, canton n° 30, rang n° 34, à l'ouest du premier méridien, se trouvant au nord de la rivière Assiniboine et appartenant à la réserve Cote.]

[post 1911]   Compiled plan. Kamsack: A subdivision of part of the S.E. Sec. 3, Twp. 30, Rge. 32, W. P.M., N.W. Sec. 34 & N.W. Sec. 35, Twp. 29, Rge. 32, W. P.M. (Gabriel Coté Indian Reserve No. 64), Saskatchewan.

1912   Plan of north limits of blocks I, II, IX, XII and XIII, Kamsack, Sections 34 and 35, Township 29, Range 32, W. P.M., Saskatchewan. . . . Winnipeg, 14th August, 1912, G.B. Bemister, D.L.S. . . .

[1912]   [North limits of/Limites septentrionales de] Kamsack.

1913   Plan of Cote Indian Reserve No. 64 showing the portion surrendered for sale 20th Nov., 1913. - as surveyed by H.K. Moberly, D.L.S. Tr. No. 4 Sask.

1913	Tr. 4. Plan of survey of park lots in E. 1/2 of N.W. 1/4 of Sec. 35, Tp. 29, R. 32, W. Pr., being in the surrendered portion of Coté I.R. No. 64, Saskatchewan. Surveyed by Donald F. Robertson, D.L.S., 1913. . . .
1913 (1916)	Amended plan of north limits of Blocks I, II, IX, XII and XIII, Kamsack, part of Secs. 34 and 35, Tp. 29, Rge. 32, W. P.M., amending regd. plans no. I.1224, No. N336, No. S.3319, Saskatchewan. . . . [Surveyed by] George Bartlett Bemister . . . Dominion Land Surveyor . . . 1913. . . . [Additions to 1916/Additions jusqu'en 1916.]
1914	Addition to Kamsack, a subdivision of part of W. 1/2, N.W. 1/4, Sec. 35, Tp. 29, R. 32, W. P.M., Saskatchewan. Surveyed by A.S. Weekes, Saskatchewan Land Surveyor. Approved, Duncan C. Scott. . . . Ottawa, Mar. 23rd, 1914. . . .
1914 (1944)	Tr. 4, Sask. Plan of Cote Indian Reserve No. 64, showing also portions surrendered for sale in 1907 and in 1913 and the portion exchanged with the Dept. of the Interior. Compiled from surveys by J. Lestock Reid, D.L.S., 1906 and H.K. Moberly, D.L.S., 1914. . . . [Additions to 1944/Additions jusqu'en 1944.]
[1915]	Kamsack, a subdivision of part of Gabriel Côté I.R. No. 64, Saskatchewan. Canadian Northern Railway System. . . .
1917	Plan showing survey of cemetery situated in S.W. ¼ Sec. 11, Twp. 30, Rge. 32, W. P.M. . . . [Surveyed by/Relevé par] H.K. Moberly, Saskatchewan Land Surveyor. . . 30th. . . November, 1917.

Cowessess No. 73

1881	See/Voir: **Ochapowace No. 71**
1889	See/Voir: **Kahkewistahaw No. 72**
[1889]	Diagram showing subdivision of a section, supposed to be Sec. 2, Tp. No. 17, Ra. 6. [2 copies]
1890	Treaty No. 4, North West Territories. Subdivision survey of part of Indian Reserve No. 73, band of Chief "Cowessess". Surveyed in Augt. & Sept. 1890 by John C. Nelson, D.L.S. in charge of Indian Reserve Surveys.
1890	Plan of the south west corner of Indian Reserve No. 73, band of Chief "O-Soup", showing the position of the road-bed of the Canadian Pacific Railway. Surveyed in Sept. 1890 by John C. Nelson, D.L.S.
1907	Plan of Township No. 17, Range 6, West of 2nd Meridian, within the Cowessess Indian Reserve No. 73 near Broadview, Sask. Surveyed in 1907 by J. Lestock Reid, D.L.S. . . . [2 copies]
1909	Plan of Cowessess Boarding School lands surrendered 1908 in Cowessess Indian Reserve No. 73, Province of Saskatchewan. Certified correct, Ottawa, Nov. 8th, 1909. J.K. McLean, D.L.S.

Crooked Lake No. 73

Refer to/Consulter: **Cowessess No. 73**

Crooked Lake No. 74

Refer to/Consulter: **Sakimay No. 74**

Cumberland No. 20

1883 (1930)*   Plan of part of Cumberland Indian Reserve shewing Chief's Island and part of Cumberland Island. Gloucester, March 1883. W.A. Austin, C.E., D.L. Sur. Treaty 5, 1882. [Additions 1930/Additions en 1930.]

1911   Plan of Cumberland House Settlement and the surrendered portion of the Cumberland Indian Reserve No. 20, Province of Saskatchewan. Compiled from official surveys by J.F. Richard, D.L.S., 3rd August, 1906. Department of the Interior, Ottawa, 8th November, 1911. [2 copies]

Cumberland No. 100A

1887   Treaty No. 6, N.W.T. Survey of Indian Reserve No. 100A (for Indians of the Cumberland District) at Carrot River. . . . Surveyed in July & August 1887 by John C. Nelson, D.L.S. in charge of Indian Res. Surveys. . . .

[1889]   See/Voir: **Fishing Lake No. 89**

1902 (1916)   See/Voir: **James Smith No. 100**

1903   See/Voir: **James Smith No. 100**

1903   Plan showing subdivision of portion of Indian Reserve No. 100A, Township 46, Range 20, W. 2nd M. Treaty No. 6, N.W.T. J. Lestock Reid, D.L.S., February 1903. [2 copies]

1905   Plan of addition to I.R. No. 100A. Treaty No. 6. J. Lestock Reid, D.L.S., January 1905.

1914   Plan of Township 46, Range 20, West of the Second Meridian, being part of Indian Reserve No. 100A, surrendered and sold. J.A. Côté, Dominion Land Surveyor. Resurvey under instructions from the Department of Indian Affairs dated April 21st, 1914.

1914   Plan of southern portion of Cumberland Indian Reserve No. 100-A, surrendered 24th July, 1902, being a portion of Township 46, R. 20., W. 2 M. Resurveyed by J.A. Côté, D.L.S., 1914. . . .

Cumberland House No. 20A

Refer to/Consulter: **Pine Bluff No. 20A**

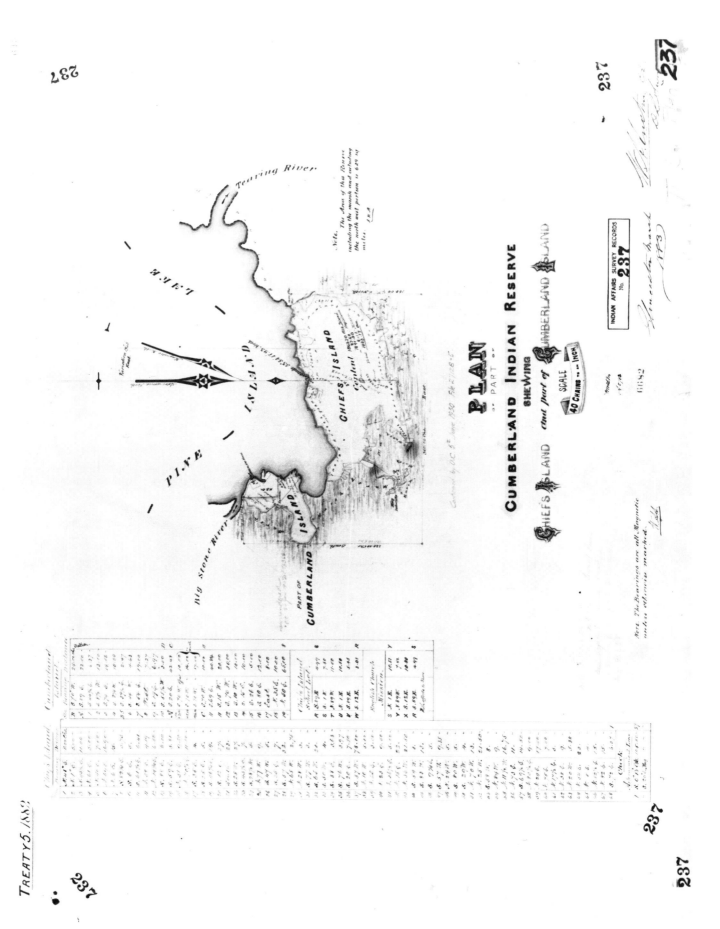

TREATY 5. 1882.

Cumberland No. 20 1883 (1930) (C 107323).

Day Star No. 87

1881	Sketch showing reserve for Day Star's band in Touchwood Hills. Touchwood Hills, Oct. 29th, 1881, J.C. Nelson, D.L.S. . . . [Sheet/Feuille] E.
1881 (1888)	Treaty No. 4, N.W.T. Survey of Indian Reservation No. 87 for the band of Chief Day Star in Big Touchwood Hills. . . . Surveyed in Oct. 1881 by J.C. Nelson, D.L.S. . . . [Additions 1888/Additions en 1888.]
1888 (1892)	Treaty No. 4, N.W.T. Plan showing the part added to the easterly side of Indian Reserve No. 87 in Big Touchwood Hills. Band of Chief "Day Star". Surveyed in 1888 by John C. Nelson, D.L.S. in charge of Indian Reserve Surveys. . . . [Additions to 1892/Additions jusqu'en 1892.]
1900	Treaty No. 4, N.W.T. Plan of resurvey of Day-Star's [corrected to/corrigé pour] Day-Star Indian Reserve No. 87. Surveyed by J. Lestock Reid, D.L.S., October 1900. . . .

Dipper Rapids No. 192C

1923 (1930)	Treaty 10. Plan of Dipper Rapids. I.R. No. 192C, Sask. for the Chipewyan band of Indians in the Ile-a-la-Crosse District. Surveyed by W.A.A. McMaster, D.L.S., 1923. [Additions 1930/Additions en 1930.]

Duck Lake

Refer to/Consulter: **Beardy No 97 & Okemasis No. 96**

Elak Dase No. 192A

1923 (1930)	Treaty 10. Plan of Elak Dase I.R. No. 192A, Sask., for the Chipewyan band of Indians in the Ile-a-la-Crosse District. Surveyed by W.A.A. McMaster, D.L.S., 1923 [Additions 1930/Additions en 1930.]

File Hill No. 81

Refer to/Consulter: **Peepeekisis No. 81**

File Hill No. 82

Refer to/Consulter: **Okanese No. 82**

File Hill No. 83

Refer to/Consulter: **Star Blanket No. 83**

File Hill No. 84

Refer to/Consulter: **Little Black Bear No. 84**

SASKATCHEWAN

Fishing Lake No. 89

1881	Sketch showing reserve for part of Yellow Quill band at Fishing Lake, N.W.T. Fishing Lake, 29th Sepr., 1881. J.C. Nelson, D.L.S. . . . [Sheet/Feuille] D.
1887	Treaty No. 4, N.W.T. Survey of Indian Reserve No. 89 at Fishing Lake for the band of Chief Yellow Quill. . . . Surveyed in September 1881 by John C. Nelson, D.L.S. . . . Examined . . . 1887.
1889	Treaty No. 4, N.W.T. Indian Reserve No. 89 at Fishing Lake. For part of the band of Chief "Yellow Quill". Surveyed in 1881 by John C. Nelson, D.L.S. Approved . . . 23rd Jan., 1889.
[1889]	[Plan showing a proposed reserve for the Fort Pelly Indians on Lake Winnipegosis, and other resrves in the area/Plan indiquant la réserve qu'on se propose de constituer à l'intention des indiens de Fort Pelly sur le lac Winnipegosis, et d'autres réserves de la région.]
1903	Plan showing Fishing Lake Indian Reserve No. 89 in Tp. 33 & 34, R. 12 & 13, W. 2nd M. Treaty No. 4, N.W.T. J. Lestock Reid, February 1903.
1909	Plan of subdivision of surrendered portion of Fishing Lake I.R. No. 89, being part of Tp. 33 and 34, Rs. 12 and 13, W. of 2nd M., Saskatchewan. Surveyed by J. Lestock Reid, D.L.S., 1908. R.G. Orr, '09. [2 copies]
1909 (1926)	Plan of subdivision of surrendered portion of Indian Reserve No. 89, Saskatchewan. Treaty No. 5 [corrected to/corrigé pour] 4. J. Lestock Reid, D.L.S., January 22nd, 1909. [Additions 1926/Additions en 1926.]
1909 (1929)	Treaty No. 4. Plan of subdivision of surrendered portion of Indian Reserve No. 89 in Townships 33 & 34, Ranges 12 & 13, W. 2nd Mer., Saskatchewan. Surveyed by J. Lestock Reid, D.L.S., Jany. 1909 . . . Certified true copy . . . Dept. of Indian Affairs . . . May 28th, 1929. . . . [2 copies]
1910	Treaty 4. Plan of the townplot of Kylemore in L.S. 9, Sec. 9, Tp. 34, R. 12, W. 2nd M., within the surrendered portion of Fishing Lake I.R. No. 89, Sask., 1910. J. Lestock Reid, D.L.S. Plotted and drawn by H. Fabien.
1915	Plan of the townplot of Kylemore, comprising that portion of L.S. 8 and L.S. 9 lying north of the station grounds of the Canadian Northern Railway in Sec. 9, Township 34, Range 12, West 2nd M., within the surrendered portion of Fishing Lake I.R. No. 89, Sask. Surveyed by J. Lestock Reid, D.L.S., 1910 and Donald F. Robertson, D.L.S., 1915. Drawn by H.W.F. . . . [2 copies]
1915	Sketch showing part of the Fishing Lake I.R., surrendered on Aug. 14th, 1915. . . .

Fishing Station No. 72A

      Refer to/Consulter: **Kahkewistahaw No. 72A**

Flying Dust No. 105

      Refer to/Consulter: **Meadow Lake No. 105**

Fort a la Corne No. 100

      Refer to/Consulter: **James Smith No. 100**

Four Portages No. 157C

1909 (1930)   Plan of Four Portages Indian Reserve No. 157c at Lac La Ronge, Sask. Treaty No. 10. Surveyed in 1909 by the late J. Lestock Reid, D.L.S. . . . [Additions 1930/Additions en 1930.]

Fox Point No. 157D

1909 (1930)   Plan of Indian Reserves No. 157D & 157E near Fox Point, Lac La Ronge, Sask. Treaty No. 10. Surveyed in 1909 by the late J. Lestock Reid, D.L.S. . . . [Additions 1930/Additions en 1930.]

Fox Point No. 157E

1909 (1930)   See/Voir: **Fox Point No. 157D**

Gabriel Cote No. 64

      Refer to/Consulter: **Cote No. 64**

George Gordon No. 86

      Refer to/Consulter: **Gordon No. 86**

Gordon No. 86

[1881]   Little Touchwood Hills. George Gordon's band. J.C. Nelson, D.L.S. . . .

1884   Treaty No. 4. George Gordon's Reserve No. 86, Touchwood Hills. . . . A.W. Ponton, D.L.S., Ottawa, February 29th, 1884.

1900 (1933)   Tr. 4. Plan of Gordons [corrected to/corrigé pour] Gordon Indian Reserve No. 86 as defined by O. in C. of the 14th day of July, 1899. Resurveyed by J. Lestock Reid, D.L.S., Augst. & Sept., 1900. [Additions to 1933/Additions jusqu'en 1933.]

[1914]   Treaty No. 4. Plan of Gordon's Indian Reserve No. 86, Saskatchewan. Compiled from surveys by the Department of the Interior and J.L. Reid, D.L.S. . . .

SASKATCHEWAN

Grant-Lebret Industrial School

1920 (1931)   Plan showing retracement survey of division line between Industrial
              School Grant-Lebret and the property of Les Reverends Peres Oblats
              de Marie Immaculée des Territoires du Nord-Ouest in Secs. 2 and 11,
              Tp. 21, R. 13, W. 2nd M. Surveyed by E.C. Brown, D. & S.L.S., 1918 and
              R.W.E. Loucks, D. & S.L.S., 1919. . . . January . . . 1920. [Additions to
              1931/Additions jusqu'en 1931.]

Grizzly Bear's Head No. 110 & Lean Man No. 111

1884   Treaty No. 6, N.W.T. Sketch showing the survey of the boundaries of
              an Indian Reserve at Eagle Hills for the bands of Grizzly Bear's Head
              & the Lean Man [and Mosquito's Reserve/et la réserve Mosquito].
              Surveyed by John C. Nelson, Dominion Land Surveyor, July 1884.

1884   Treaty No. 6, N.W.T. Plan of Indian Reserve No. 110, Chiefs Grizzly
              Bear's Head & Lean Man. Surveyed in July and August 1884 by J.C.
              Nelson, D.L.S. . . . Surveyor in charge I.R. Surveys. . . .

1903 (1905)   See/Voir: **Red Pheasant No. 108**

1905   Plan of part of Township No. 41, Range 17, West of 3d. M. in Indian
              Reserve No. 110 and 111 (undivided). Chiefs Grizzly Bears Head and
              Lean Man. Surveyed by J.K. McLean, D.L.S., Sept. 1905. . . .

Hay Lands No. 75A

1885 (1947)   See/Voir: **Piapot No. 75**

1885 (1950)   See/Voir: **Piapot No. 75**

1919   See/Voir: **Piapot No. 75**

Hay Lands No. 112A

              Refer to/Consulter: **Moosomin No. 112A**

Hay Lands No. 113B

              Refer to/Consulter: **Sweet Grass No. 113B**

Indian Head No. 76

              Refer to/Consulter: **Assiniboine No. 76**

Indian School Lands No. A

1909   Plan of Indian school lands No. A (Treaty 10) at Lac La Ronge,
              Saskatchewan. Surveyed in 1909 by the late J. Lestock Reid, D.L.S. . . .

Jack No. 76

Refer to/Consulter: **Assiniboine No. 76**

James Smith No. 100

1885*   Plan, Indian Reserve, Chief James Smith, at Fort a la Corne. Treaty No. 6, Carlton District. I.R. No. 100. Certified correct, A.W. Ponton, Dominion Land Surveyor, Indian Office, Regina, Assa., March 19th, 1885.

[1889]   See/Voir: **Fishing Lake No. 89**

1902 (1916) Plan showing the La Corne Indian Reserves No. 100 & 100A, Tps. 46, 47 & 48, R. 19, 20 & 21, W. 2nd M. Treaty No. 6, N.W.T. Survey retraced Sept. — October 1902. J. Lestock Reid, D.L.S. . . . [Additions 1916/Additions en 1916.]

1903   Plan of Neesh-ah-pah-tow-an Marsh in La Corne Indian Reserves. Treaty No. 6. No. 100 & 100A. J. Lestock Reid, D.L.S., February 1903.

1916   See/Voir: **Beardy No. 97 & Okemasis No. 96**

James Smith No. 100A

Refer to/Consulter: **Cumberland No. 100A**

John Smith No. 99

Refer to/Consulter: **Muskoday No. 99**

Kahkewistahaw No. 72

1881   See/Voir: **Ochapowace No. 71**

1888   [Plan showing a part of the Kahkewistahaw Indian Reserve/Plan indiquant une partie de la réserve indienne Kahkewistahaw.] Dominion Lands Office, Ottawa, 4th February, 1888. . . .

1889   Treaty No. 4. N.W.T. Subdivision survey of portions of Indian Reserves Nos. 72 & 73 Chiefs Kakewistahaw & O'Soup. Surveyed in September & November 1889 by Chas. P. Aylen, D.L.S. . . .

1907   Plan of Township No. 17, Range 4, West of 2nd Meridian, within the Kakeewistahaw Indian Reserve No. 72 near Broadview, Sask. Surveyed in 1907 by J. Lestock Reid, D.L.S. . . . [2 copies]

1907   Plan of Township No. 17, Range 5, West of 2nd Meridian, within the Kakeewistahaw Indian Reserve No. 72, near Broadview, Sask. Surveyed in 1907 by J. Lestock Reid, D.L.S. . . . [2 copies]

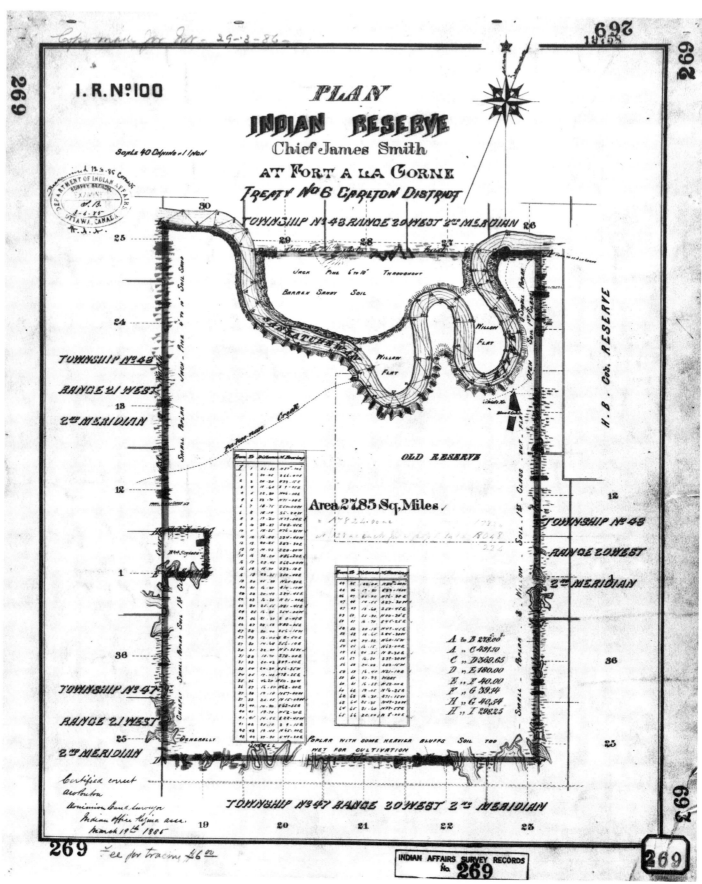

James Smith No. 100 1885 (NMC 5691).

1916   Treaty No. 4. Plan of the Kakiwistahaw [corrected to/corrigé pour] Kahkewistahaw Indian Reserve No. 72, Tp's. 17 & 18, R's 4 & 5, W. 2 M. 14/11/16, J.P. McD.

1919   See/Voir: **Ochapowace No. 71**

Kahkewistahaw No. 72A

1884   Copy of sketch of fishing station at Crooked Lake, accompanying my report of June 5th, 1884 to. . . the Commissioner of Indian Affairs. John C. Nelson.

[1884]

              Sketch showing a fishing station at Crooked Lake, fractional part of Sec. 5, Township 19, Range 5, W. of 2nd P.M. J.C. Nelson.

1885 (1924) Kahkewistahaw I.R. 72A. Proposed fishing station at Crooked Lake. John C. Nelson, D.L.S. . . . Examined. . . 12-6-85. . . . [Additions 1924/Additions en 1924.]

Kakeesheway No. 71

              Refer to/Consulter: **Ochapowace No. 71**

Kawkewistahaw No. 72

              Refer to/Consulter: **Kahkewistahaw No. 72**

Kawkewistahaw No. 72A

              Refer to/Consulter: **Kahkewistahaw No. 72A**

Keeseekoose No. 66

1884   Treaty No. 4. Kee-see-kons' Reserve, Pelly, shewing the portion surveyed by A.W. Ponton, D.L.S. . . . Ottawa, February 29th, 1884.

1884 (1916) Treaty No. 4, N.W.T. Survey of Indian Reserve No. 66 for the band of Chief Keeshekonse [corrected to/corrigé pour] Keeseekoose on the east side to the Assiniboine River, near Pelly. . . . Surveyed in Dec. 1883 & Jany. 1884 by John C. Nelson, D.L.S. in charge of Indian Reserve Surveys. . . . [Additions to 1916/Additions jusqu'en 1916.]

[1889]   Rough sketch of Kee-see-kouse's Reserve showing approximate position of Indian Settlement.

1897 (1902) See/Voir: **Cote No. 64**

1906   Mossy Portage Sheet, West of Principal Meridian. Sectional map [showing Porcupine Reserves No. 1 and 2 and other reserves in the area/montrant les réserves Porcupine Nos 1 et 2 et les autres réserves de la région.] Revised to the 31st August, 1906.

SASKATCHEWAN

1907   Plan of portion of east boundary of Keeseekoose Indian Reserve No. 66. Treaty No. 4. J. Lestock Reid, D.L.S., February 1907.

1910   Treaty No. 4. Plan of the subdivision of the portion surrendered in 1909 of the Keeseekoose I.R. No. 66, Sask. Surveyed by J. Lestock Reid, D.L.S., May 1910. . . . [2 copies]

1910 (1927)   Tr. 4. Plan of subdivision of a portion of the Keeseekoose Indian Reserve No. 66, for Indian purposes. Sask. Surveyed by J. Lestock Reid, D.L.S., 1910. [Additions 1927/Additions en 1927.]

Keeseekoose No. 66A

1910   See/Voir: **Keeseekoose No. 66**

Kenemotayoo No. 118

Refer to/Consulter: **Big River No. 118**

Kenemotayoo No. 118A

Refer to/Consulter: **Big River No. 118A**

Kesickonse No. 66

Refer to/Consulter: **Keeseekoose No. 66**

Kesickonse No. 66A

Refer to/Consulter: **Keeseekoose No. 66A**

Key No. 65

Refer to/Consulter: **The Key No. 65**

Kinistino No. 91

1900 (1925)   . . . Plan of Kinistino Indian Reserve No. 91. Treaty No. 6, N.W.T. Surveyed by J. Lestock Reid, D.L.S., July 1900. [Additions to 1925/ Additions jusqu'en 1925.]

Kitsakie No. 156B

1909 (1923)   Plan of Kitsakie Indian Reserve No. 156B at Lac La Ronge, Saskatchewan. Treaty No. 10. Surveyed in 1909 by the late J. Lestock Reid, D.L.S. . . . [Additions 1923/Additions en 1923.]

1920 (1930)   Plan of Kitsakie Indian Reserve No. 156B, La Ronge Settlement, Saskatchewan. Compiled from surveys made by J.L. Reid, D.L.S., 1910; S.D. Fawcett, D.L.S., 1920. Treaty 10. . . . Drawn by G.P. . . . [Additions 1930/Additions en 1930.]

Knee Lake No. 192B

1923 (1930)   Treaty 10. Plan of Knee Lake I.R. No. 192B, Sask., for the Chipewyan band of Indians in the Île-a-la-Crosse District. Surveyed by W.A.A. McMaster, D.L.S., 1923. [Additions 1930/Additions en 1930.]

Lac la Ronge No. A

Refer to/Consulter: **Indian School Lands No. A**

Lac la Ronge No. 156

1909 (1930)   Plan of Indian Reserve No. 156 at Lac La Ronge, Saskatchewan. Treaty No. 10. Surveyed in 1909 by the late J. Lestock Reid, D.L.S. . . . [Additions 1930/Additions en 1930.]

Lac la Ronge No. 156C

Refer to/Consulter: **Sucker River No. 156C**

Lac la Ronge No. 157A

Refer to/Consulter: **Stanley No. 157A**

La Corne No. 100

Refer to/Consulter: **James Smith No. 100**

La Corne No. 100A

Refer to/Consulter: **Cumberland No. 100A**

La Plonge No. 192

1923 (1930)   Treaty 10. Plan of La-Plonge I.R. No. 192, Sask., in Townships 71 and 72, Range 11, West 3 Mer., for the Chipewyan band of Indians in the Île-a-la-Crosse District. Surveyed by W.A.A. McMaster, D.L.S., 1923. [Additions 1930/Additions en 1930.]

Last Mountain Lake No. 80A

1884   Copy of sketch of proposed fishing station at Long or Last Mountain Lake, accompanying report of June 5th, 1884 to the Commissioner of Indian Affairs. John C. Nelson.

[1884]   Sketch accompanying report on proposed fishing stations at Long or Last Mountain Lake for the Touchwood Hills and Qu'Appelle Indians. J.C. Nelson, D.L.S. (in charge of Indn. Res. Surveys).

1885 (1921)   Treaty No. 4 N.W.T. Fishing ground at Long or Last Mountn. Lake. . . . Surveyed in June 1885 by J.C. Nelson, D.L.S. in charge I.R. Surveys. [Additions to 1921/Additions jusqu'en 1921.]

1919	Plan of Lakeview at Regina Beach, Sask., being a subdivision of fractional Section 21, Township 21, Range 22, West 2nd Meridian, in Last Mountain Lake Indian Reserve No. 80-A, — surveyed by T.D. Green, D.L.S., Sept. 1918. . . . Approved . . . The Canadian Pacific Railway Company . . . Winnipeg, Sept. 1919. . . . [2 copies]
1958	Canadian Pacific Railway. Regina, Saskatoon & North Saskatchewan Br. Colonsay Subdivision. . . . Plan and field notes of survey of extra right of way in Last Mountain Lake Indian Reserve No. 80A, N.W. 1/4 Sec. 17 & N.E. 1/4 Sec. 18, Tp. 21, R. 22, W. 2 M, Saskatchewan, 1958. [Surveyed by/Relevé par] R.G. Cairns, S.L.S. . . .

Lean Man No. 111

Refer to/Consulter: **Grizzly Bear's Head No. 110 & Lean Man No. 111**

Leech Lake No. 73A

1884 (1899)	Treaty 4. Survey of a proposed reserve for Little Bones band at Leech Lake or Crescent Lake. Surveyed in January 1884 by John C. Nelson, Dominion Land Surveyor. [Additions to 1899/Additions jusqu'en 1899.]
1899	Plan showing survey of new road through Leech Lake Indian Reserve, by W.T. Thompson, D.T.S., 1899. . . .
1907	Plan of resurvey of Indian Reserve No. 73A "The Little Bone". Treaty No. 4, Saskatchewan. Surveyed by J. Lestock Reid, 1906. J. Lestock Reid, D.L.S., February 1907.
1908	Treaty No. 4. Plan of subdivision of Indian Reserve 73A, Little Bone, in Townships 23 & 24, Ranges 3 & 4, W. 2 M., Saskatchewan. Surveyed by J.L. Reid, D.L.S., in 1908. . . . [2 copies]
1909 (1946)	Plan of subdivision of Indian Reserve 73A, Little Bone, in Townships 23 and 24, Ranges 3 an[d] 4, West of 2nd M., Saskatchewan. Surveyed by J.L. Reid, D.L.S. in 1908. Treaty No. 4. J. Lestock Reid, D.L.S., 9th February, 1909. [Additions to 1946/ Additions jusqu'en 1946.]

Little Black Bear No. 84

[1885] (1889)	See/Voir: **Peepeekisis No. 81**
1903	Plan showing File Hill Indian Reserves in Tps. 21, 22, 23 & 24, R. 10 & 11, W. 2nd M. Survey retraced May-June 1902. Treaty No. 4, N.W.T. J. Lestock Reid, D.L.S., February 1903.
1928	Plan of subdivision of the northern portion of Little Black Bear I.R. No. 84 in Tps. 23 & 24, Rgs. 10 & 11, W. 2nd Mer., Saskatchewan. Surveyed by D. Alpine Smith, D.L.S., 1928. [2 copies]

Little Bone No. 73A

Refer to/Consulter: **Leech Lake No. 73A**

Little Hills No. 158

1909 (1930)   Plan of Indian Reserves No. 158, 158A & 158B, Little Hills, Montreal River, Sask. Treaty No. 10. Surveyed in 1909 by the late J. Lestock Reid, D.L.S. . . . [Additions 1930/Additions en 1930.]

Little Hills No. 158A

1909 (1930)   See/Voir: **Little Hills No. 158**

Little Hills No. 158B

1909 (1930)   See/Voir: **Little Hills No. 158**

Little Pine & Lucky Man No. 116

1887 (1927)   Treaty No. 6, North West Territory. Survey of Indian Reserve No. 116 on Battle River for the band of Chief Little Pine. . . . Surveyed in September 1887 by John C. Nelson, D.L.S. in charge of Indian Res. Surveys. [Additions to 1927/Additions jusqu'en 1927.]

1904 (1927)   See/Voir: **Poundmaker No. 114**

Little Red River No. 106A

1897 (1938)   Treaty No. 6, N.W.T. Plan of Indian Reseve [sic] No. 106A on Little Red River for the Montreal Lake and Lac la Ronge Indians. . . . Surveyed by A.W. Ponton, D.L.S., in June & July 1897. . . . [Additions to 1938/Additions jusqu'en 1938.]

Long Lake No. 80A

Refer to/Consulter: **Last Mountain Lake No. 80A**

Lucky Man No. 116

Refer to/Consulter: **Little Pine & Lucky Man No. 116**

Makaoo No. 120

1904 (1927)   See/Voir: **Seekaskootch No. 119**

[1904]   See/Voir: **Seekaskootch No. 119**

1914 [1915]   See/Voir: **New Thunderchild No. 115B**

SASKATCHEWAN

1915   Tr. No. 6. Plan of proposed lands for Roman Catholic and English missions in Indian Reserve No. 120, Sask. Surveyed by D.F. Robertson, D.L.S., 1915.

Makwa Lake No. 129

1915 (1919)   Tr. 6. Plan of Makwa Lake Indian Reserve No. 129 for the Indians of the Cree band, situate in Township 58, Range 23, West 3 M. Surveyed by A. Fawcett, D.L.S., 1910 and Donald F. Robertson, D.L.S., 1915. . . . [Additions 1919/Additions en 1919.]

Makwa Lake No. 129A

1915 (1919)   Tr. 6. Plan of Makwa Lake Indian Reserve No. 129A for the Indians of the Cree band. Surveyed by W. Waddell, D.L.S. 1912 and Donald F. Robertson, D.L.S., 1915. [Additions 1919/Additions en 1919.]

Makwa Lake No. 129B

1935   Loon Lake townplot, Makwa Lake Indian Reserve No. 129B in E. 1/2 Sec. 23, Twp. 58, Rge. 22, W. 3 Mer., Saskatchewan. Surveyed by E.C. Brown, S.L.S., November 1931. . . . January 12th, 35. . . .

1941 (1958)   Plan of addition to Loon Lake townplot, Makwa Lake Indian Reserve No. 129B . . . Saskatchewan. . . . [surveyed by/relevé par] Cecil B.C. Donnelly, D.L.S. . . . 1941. [Addition:] Plan of survey of part of Makwa Lake Indian Reserve No. 129B . . . being an addition to Loon Lake subdivision, Saskatchewan. . . . [Surveyed by/relevé par] D.A. Ferguson, S.L.S. . . . 1957. . . . Department of Mines and Technical Surveys . . . 1958. . . .

Meadow Lake No. 105

[1881]   Treaty No. 6, Carlton District. Flying Dust's Reserve. . . . Geo. A. Simpson, D.L.S. . . . Sheet 7.

1908 (1953)*   Treaty No. 6. Plan of resurvey of Meadow Lake Indian Reserve No. 105, Saskatchewan. J. Lestock Reid, D.L.S., March 1908. [Additions to 1953/Additions jusqu'en 1953.]

1959   Plan showing survey of parcel "B", Meadow Lake Indian Reserve No. 105, N.E. 1/4 Sec. 25, Tp. 59, R. 17, W. 3rd M., Saskatchewan. . . . [Surveyed by/Relevé par] D.A. Ferguson, S.L.S. . . . 12th . . . May . . . 1959. . . .

Ministikwan No. 161

[1914]   Plan of Ministikwan Lake Indian Reserve. Treaty No. 6. Province of Saskatchewan, Townships 58, 59 & 60, Ranges 25 & 26, W. 3rd M.

Tr 6

Meadow Lake No. 105 1908 (1953) (NMC 8384).

SASKATCHEWAN

1914 (1943)   Treaty No. 6. Plan of Ministikwan Lake Indian Reserves Nos. 161 & 161A situated in Tps. 58, 59 & 60, Ranges 24, 25 & 26, W. of 3rd Meridian, Sask. . . . Donald F, Robertson, D.L.S., 8th Oct., 1914. . . . [Additions to 1943/Additions jusqu'en 1943.]

Ministikwan No. 161A

[1914]   See/Voir: **Ministikwan No. 161**

1914 (1943)   See/Voir: **Ministikwan No. 161**

Mirond Lake No. 184E

1919 (1930)   Treaty 6, Sask. Plan of Mirond Lake Indian Reserve No. 184-E. Timber reserve for Pelican Narrows band. Situated about 6 miles north-east of Pelican Narrows Settlement in unsurveyed territory. Surveyed by W.R. White, Sept. 1919. [Additions 1930/Additions en 1930.]

Mistawasis No. 103

1891 (1916)   Treaty No. 6 N.W.T. Subdivision survey of part of Indian Reserve No. 103 into 40 acre lots. Chief Mistawasis. Surveyed in Aug. & Sept. 1891 by A.W. Ponton, D.L.S. [Additions 1916/Additions en 1916.]

1906 (1911)   Plan of re-survey of Mistowasis [corrected to/corrigé pour] Snake Plain Indian Reserve No. 103. Treaty No. 6. Boundaries re surveyed summer season 1906 . . . J. Lestock Reid, D.L.S. [Additions 1911/ Additions en 1911.]

1907 (1919)   Plan of subdivision or portion of Mistawasis Indian Reserve No. 103. Treaty No. 6, Saskatchewan. Surveyed by J. Lestock Reid, 1907. . . .

1908 (1916)   Plan of subdivision of portion of Mistawasis Indian Reserve No. 103. Treaty No. 6, Saskatchewan. J. Lestock Reid, D.L.S., January 31st, 1908. [Additions to 1916/Additions jusqu'en 1916.]

1911   Plan of portion of Mistawasis I.R. No. 103 surrendered for sale in 1911. Surveyed by J.L. Reid, D.L.S., 1907. . . . W.R. White. [2 copies]

1919   Part of trail Carlton to Green Lake [through Mistawasis Indian Reserve/traversant la réserve indienne Mistawasis], by John Bourgeois, D.L.S., 1888. . . . 17/7/19, J.P.M.

1920   See/Voir: **Muskeg Lake No. 102**

1922   Treaty 6, Saskatchewan. Plan of Mistawasis Indian Reserve No. 103, subdivided by J.E. Underwood, D.L.S., 1921. Approved, Ottawa, Mar. 1st, 1922, Donald F. Robertson, D.L.S., for Chief Surveyor. . . . Drawn by W.R.W.

Mistawasis Timber Berth

1908   Plan of timber berth for Mistawasis Indian Reserve No. 103. Treaty No. 6, Saskatchewan. J. Lestock Reid, D.L.S., January 31st, 1908.

Montreal Lake No. 106

1889 (1951)   Treaty No. 6, N.W.T. Survey of Indian Reserve No. 106 at Montreal Lake. Chief William Charles. . . . Surveyed in October 1889 by A.W. Ponton, D.L.S. [Additions to 1951/Additions jusqu'en 1951.]

Moose Mountain No. 68

          Refer to/Consulter: **Pheasant Rump No. 68**

Moose Mountain No. 69

          Refer to/Consulter: **Ocean Man No. 69**

Moose Mountain No. 70

          Refer to/Consulter: **White Bear No. 70**

Moose Woods No. 94

          Refer to/Consulter: **White Cap No. 94**

Moosomin No. 112

[1881]   Treaty No. 6, Battleford District. Moosomin's Reserve. . . . Geo. A. Simpson, D.L.S. . . . Sheet 1.

1885   See/Voir: **Thunderchild No. 115A**

1887   Treaty No. 6, North West Territories. Survey into lots of part of Indian Reserve No. 112, band of Chief Moosomin. Surveyed in September 1887 by John C. Nelson, D.L.S. in charge of Indian Res. Surveys.

1904   Resurvey plan of Moosomin & Thunder-Child Indian Reserves No. 112 & 115. Treaty No. 6, N.W.T. Portion of Township 44 - 46, Range 17 - 19, W. 3rd M. J. Lestock Reid, D.L.S., January 1904.

1909   Plan . . . of subdivision of Thunderchild and Moosomin Indian Reserves Nos. 112, 115 and 115A, Sask. Surveyed by J. Lestock Reid, D.L.S., 1909. R.G. Orr, Sept. '09.

1909   Plan of subdivision of Moosomin Indian Reserve No. 112, Sask. Surveyed by J. Lestock Reid, D.L.S., 1909. . . . H. Fabien, Draughtsman.

SASKATCHEWAN

[1909]   [Map showing portion of surveyed roadway through Moosomin and
            Thunderchild Reserves/Carte indiquant une partie de la route étudiée
            qui traverse les réserves Moosomin et Thunderchild.]

1910   Plan showing survey of new road in Township 44, Range 17, West of
            3rd M. [through Moosomin Reserve/traversant la réserve Moosomin].
            By J.D. Shepley, D.L.S. . . . 1907. . . . 20:1:10. [2 copies]

1913   Plan of the town-plot of Highgate in frac. south half of Sec. 17, Tp.
            45, R. 17, W. 3 M. in the Moosomin I.R. (surrendered), Sask. I.J.
            Steele, D.L.S., S.L.S., Ottawa, Nov. 6th, 1913.

1933   Plan of the town plot of Highgate in frac. south half of Sec. 17, Tp.
            45, R. 17, W. 3 M., in the surrendered portion of Moosomin Indian
            Reserve No. 112, Sask. Compiled from surveys . . . 1909 . . . [to/
            jusqu'en] 1927. Traced by G.P. . . . 1-12-33. . . .

Moosomin No. 112A

1909   Battleford Land District. [Map showing location of Reserve No.
            112A, held in common by the Thunderchild and Moosomin bands, and
            other reserves in the area/Carte indiquant l'emplacement de la
            réserve n° 112A, détenue en commun par les bandes Thunderchild
            et Moosomin, ainsi que d'autres réserves de la région.] Department
            of the Interior . . . 1909.

1909   Plan of Section 14, Tp. 46, R. 16, W. 3rd Miridian [sic]. Surrendered
            for sale by the Moosomin and Thunderchild . . . band of Indians.
            Resurveyed by J. Lestock Reid, D.L.S., July 1909. . . .

1912 [1915] Saskatchewan. Battleford Sheet, West of Third Meridian. Sectional
            map [showing lands required for Thunderchild and Moosomin bands,
            and other reserves in the area/indiquant les terrains demandés pour
            les bandes Thunderchild et Moosomin, ainsi que d'autres réserves
            de la région.] Revised to the 29th August, 1912. . . .

Moosomin No. 112B

1909 (1926) Plan of Moosomin "New" Indian Reserve No. 112B, Townships 47 &
            48, Ranges 16 & 15, W. 3 M., Saskatchewan. Treaty No. 6. J.
            Lestock Reid, D.L.S., December 1909. [Additions to 1926/Additions
            jusqu'en 1926.]

[1909]   [Map showing location of proposed new reserve for the Moosomin
            band, at Murray Lake, and other reserves in the area/Carte indiquant
            l'emplacement de la nouvelle réserve qu'on se propose de donner
            à la bande Moosomin, au lac Murray, ainsi que d'autres réserves de
            la région.]

1912 [1915] See/Voir: **Moosomin No. 112A**

Moosomin No. 112E

1914 [1915]   See/Voir: **New Thunderchild No. 115B**

Moosomin No. 112F

1914 [1915]   See/Voir: **New Thunderchild No. 115B**

Moosomin's Hay Grounds No. 112A

Refer to/Consulter: **Moosomin No. 112A**

Mosquito No. 74

Refer to/Consulter: **Sakimay No. 74**

Mosquito No. 109

1884   See/Voir: **Grizzly Bear's Head No. 110 & Lean Man No. 111**

1903 (1905)   See/Voir: **Red Pheasant No. 108**

Muscowequan No. 85

Refer to/Consulter: **Muskowekwan No. 85**

Muscowpetung No. 80

N.D./S.D.   Plan of R.C. mission property in Sec. 18, Tp. 21, R. 16, W. 2 Mer., Muscowpetung Indian Reserve No. 80, Sask.

1881   Muskowpeetung's Reserve. Qu'Appelle, 18th Nov., 1881. J.C. Nelson, D.L.S. . . . [Sheet/Feuille] G.

1882 (1889)   Treaty No. 4. Plan, Indian Reserve No. 80, Qu'Appelle Valley. Chief Muskowpeetung. . . . Surveyed in June 1882 by J.C. Nelson, D.L.S. . . . [Additions to 1889/Additions jusqu'en 1889.]

1884   See/Voir: **Piapot No. 75**

1889   Treaty No. 4, N.W.T. Indian Reserve No. 80, Chief "Muscowpetung". Surveyed by J.C. Nelson, D.L.S., Nov. 1881 & June 1882. Approved . . . 6th Feb., 1889. . . . [2 copies]

1889   Treaty No. 4, N.W.T. Subdivision survey of Indian Reserve No. 80. Chief Muskowpetung. Surveyed in July 1889 by Chas. P. Aylen, D.L.S.

1889   Treaty No. 4, North West Territories. Subdivision survey of part of Indian Reserve No. 80. Chief "Muskowpetung". Surveyed in July 1889 by John C. Nelson, D.L.S. in charge of Indian Reserve Surveys.

SASKATCHEWAN

[1896] See/Voir: **Piapot No. 75**

1901 Plan of east boundary of Muscowpeetung Indian Reserve No. 80. Treaty No. 4. T. 20 & 21, R. 16 & 17, W. 2nd M. J. Lestock Reid, D.L.S., Sept. 1901.

[1906] Indian Reserve No. 80, Chief Muscowpetung [showing north limit of part covered by O.C. and north limit of part first proposed to be surrendered/indiquant la limite septentrionale de la partie couverte par O.C. et la limite septentrionale de la partie qu'on se proposait tout d'abord de céder].

[1908] [Map of Muscowpetung, Piapot and Pasqua Reserves, showing the portion of Muscowpetung Reserve proposed to be surrendered/Carte des réserves Muscowpetung, Piapot et Pasqua, indiquant la partie de la réserve Muscowpetung qu'on se propose de céder.]

1909 Plan of subdivision of part of Muscowpeetung [corrected to/corrigé pour] Muscowpetung I.R. No. 80, being part of Township 20, Ranges 16 and 17, West of 2nd M., Sask. Treaty 4. Certified correct. Hobbema, Alta., June 1st, 1909. J.K. McLean, Dominion Land Surveyor. [3 copies]

1921 Plan of Muscowpetung Indian Reserve No. 80, being parts of Townships 20 and 21, R's 16 and 17, W. 2 M., Sask. Compiled from surveys by J.K. McLean, D.L.S., 1909 & 1911 and K.N. Crowther, D.L.S., 1920. W.R.W., May 1921. . . .

Muskeg Lake No. 20C

Refer to/Consulter: **Muskeg River No. 20C**

Muskeg Lake No. 102

[1881] Treaty No. 6, Carlton District. Pet-ty-quaw-ky's. . . . Geo. A. Simpson, D.L.S. . . . Sheet 6.

1891 Treaty No. 6, N.W.T. Subdivision survey of part of Indian Reserve No. 102 into 40 acre lots. Chief Pettyquawky. Surveyed in October 1891 by A.W. Ponton, D.L.S. . . . [2 copies]

1906 (1919) Plan of re-survey of Pettyquawky [corrected to/corrigé pour] Muskeg Lake Indian Reserve No. 102. Treaty No. 6. Boundaries re surveyed summer season 1906 by J. Lestock Reid, D.L.S. [Additions 1919/ Additions en 1919.]

1920 Plan showing surrendered portions, Muskeg Lake I.R. 102 and Mistawasis I.R. 103. . . . Dept. of the Interior, Ottawa, 19th January, 1920. . . .

1922 Treaty No. 6. Plan of Muskeg Lake Indian Reserve No. 102, Sask. Subdivided ey [by/par] J.E. Underwood, D.L.S., 1921. Approved March 1st, 1922. . . .

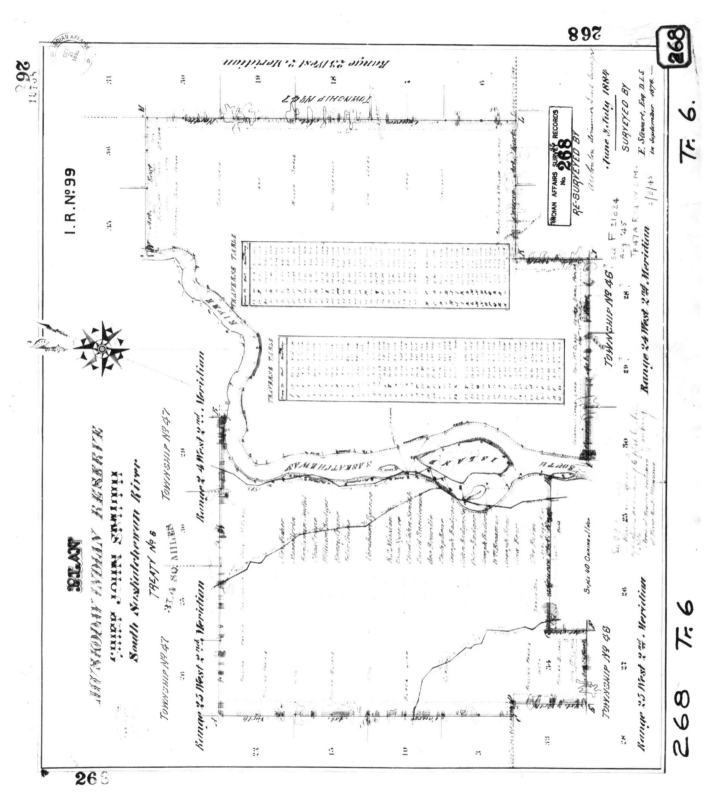

Muskoday No. 99 1884 (1945) (NMC 8387).

SASKATCHEWAN

Muskeg River No. 20C

1919   Treaty 5. Plan of Muskeg River Indian Reserve No. 20-C. Timber limit for Cumberland band. Surveyed by W.R. White, O. & D.L.S., June 1919.

Muskoday No. 99

1884 (1945)*   Plan, Muskoday Indian Reserve, Chief John Smith, South Saskatchewan River. Treaty No. 6. . . . Surveyed by E. Stewart, Esq., D.L.S. in September 1876. Re-surveyed by A.W. Ponton, Dominion Land Surveyor, June & July 1884. [Additions to 1945/Additions jusqu'en 1945.]

[1889]   See/Voir: **Fishing Lake No. 89**

1908   Plan of Muskoday Indian Reserve [No. 99/n° 99], Chief John Smith, Treaty No. 6, on east side of river. Re-surveyed by A.W. Ponton, D.L.S., 1884. E.C.R., 26/11/08.

[1909]   Plan of resurvey of Indian Reserve No. 99, "John Smith", Treaty No. 6, on west side of river. J. Lestock Reid, D.L.S.

1916   See/Voir: **Beardy No. 97 & Okemasis No. 96**

Muskowekwan No. 85

1884   Plan of Indian Reserve (Treaty No. 4) at Little Touchwood Hills. Surveyed in March 1884. No. 85. John C. Nelson, D.L. Surveyor in charge I.R. Surveys. . . .

1889   Treaty No. 4, N.W.T. Indian Reserve No. 85 at Little Touchwood Hills. Chief "Muskowekwun". Surveyed by J.C. Nelson, D.L.S., March 1884. Approved . . . 23rd Jan., 1889. . . .

1900   Plan of Muscowequan Indian Reserve No. 85, Saskatchewan. Compiled from surveys by J.L. Reid, D.L.S., 1880, 1881, 1900, and J.C. Nelson, D.L.S., 1884. . . . [2 copies]

1900 (1919)   Treaty No. 4. Plan of Muskowekwun [corrected to/corrigé pour] Muskowekwan Indian Reserve No. 85. Resurveyed by J. Lestock Reid, D.L.S., September 1900. [Additions to 1919/Additions jusqu'en 1919.]

[1905]   Plan of Muscowequan's Indian Reserve No. 85. (Copy).

[1907]   Sec. 6, Tg. [Tp.] 27, Ranges 14 & 15, 2nd Meridian. [Plan showing land that the Grand Trunk Railway wishes to obtain in Muskowekwan Reserve No. 85/Plan indiquant les terrains que la *Grand Trunk Railway* souhaite obtenir dans la réserve Muskowekwan n° 85.]

1908   Map showing location of proposed pipe line at Mostyn. . . . Nov. 20, 08. L.M. Bidwell, Res. Eng.

1909 (1910)	Grand Trunk Pacific Railway. Proposed pipe line for water supply, Mostyn, Province of Saskatchewan . . . Feb. 8, 1909. [Additions 1910/Additions en 1910.]
1910	Treaty No. 4. Plan of part of the town-plot of Mostyn in the Muscowequan I.R. No. 85, Sask. Surveyed by J. Lestock Reid, D.L.S., 1910. . . . R.G. Orr, '10. [2 copies]
1910	Grand Trunk Pacific Railway Company. Mostyn water supply, N.W. 1/4 Sec. 6, T. 27, R. 14, W. 2nd Mer., Muskowekwun Indian Reserve, District of Saskatoon, Province of Saskatchewan . . . August 17th, 1910. . . .
1910	Treaty No. 4. Plan of part of the town-plot of Mostyn [corrected to/corrigé pour] Lestock in the Muscowequan [corrected to/corrigé pour] Muskowekwan I.R. No. 85, Sask. Surveyed by J. Lestock Reid, D.L.S., 1910. . . . [2 copies]
[1910]	Plan of townsite, Mostyn. . . .
[1910]	[Plan showing the Muskowekwan Indian Reserve No. 85/Plan indiquant la réserve indienne Muskowekwan nᵒ 85.]
1921 (1927)	Plan of part of Township 27, Range 14, West of the 2nd Meridian, in Muscowequan Indian Reserve No. 85, Saskatchewan. Surrendered 4th November, 1920. Surveyed by W.R. White, D.L.S., October 1921. . . . [Additions to 1927/Additions jusqu'en 1927.] [2 copies]
1936	Plan of subdivision of that part of the N.W. 1/4 of Sec. 6, T. 27., R. 14, W. of 2 M. lying south of the station grounds of the Grand Trunk Pacific Railway. Survey made by S. Harding, S.L.S., 1936. . . .

Muskowpeetung No. 80

    Refer to/Consulter: **Muscowpetung No. 80**

Nemeiben No. 156C

    Refer to/Consulter: **Sucker River No. 156C**

New Moosomin No. 112A

    Refer to/Consulter: **Moosomin No. 112A**

New Moosomin No. 112B

    Refer to/Consulter: **Moosomin No. 112B**

New Thunderchild No. 115B

1911	Battleford Land District. [Map showing timber lands for Thunderchild's band, and other reserves in the area/Carte indiquant les concessions forestières de la bande Thunderchild et d'autres réserves de la région.] Department of the Interior . . . 1911. . . .

SASKATCHEWAN

1914 [1915]   Saskatchewan. Fort Pitt Sheet, West of Third Meridian. Sectional map [showing lands required by Thunderchild and Moosomin bands/ indiquant les terrains demandés par les bandes Thunderchild et Moosomin]. Revised to the 1st May, 1914. . . .

New Thunderchild No. 115C

1909 (1914)   Plan of Thunderchild's Hay Reserve 115C at Turtle Lake, Saskatchewan. Treaty No. 6. J. Lestock Reid, D.L.S., November 25th, 1909. [Additions to 1914/Additions jusqu'en 1914.]

1911   Plan of Township 54, Range 18, West of the 3rd Meridian [showing Thunderchild's hay reserve/indiquant la réserve de foin de la bande Thunderchild.] Department of the Interior, Ottawa . . . 17/2/11.

1914 [1915]   See/Voir: **New Thunderchild No. 115B**

Nut Lake No. 90

1881   Rough sketch on a scale of 2 miles to the inch, showing reserve for part of Yellow Quill's band, at Nut Lake. . . . Nut Lake, Sepr. 15th, 1881. J.C. Nelson, D.L.S. . . . [Sheet/Feuille] C.

[1889]   See/Voir: **Fishing Lake No. 89**

1903 (1911)   Plan showing Nut Lake Indian Reserve No. 90 in T. 38 & 39, R. 12, W. 2nd M. Treaty No. 4, N.W.T. J. Lestock Reid, D.L.S., February 1903. . . . [Additions 1911/Additions en 1911.]

Ocean Man No. 69

1881   See/Voir: **Pheasant Rump No. 68**

1883   See/Voir: **Pheasant Rump No. 68**

1886   See/Voir: **Pheasant Rump No. 68**

1901   See/Voir: **Pheasant Rump No. 68**

1901 (1905)   See/Voir: **Pheasant Rump No. 68**

1902   See/Voir: **Pheasant Rump No. 68**

Ochapowace No. 71

1881   Sketch showing Indian reserves on Crooked and Round Lakes. . . . Crooked Lake, August 20th, 1881. J.C. Nelson, D.L.S. . . . [Sheet/Feuille] B.

1890   Sketch of survey of wagon road through easterly part of Indian Reserve No. 71 . . . for the bands of Chiefs "Loud-Voice" & "Chacachas," now "Ochapawace".

1919	[Saskatchewan. Plans of Township 17, Range 3 and Township 17, Range 4, West of the Second Meridian, including Ochapowace Reserve No. 71 and part of Kahkewistahaw Reserve No. 72/Saskatchewan. Plans des cantons n° 17, rang n° 3, et n° 17, rang n° 4 à l'ouest du deuxième méridien, incluant la réserve Ochapowace n° 71 et une partie de la réserve Kahkewistahaw n° 72.] Department of the Interior, Ottawa . . . December 1919. . . .
1922	Plan of Ochapowace Indian Reserve No. 71. Treaty No. 4, Saskatchewan. Compiled from plans of the adjoining townships. Donald Robertson, D.L.S., Chief Surveyor, Dept. of Indian Affairs. . . . G.P., 11th Oct., 1922. . . .

Ogemasis No. 96

Refer to/Consulter: **Beardy No. 97 & Okemasis No. 96**

Okanese No. 82

[1881]	See/Voir: **Peepeekisis No. 81**
[1885] (1889)	See/Voir: **Peepeekisis No. 81**
1903	See/Voir: **Little Black Bear No. 84**

Okemasis No. 96

Refer to/Consulter: **Beardy No. 97 & Okemasis No. 96.**

Old Fort No. 157B

1909 (1930)	Plan of Old Fort Indian Reserve No. 157B at Lac La Ronge, Sask. Treaty No. 10. Surveyed in 1909 by the late J. Lestock Reid, D.L.S. . . . [Additions 1930/Additions en 1930.]

One Arrow No. 95

1881 (1883)*	One Arrow's Reserve [showing lot owners' names in the St. Laurent Settlement/indiquant le nom des propriétaires de lots dans la zone de peuplement du Saint-Laurent]. . . . Surveyed in June & July 1881. Township 43, Range 1, West of 3rd Meridian. [Additions to 1883/Additions jusqu'en 1883.]
[1881]	Treaty No. 6, Carlton District. One Arrow's Reserve. . . . Geo. A. Simpson, D.L.S. . . . Sheet 5.
1884	[Part of/Partie de la] One Arrows Reserve, Tp. 43, R. 1, W. 3 Mdn. A.W. Ponton, Indian Reserve Surveyor, August 1884. [2 copies]
1888	Treaty No. 6, North West Territories. Plan showing alterations effected in the boundaries of Indian Reserve No. 95, band of Chief "One Arrow", near Batoche. Surveyed in July 1888 by John C. Nelson, D.L.S. in charge of Indian Reserve Surveys.

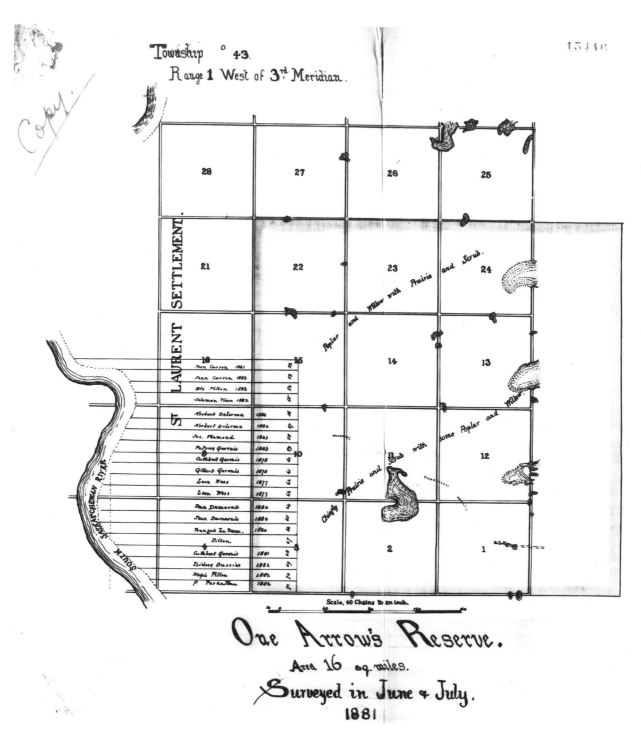

One Arrow No. 95 1881 (1883) (NMC 12125).

[1893]   [Proposed road through/Tracé proposé d'une route traversant] One Arrow Reserve. Band No. 95.

[1894]   Plan of resurvey of Indian Reserve No. 95, "One Arrow". Treaty No. 6. J. Lestock Reid, D.L.S.

1916   See/Voir: **Beardy No. 97 & Okemasis No. 96**

Onion Lake No. 119

              Refer to/Consulter: **Seekaskootch No. 119**

O'Soup No. 73

              Refer to/Consulter: **Cowessess No. 73**

Paddling Lake No. 102

              Refer to/Consulter: **Muskeg Lake No. 102**

Pas Mission

              Refer to/Consulter: **Pas Mountain No. 30**

Pas Mountain No. 30

1884 (1895)   . . . Plan of part, Indian Reserve for band at Pas Mission, Treay [sic] No. 5, Saskatchewan District. Surveyed by T.D. Green, D.L.S. . . . 1884. . . . [Additions 1895/Additions en 1895.]

Pasqua No. 79

1884   See/Voir: **Piapot No. 75**

1889   Treaty No. 4, N.W.T. Subdivision survey of Indian Reserve No. 79, Chief Pasqua. Surveyed in August 1889 by Chas. P. Aylen, D.L.S.

1889 (1905)   Treaty No. 4, N.W.T. Indian Reserve No. 79, Chief "Pasquaw". Surveyed by William Wagner, D.L.S., October 1876. Approved. . . 23rd Jan., 1889. . . . [Additions 1905/Additions en 1905.]

[1896]   See/Voir: **Piapot No. 75**

1906   Plan of subdivision of south portion of Pasqua Indian Reserve No. 79, Treaty No. 4. . . . Surveyed by J. Lestock Reid, D.L.S., July 1906. . . . [2 copies]

1906   [Sketch showing Assinee Cappo's land on Pasqua Indian Reserve No. 79/Croquis indiquant le terrain d'Assinee Cappo sur la réserve indienne Pasqua n° 79.] . . . Aug. 29-06.

SASKATCHEWAN

[1906]   Treaty No. 4, N.W.T. Indian Reserve No. 79, Chief "Pasquaw" [showing the north boundary of surrender/indiquant l'extrémité nord de la partie cédée].

[1906]   [Sketch/Croquis] showing position of government farm house [Pasqua Reserve No. 79/réserve Pasqua n° 79].

1907   Plan of subdivision of south portion of Pasqua Indian Reserve No. 79. Treaty No. 4. Township 20, Ranges 14, 15 & 16, W. 2nd M. J. Lestock Reid, D.L.S., February 1907. [2 copies]

[1908]   See/Voir: **Muscowpetung No. 80**

Peepeekisis No. 81

[1881]   Sketch showing reserves in the File Hills; the dotted lines are yet to be run. J.C. Nelson, D.L.S. . . . [Sheet/Feuille] I.

[1885] (1889)   Treaty No. 4. Plan of Indian Reserves at the File Hills, N.W.T. Surveyed by A.P. Patrick & J.C. Nelson, Dominion Land Surveyors. John C. Nelson, Surveyor in charge I.R. Surveys. [Additions to 1889/Additions jusqu'en 1889.]

1887   Plan of south boundary of Indian Reserve No. 81 at File Hills. Resurveyed in July 1887 by John C. Nelson, D.L.S. in charge of Indian Res. Surveys.

1903   Plan showing the sub-division of portion of Indian Reserve No. 81. Treaty No. 4, N.W.T. J. Lestock Reid, D.L.S., February 1903. . . . [2 copies]

1903   See/Voir: **Little Black Bear No. 84**

1906   Plan of sub-division of part of Pepeekesis I.R. No. 81 into 80 acre lots. Surveyed by J.L. Reid, D.L.S., 1903 and J.K. McLean, D.L.S., 1906. . . . W.R. White, Dec. 1906.

Pelican Narrows No. 184B

1919 (1930)   Treaty 6. Plan of Pelican Narrows Indian Reserve No. 184B for Pelican Narrows band, Sask. Surveyed by W.R. White, D.L.S., Aug 1919. [Additions 1930/Additions en 1930.]

Peter Pond Lake No. 193

1923 (1930)   Treaty 10. Plan of Peter Pond Lake I.R. No. 193, Sask., for the Chipewyan Indians of the Peter Pond Lake band. Surveyed by W.A.A. McMaster, D.L.S., 1923. [Additions 1930/Additions en 1930.]

Pettyquawky No. 102

Refer to/Consulter: **Muskeg Lake No. 102**

Pheasant Rump No. 68

1881	Sketch shewing Indian Reserves [Pheasant Rump, Ocean Man and White Bear/Pheasant Rump, Ocean Man et White Bear], Moose Mountn. Moose Mountain, July 21st, 1881. J.C. Nelson, D.L.S. [Sheet/Feuille] A.
1883	Treaty No. 2, N.W.T. Survey of Indian Reserves at Moose Mountain for the bands of Pheasant's Rump [and/et] the Ocean Man, Nos. 68 & 69. . . . John C. Nelson, D.L.S., Ottawa, November 2nd, 1883.
1886	Treaty No. 4 [corrected to/corrigé pour] 2, N.W.T. Survey of Indian Reserves Nos. 68 & 69 at Moose Mountain for the bands of Chief's Pheasant Rump & the Ocean Man. . . . Boundaries surveyed in July 1881 by John C. Nelson, D.L.S. Dividing line surveyed in July 1886 by A.W. Ponton. John C. Nelson, D.L.S.
1901	Plan of the subdivision survey of Pheasant-Rump & Ocean-Man's Indian Reserve No. 68 & 69. Surveyed by J. Lestock Reid, D.L.S. May — July, 1901.
1901 (1905)	Plan of Indian graveyard on N.E. ¼ Sec. 6, Tp. 10, R. 5, W. 2nd M., from field notes filed in Dept. of Indian Affairs in 1901 by J.L. Reid, D.L.S. Pheasant Rump & Ocean-Man I.R.'s 68 & 69. . . . [Additions 1905/Additions en 1905.]
1902	Plan of subdivision of Pheasant-Rump & Ocean-Man Indian Reserve (Nos. 68 and 69), situated in Townships 9 & 10, Ranges 5, 6 & 7, W. 2 M., Saskatchewan. Surveyed by J. Lestock Reid, D.L.S., May — July 1901. A.S., Jan. 1902. . . .

Piapot No. 75

1882 (1885)	Plan of Township[s] No. 21 [and 20/et n° 20] Range 18, West of Second Meridian [showing the Piapot Reserve/indiquant la réserve Piapot]. . . . Dominion Lands Office . . . 16th November, 1882. [Additions 1885/Additions en 1885.]
1884	Sectional map No. 1 of Manitoba and Northwestern Railway of Canada. Land grant [showing the location of Piapot Reserve and other reserves in the area/indiquant l'emplacement de la réserve Piapot et d'autres réserves de la région]. . . . Map accompanying . . . letter of 19th Sept., 1884.
1884	Sectional map No. 2 of Canadian Pacific Railway lands, from Second to Third Initial Meridian. Map . . . showing position of Piapots old Reserve, [new Reserve and other reserves in the area/de la nouvelle réserve et d'autres réserves de la région], accompanying letter of 20th Oct., 1884. W.K. Jaudowski, Draughtsman. . . .

1885 (1927 Treaty No. 4, N.W.T. Indian Reserve No. 75 on Qu'Appelle River. Chief Pie-a-pot. . . . Surveyed in July 1885 by . . . John C. Nelson, D.L.S. [Additions to 1927/Additions jusqu'en 1927.]

1885 (1947) Treaty No. 4. Plan of Piapot Indian Reserve No. 75 & 75A, Sask. Surveyed by J.C. Nelson, D.L.S., 1885. . . . [Additions to 1947/Additions jusqu'en 1947.]

1885 (1950) Piapot Indian Reserve No. 75 and 75A, Sask. Surveyed by J.C. Nelson, D.L.S., 1885. . . . [Additions to 1950/Additions jusqu'en 1950.]

1889 Treaty No. 4, N.W.T. Indian Reserve No. 75, Chief "Pi-a-pot's" band. Surveyed by John C. Nelson, D.L.S., June 1885. Approved . . . 23rd Jan., 1889. [2 copies.]

1889 Treaty No. 4, N.W.T. Subdivision survey of part of Indian Reserve No. 75. Chief Piapot. Surveyed in June and July 1889 by Chas. P. Aylen, D.L.S.

[1896] [Sketch showing the lands required as an addition to the Piapot Reserve/Croquis indiquant les terrains qu'il faut ajouter à la réserve Piapot.]

[1896] [Plan showing the location of Piapot, Muscowpetung, Pasqua and Standing Buffalo Reserves on the Qu'Appelle River/Plan indiquant l'emplacement des réserves Piapot, Muscowpetung, Pasqua et Standing Buffalo sur la rivière Qu'Appelle.] [Surveyed/Levés] . . . 1876, 1881, 1881-2, 1885.

[1908] See/Voir: **Muscowpetung No. 80**

1914 Tr. 4. Piapot Indian Reservation No. 75. Resurveyed by W.R. Reilly, D.L.S., 1914. Tp. 20, R. 18, W. 2. Certified correct, Wm. R. Reilly, Saskatchewan and Dominion Land Surveyor.

1919* Plan of surrendered portion of Piapot I.R. No. 75 and 75A. Tr. 4, Sask. Surveyed by T.D. Green, D.L.S., 1918. Drn. by H.F., 16 May, 1919. . . .

Piapot No. 75A

Refer to/Consulter: **Hay Lands No. 75A**

Piapot No. 76

Refer to/Consulter: **Assiniboine No. 76**

Pine Bluff No. 20A

1912 (1930) Tr. 5. Plan of part of Cumberland House Indian Reserve No. 20A, showing Pine Bluff. Surveyed by Donald F. Robertson, D.L.S., September 1912. . . . [Additions 1930/Additions en 1930.]

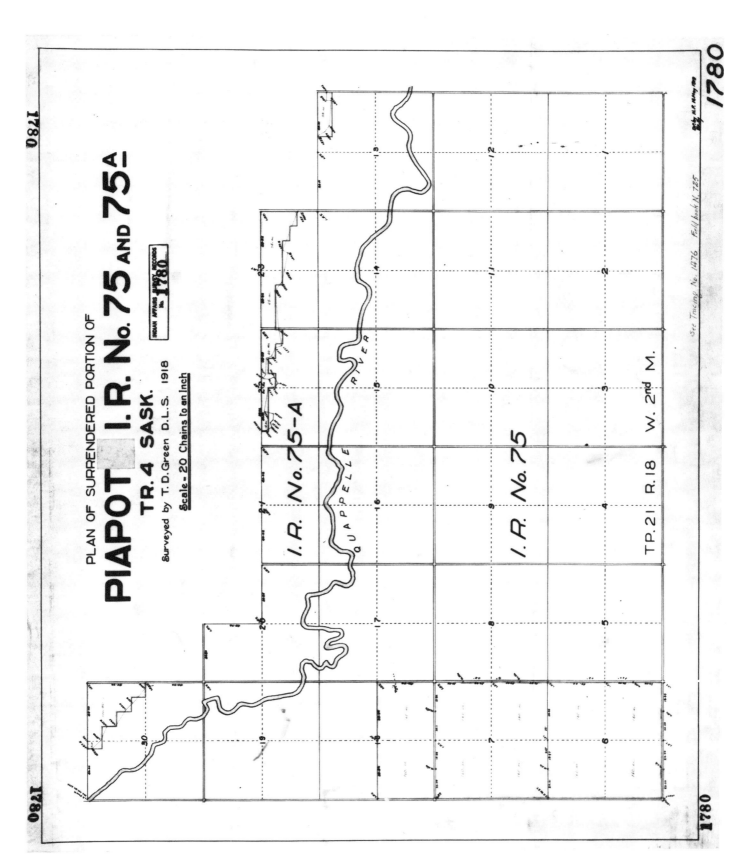

PLAN OF SURRENDERED PORTION OF

PIAPOT I.R. No. 75 AND 75A

TR. 4 SASK.

Surveyed by T. D. Green D.L.S. 1918

Scale — 20 Chains to an Inch

INDIAN AFFAIRS SURVEY RECORDS No. **1780**

I.R. No. 75-A

I.R. No. 75

QUAPPELLE RIVER

TP. 21 R. 18 W. 2nd M.

See Tracing No. 1476 Field book No. 725

1780

Piapot No. 75 1919 (C 10735).

SASKATCHEWAN

Pine Bluff No. 20B

1919 (1930)   Treaty 5. Plan of Indian Reserve No. 20-B, addition to I.R. No. 20A at Pine Bluff, Sask. Surveyed by W.R. White, O. & D.L.S., June 1919. [Additions 1930/Additions en 1930.]

Poor Man No. 88

1917 (1918)   Poor Man Indian Reserve No. 88, Townships 29 & 30, Ranges 17 & 18, West 2nd Meridian. Treaty 4. J.P. McD., 11/6/17. . . . [Additions 1918/Additions en 1918.] [2 copies]

1918   Plan of that part of the Poorman Indian Reserve No. 88, Province of Sasketchawan [sic], surrendered 13th April, 1918. Surveyed by T.D. Green, D.L.S., dated July 1st, 1918. . . . Traced by W.R.W. . . .

Potato River No. 156A

1909 (1930)   Plan of Indian Reserve No. 156A at Potato River — Lac La Ronge, Saskatchewan. Treaty No. 10. Surveyed in 1909 by the late J. Lestock Reid, D.L.S. . . . [Additions 1930/Additions en 1930.]

Poundmaker No. 114

[1881]   Treaty No. 6, Battleford District. Pound Maker's Reserve. . . . Geo. A. Simpson, D.L.S. . . . Sheet 3.

1904 (1927)   Resurvey plan of Poundmaker & Little Pine Indian Reserves No. 114 & 116. Treaty No. 6, N.W.T. J. Lestock Reid, D.L.S., January 1904. [Additions to 1927/Additions jusqu'en 1927.]

Qu'Appelle

[1881]   Rough sketch shewing Hudson Bay Co. and Indian Department reserves at Qu'Appelle, N.W.T. J.C. Nelson, D.L.S. . . . [2 copies]

[1881]   Rough sketch shewing Indian Department & Hudson's Bay Company Reserves at Qu'Appelle, N.W.T. Enlarged from Mr. Nelson's sketch.

[1881]   [Sketch showing Hudson Bay Company Reserve and proposed reserve for the paying of annuities to the Plains Indians./Croquis indiquant la réserve de la Compagnie de la baie d'Hudson et la réserve qu'on se propose de constituer pour le versement de rentes aux Indiens des plaines.]

Qu'Appelle Industrial School

[1910]   [Two sketches showing proposed railway line to be built through the grounds of Qu'Appelle Industrial School/Deux croquis indiquant la voie ferrée qu'on se propose de construire et qui traversera les terrains de l'école industrielle Qu'Appelle.]

1911   [Plan and profile of Grand Trunk Pacific Railway right-of-way and abutting land in the vicinity of Qu'Appelle Industrial School./Plan et configuration de l'emprise du *Grand Trunk Pacific Railway* et des terrains limitrophes situés dans le voisinage de l'école industrielle Qu'Appelle.] G.T.P.B.L. Co., Melville-Regina Branch. Office of Chief Engineer, November 29, 1911.

[1911]   [Sketch showing proposed subway to be constructed under the Grand Trunk Pacific Railway near/Croquis indiquant le passage souterrain qu'on se propose de construire sous le *Grand Trunk Pacific Railway* à proximité de] Qu'Appelle Industrial School. [2 copies]

Red Earth No. 29

1885   Treaty No. 5. Plan of the Indian Reserve at Red Earth No. 29, Saskatchewan District. This plan is correct and is prepared under instructions from the . . . Supt. Genl. of Indian Affairs. Ottawa, Jany. 1885. T.D. Green, D.L.S.

1911   Tr. 5. Plan showing Indian Reserve No. 29, Red Earth, and the tieline connecting that Reserve with I.R. 29A Carrot River; also tieline from Indian Reserve 29A Carrot River to 14th base line. The plan also shows the old position of Indian Reserve No. 29. Surveyed and certified correct by H.B. Proudfoot, D.L. Surveyor, Nov. 1st, 1911.

Red Earth No. 29A

Refer to/Consulter: **Carrot River No. 29A**

Red Pheasant No. 108

1884   See/Voir: **Grizzly Bear's Head No.110 & Lean Man No. 111**

1903 (1905)   Resurvey plan of Indian Reserves No. 108, 109, 110 & 111. Treaty No. 6, N.W.T. J. Lestock Reid, D.L.S., 1903. [Additions 1905/Additions en 1905.]

Regina Industrial School

1902   Plan of road diversion in Secs. 27 and 26 in Township 20, Range 21, W. 2nd M. [relating to Regina Industrial School/relatif à l'école industrielle Regina] 1902. By E.E. Farncomb, D.L.S. . . . [2 copies]

1905   Detail of part of Plan 292 [relating to Regina Industrial School/relatif à l'école industrielle Regina]. I.J. Robinson, D.C. H.D., Decr. 15th, 1905.

Round Lake No. 71

Refer to/Consulter: **Ochapowace No. 71**

SASKATCHEWAN

Round Plain No. 94A

        Refer to/Consulter: **Wahpaton No. 94A**

Sakimay No. 74

1881   See/Voir: **Ochapowace No. 71**

1889 (1911)   Treaty No. 4, N.W.T. Subdivision survey of part of Indian Reserve No. 74, Chief Sakimay. Surveyed in October 1889 by Chas. P. Aylen, D.L.S. [Additions to 1911/Additions jusqu'en 1911.]

1916 (1939)   Plan of Sakimay I.R. No. 74 in Townships 18, 19, 19A, Range 6, East of Principal Meridian [corrected to/corrigé pour] West of 2nd Meridian. Treaty 4. . . . Compiled . . . from information given by O.C. of May 17th, 1889. 17/11/16, J.P. McD. . . . [Additions to 1939/Additions jusqu'en 1939.]

Sandy Lake No. 104

        Refer to/Consulter: **Atakakup No. 104**

Sandy Narrows No. 184C

1919 (1930)   Treaty 6. Plan of Sandy Narrows Indian Reserve No. 184C for Pelican Narrows band situated about 6 miles south-west of Pelican Narrows Settlement, Sask., in unsurveyed territory. Surveyed by W.R. White, Aug. 1919. [Additions 1930/Additions en 1930.]

Saulteaux No. 159

[1910] (1922)   Treaty 6. Plan of Saulteaux Indian Reserve No. 159, Townships 47 & 48, Ranges 16 & 17, W. 3 M., Saskatchewan. . . . J. Lestock Reid, D.L.S. [Additions 1922/Additions en 1922.]

Seekaskootch No. 119

1904 (1927)   . . . Plan of resurvey of Seekaskootch & Makaoo Indian Reserves No. 119 & 120. Treaty No. 6, N.W.T. J. Lestock Reid, D.L.S., February 1904. [Additions to 1927/Additions jusqu'en 1927.]

[1904]   [Plan showing the approximate position of the Kehiwin Reserve and other reserves in the area./Plan indiquant l'emplacement approximatif de la réserve Kehiwin et d'autres réserves de la région.]

1914 [1915]   See/Voir: **New Thunderchild No. 115B**

Shesheep No. 74A

1884   Treaty No. 4, N.W.T. Plan of Indian Reserve (Shesheep) No. 74a at Crooked Lake for the part of the band of Chief Mosquito (Sakimay) under Shesheep. . . . Surveyed in February 1884 by John C. Nelson, D.L.S. in charge of I.R. Surveys.

Shoal Lake No. 28

1894 (1895)   Treaty No. 5, Saskatchewan. Shoal Lake Indian Reserve. Situated near the Carrot River about ten miles east from Red Earth. Surveyed for the Shoal Lake band of Indians, a branch of The Pas Mountain band. The portion coloured red together with the graveyard is substituted for the reserve as surveyed by T.D. Green, D.L.S. in January 1885. Surveyed by S. Bray, C.E., D.L.S., Asst. Chief Surveyor, Dept. of Indian Affairs, 30th Nov., 1894. [Additions 1895/Additions en 1895.]

Shoal Lake No. 28A

1885   Treaty No. 5. Plan of the Indian Reserve at Shoal Lake, Saskatchewan District. This plan is correct and is prepared under instructions from. . . the Supt. Genl. of Indian Affairs. T.D. Green, D.L.S., Ottawa, Jany. 1885.

1894 (1895)   See/Voir: **Shoal Lake No. 28**

1911 (1927)   Indian Reserve 28A, Carrot River [corrected to/corrigé pour] Shoal Lake. Plan showing the addition to Indian Reserve 28A and the tie line between I.R. 28A and the 14th baseline as surveyed by J.N. Wallace, D.L.S., 1906, and the correction to be applied to Wallace's tie line. Surveyed by H.B. Proudfoot, Dominion Land Surveyor, November 1911. Tr. 5. [Additions to 1927/Additions jusqu'en 1927.]

1921   Plan of Shoal Lake Reserve No. 28A H.J. Bury, Oct. 1921.

Snake Plain No. 103

Refer to/Consulter: **Mistawasis No. 103**

Standing Buffalo No. 78

1881   Standing Buffalo's Reserve. Qu'Appelle, Nov. 18th, 1881. J.C. Nelson, D.L.S. . . . [Sheet/Feuille] F.

[1896]   See/Voir: **Piapot No. 75**

1902 (1933)   Plan of Indian Reserve No. 78, "Standing Buffalo". Survey — retraced July 1902. J. Lestock Reid, D.L.S., July 1902. [Additions to 1933/ Additions jusqu'en 1933.]

Stanley No. 157

1909 (1930)   Plan of Stanley Indian Reserve No. 157, Saskatchewan. Treaty No. 10. Surveyed in 1909 by the late J. Lestock Reid, D.L.S. . . . [Additions 1930/Additions en 1930.]

SASKATCHEWAN

Stanley No. 157A

1909 (1930)   Plan of Indian Reserve No. 157A at Lac La Ronge, Sask. Treaty No. 10. Surveyed in 1909 by the late J. Lestock Reid, D.L.S. . . . [Additions 1930/Additions en 1930.]

Star Blanket No. 83

[1881]   See/Voir: **Peepeekisis No. 81**

[1885] (1889)   See/Voir: **Peepeekisis No. 81**

1903   See/Voir: **Little Black Bear No. 84**

Strike Him on the Back No. 113A

Refer to/Consulter: **Sweet Grass No. 113A**

Strike Him on the Back No. 113B

Refer to/Consulter: **Sweet Grass No. 113B**

Sturgeon Lake No. 101

1878 (1913)   Plan of the Sturgeon Lake Indian Reserve No. 10, north of the Prince Albert Settlement in Treaty No. 6, North West Territory. Surveyed by E. Stewart, D.L.S. in August and September 1878. [Additions to 1913/Additions jusqu'en 1913.]

Sucker River No. 156C

1909 (1930)   Plan of Sucker River Indian Reserve No. 156C at Lac La Ronge, Sask. Treaty No. 10. Surveyed in 1909 by the late J. Lestock Reid, D.L.S. . . . [Additions 1930/Additions en 1930.]

Swan Lake No. 7A

1905   Saskatchewan. Plan of Township 36, Range 20, West of the Third Meridian. . . [showing Swan Lake Reserve No. 7A received in lieu of land eliminated from the Swan Lake Reserve No. 7, Manitoba/ indiquant la réserve Swan Lake nº 7A reçue en contrepartie des terrains retranchés de la réserve Swan Lake nº 7, Manitoba]. . . . Department of the Interior, Ottawa, 25th February, 1905. . . . [2 copies]

Sweet Grass No. 30

Refer to/Consulter: **Sweet Grass No. 113A**

Sweet Grass No. 31

Refer to/Consulter: **Sweet Grass No. 113**

Sweet Grass No. 113

1884	Treaty No. 6, N.W.T. Plan of Indian Reserve No. 113, Chief Sweet Grass. Surveyed in July 1884 by . . . John C. Nelson, D.L.S. in charge I.R. Surveys.
1884	Sketch . . . showing Indian Reserve No. 31 [i.e. 113] south of Battle River, N.W.T., for the bands of Chiefs "Strike-him on the back" and Sweet Grass. Surveyed in July 1884 by John C. Nelson, Dominion Land Surveyor.
1904 (1951)	Resurvey plan of Sweetgrass Indian Reserve No. 113. Treaty No. 6, N.W.T. J. Lestock Reid, D.L.S., January 1904. [Additions to 1951/ Additions jusqu'en 1951.]

Sweet Grass No. 113A

1884	Treaty No. 6, N.W.T. Plan, Indian Reserve No. 113a, Chief Strike Him on the Back. Surveyed in July 1884 by J.C. Nelson, D.L.S. . . . Surveyor in charge I.R. Surveys.
1884	Sketch of a small Indian Reserve on the north side of the "Sand Hills", between Manitou Creek and Battle River, covering the farms and improvements made there by the bands of Chiefs "Strike-him-on-the-back" and "Sweet-Grass". Surveyed in July 1884 by John C. Nelson, D.L.S.
1904 (1951)	See/Voir: **Sweet Grass No. 113**

Sweet Grass No. 113B

1904 (1951)	See/Voir: **Sweet Grass No. 113**

The Key No. 65

1884	Treaty No. 4. Key's Reserve, Pelly. . . . A.W. Ponton, D.L.S., Ottawa, February 29th, 1884.
1910*	Treaty No. 4 (Sask.). Plan of The Key I.R. No. 65, showing subdivision of the portions surrendered in 1909. Surveyed in 1910. J. Lestock Reid, D.L.S. . . . [2 copies]

The Little Bone No. 73A

Refer to/Consulter: **Leech Lake No. 73A**

The-Man-Who-Took-The-Goat No. 76

Refer to/Consulter: **Assiniboine No. 76**

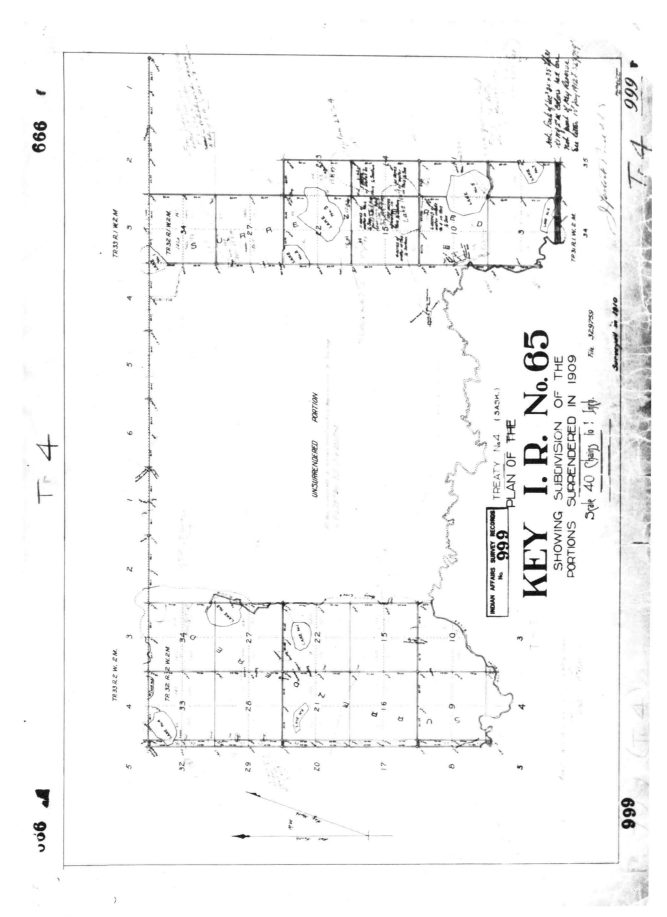

The Key No. 65 1910 (NMC 8379).

The Ocean Man No. 69

> Refer to/Consulter: **Ocean Man No. 69**

The Poor Man No. 88

> Refer to/Consulter: **Poor Man No. 88**

Thunderchild No. 112A

> Refer to/Consulter: **Moosomin No. 112A**

Thunderchild No. 115

[1881]	Treaty No. 6, Battleford District. Thunderchild's Reserve. . . . Geo. A. Simpson, D.L.S. . . . Sheet 2.
1885	See/Voir: **Thunderchild No. 115A**
1904	See/Voir: **Moosomin No. 112**
1909	Treaty 6. Plan of subdivision of Thunderchild Indian Reserves Nos. 115 and 115A, Sask. Surveyed by J. Lestock Reid, D.L.S., 1909. . . . H. Fabien, Draughtsman.
1909	See/Voir: **Moosomin No. 112**
[1909]	See/Voir: **Moosomin No. 112**

Thunderchild No. 115A

1885	Plan of Indian Reserve, Treaty No. 6, North Saskatchewan River, Chief Thunderchild, shewing addition of 8.5 sq. miles. Surveyed by A.W. Ponton, D.L.S., 1884. . . . Indian Office, Regina, Assa., March 19th, 1885. . . .
1904	Resurvey plan of Indian Reserve No. 115A, "Thunderchild". Treaty No. 6, N.W.T. J. Lestock Reid, D.L.S., January 1904.
1909	See/Voir: **Moosomin No. 112**
1909	See/Voir: **Thunderchild No. 115**

Thunderchild No. 115B

> Refer to/Consulter: **New Thunderchild No. 115B**

Thunderchild No. 115C

> Refer to/Consulter: **New Thunderchild No. 115C**

SASKATCHEWAN

Thunderchild No. 115D

1910 — Battleford Land District. [Map showing present and proposed timber lands for Thunderchild's band, and other reserves in the area/Carte indiquant les concessions forestières actuelles de la bande Thunderchild et celles qu'on se propose de lui donner, ainsi que d'autres réserves de la région.] Department of the Interior . . . 1910. . . .

1914 [1915] — See/Voir: **New Thunderchild No. 115B**

Thunderchild's Hay No. 115C

Refer to/Consulter: **New Thunderchild No. 115C**

Timber Berth No. 27A

Refer to/Consulter: **Carrot River No. 27A**

Timber Berth (Mistawasis)

Refer to/Consulter: **Mistawasis Timber Berth**

Turnor Lake No. 193B

1923 (1930) — Treaty 10. Plan of Turnor Lake I.R. No. 193B, Sask., for the Chipewyan Indians of the Peter Pond Lake band. Surveyed by W.A.A. McMaster, D.L.S., 1923. [Additions 1930/Additions en 1930.]

Wahpaton No. 94A

1895 — Treaty No. 6. Survey of Indian Reserve No. 94A on Sturgeon River, Tp. 49, Ra. 27, W. 2nd Mer. for Sioux refugees. . . . Surveyed in August 1894 by A.W. Ponton, D.L.S. . . . Regina, 23rd April, 1895. . . .

1899 — Treaty No. 6. Plan of subdivision survey of Indian Reserve No. 94A at Round Plain on Sturgeon River for Sioux refugees. . . . Department of Indian Affairs, Ottawa, Ont., 1st Feb'y., 1899. T.D. Green, D.L.S.

Wapachewunak No. 192D

1923 (1933) — Treaty 10. Plan of Wapachewunak I.R. No. 192D, Sask., for the Chipewyan band of Indians in the Ile-a-la-Crosse District. Surveyed by W.A.A. McMaster, D.L.S., 1923. [Additions 1933/Additions en 1933.]

White Bear No. 70

1881 — See/Voir: **Pheasant Rump No. 68**

1890	Treaty No. 4 [corrected to/corrigé pour] 2, North West Territories. Subdivision survey of part of Indian Reserve No. 70 at Moose Mountain, band of Chief "White Bear". Surveyed in August 1890 by John C. Nelson, D.L.S. in charge of Indian Reserve Surveys.
1902	Treaty No. 2. Plan of White Bear Indian Reserve No. 70. Surveyed by J. Lestock Reid, D.L.S., July-August 1901. J. Lestock Reid, D.L.S., January 1902. [2 copies]
1902	Treaty No. 2. Plan of big meadow in the White Bear Reserve No. 70. J. Lestock Reid, D.L.S., January 1902.
1905	Plan of addition to White Bear Indian Reserve No. 70. Treaty No. 4 [corrected to/corrigé pour] 2. J. Lestock Reid, D.L.S., January 11th, 1905.
1923 (1933)	Plan of White Bear Lake and land leased to Town of Carlyle in White Bear I.R. No. 70, Sask. Surveyed 1922. Donald F. Robertson, D.L.S., Chief Surveyor, Dept. of Indian Affairs. H.W.F., 22 Jan., 1923. . . . [Additions to 1933/Additions jusqu'en 1933.]

White Cap No. 94

[1881]	Treaty No. 6, Carlton District, White Cap (Sioux) Reserve. . . . Geo. A. Simpson, D.L.S. . . . Sheet 4.
1888 (1941)	Treaty No. 6, N.W.T. Indian Reserve No. 94 at Moose Woods, band of Chief White Cap (Sioux). . . . Resurveyed by John C. Nelson, D.L.S., June 1888. [Additions to 1941/Additions jusqu'en 1941.]
1889	Treaty No. 6, N.W.T. Subdivision survey of Indian Reserve No. 94, Chief White Cap (Sioux), at Moose Woods. Surveyed in June 1889 by A. W. Ponton, D.L.S.
[1903] (1941)	Treaty No. 6. Moose Woods Indian Reserve No. 94, Chief White Cap (Sioux), Assiniboia, N.W.T. W. Mackenzie, Draughtsman. [Additions to 1941/Additions jusqu'en 1941.]

William Charles No. 106

Refer to/Consulter: **Montreal Lake No. 106**

William Charles & James Roberts No. 106A

Refer to/Consulter: **Little Red River No. 106A**

William Twatt No. 101

Refer to/Consulter: **Sturgeon Lake No. 101**

SASKATCHEWAN

Woody Lake No. 184D

1919 (1930)   Treaty 6, Sask. Plan of Woody Lake Indian Reserve No. 184D for Pelican Narrows band. Situated about 15 miles north-west of Pelican Narrows Settlement in unsurveyed territory. Surveyed by W.R. White, Aug. 1919. [Additions 1930/Additions en 1930.]

Yellow Quill No. 7A

Refer to/Consulter: **Swan Lake No. 7A**

Yellow Quill No. 89

Refer to/Consulter: **Fishing Lake No. 89**

Yellow Quill No. 90

Refer to/Consulter: **Nut Lake No. 90**

Young Chipewyan No. 107

1888   Treaty No. 6, N.W.T. Survey of Indian Reserve No. 107 at Stony Knoll "Opwa-she-mocha-katinaw" for the band of Chief "Young Chipewyan". . . . Surveyed in July 1888 by John C. Nelson, D.L.S. in charge of Indian Reserve Surveys.

MANITOBA - GENERAL MAPS/
MANITOBA - CARTES GÉNÉRALES

1817   Plan of land bought by the Earl of Selkirk from Pegius and other Indians, 18th July, 1817 [showing names and marks of Indian participants/indiquant les noms et les signatures distinctives des participants indiens.]

[1884]   [Plan showing the allotment of land to the Manitoba and North Western Railway/Plan indiquant les terrains cédés à la *Manitoba and North Western Railway.*]

[1889]*   [Map showing reserves in Manitoba/Carte indiquant les réserves du Manitoba.]

[1908]   Map of part of the Dominion of Canada showing Treaty No. 3. S. Bray, Chief Surveyor, Dept. I.A.

1968   Map of Manitoba showing areas populated by Indians and Metis. Prepared by The Community Welfare Planning Council [City of Winnipeg/municipalité de Winnipeg] . . . Winnipeg . . . Manitoba. [First published/Première édition] Feb. 1959. [Revised/Revisé] June 1968.

MANITOBA - AGENCIES/
MANITOBA - AGENCES

Fort Frances

[1893]   See/Voir: **Kenora**

Kenora

[1893]   Lake of the Woods. [Plan showing the location of Indian reserves in the area/Plan indiquant l'emplacement des réserves indiennes de la région.]

Manitoba House

Refer to/Consulter: **Manitowapah**

Manitowapah

1882   Mr. Martineau's map showing the proposed fishery reserves in his Agency. . . . Manitoba House Indian Agency, 30th January, 1882, H. Martineau, Indian Agent.

[1897]   [Plan showing the proposed amalgamation of the bands of Indians of Manitowapah Agency and the portions proposed to be exchanged/ Plan indiquant le regroupement suggéré des bandes d'Indiens de l'agence Manitowapah et les parties qu'on se propose d'échanger.] [2 copies]

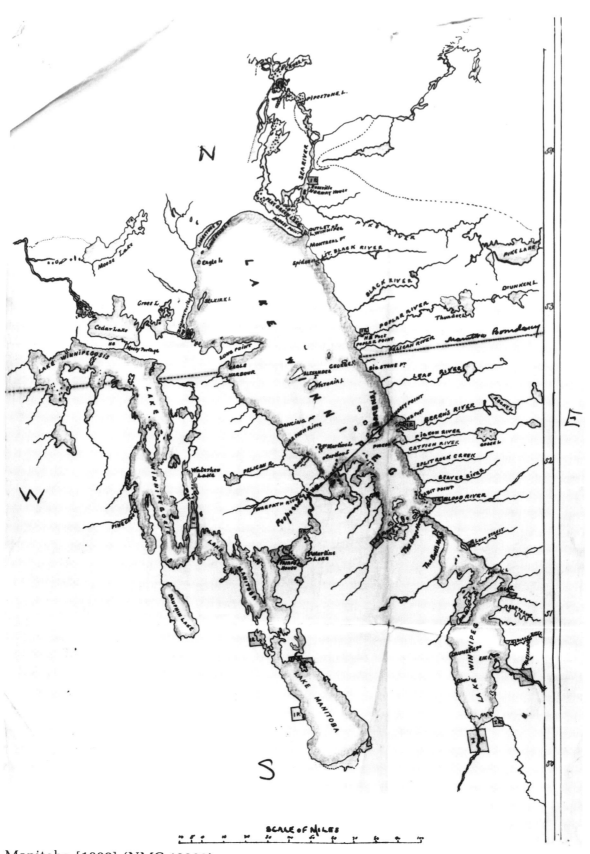

Manitoba [1889] (NMC 12263).

MANITOBA - RESERVES AND SETTLEMENTS
MANITOBA - RÉSERVES ET AGGLOMÉRATIONS

Battle Lake No. 61B

Refer to/Consulter: **Bottle Lake No. 61B**

Berens River No. 13

1885 [1896]   Plan showing changes in the north, south and east boundaries of the eastern portion of the Berens River Indian Reserve. Treaty No. 2 [corrected to/corrigé pour] 5. Jacob Berens, Chief of Reserve. Surveyed by . . . J.I. Dufresne, D.T.S., September 1885. [Additions to 1896/Additions jusqu'en 1896.]

1911   Treaty No. 5. Plan of Berens River Indian Reserve No. 13, Manitoba. Resurveyed by J.K. McLean, D.L.S. 1910. . . . Ottawa, 20th January, 1911. Certified correct, J.K. McLean, D.L.S.

1911   Treaty 5. Plan of land leased to Dept. of Marine & Fisheries for fish hatchery on Berens River Indian Reserve. Surveyed by J.K. McLean, D.L.S., 1910. Ottawa, 23rd January, 1911. Certified correct, J.K. McLean, D.L.S.

Big Jackhead No. 43

Refer to/Consulter: **Jackhead No. 43**

Bignell No. 21M

1919 (1930)   Treaty 5, Manitoba. Plan of Bignell Indian Reserve No. 21M for The Pas band. Surveyed by W.R. White . . . O. & D.L.S., Sept. 1919. . . . [Additions to 1930/Additions jusqu'en 1930.]

Birdtail Creek No. 57

1886*   Treaty No. 2, Manitoba. Subdivision survey of part of Indian Reserve No. 57 at Bird-Tail Creek. Chief Enoch. Surveyed in July & Aug. 1886 by A.W. Ponton, D.L.S.

Black River No. 9

1928   Plan of Black River Reserve. H.J. Bury, July 1928.

Bloodvein River No. 12

1884   Plan of Indian Reserve, Blood Vein River, Lake Winnipeg, Province of Manitoba. Treaty No. 2. Surveyed by T.D. Green, D.L.S. . . . 1884.

Bottle Lake No. 61B

1917   Plan of the Battle [i.e. Bottle] Lake Indian Reserve No. 61B situated in the W. 1/2 of Sec. 15, Tp. 19 - R. 20, W. 1 M., Man. [Surveyed by/Relevé par] . . . Richard Jermy Jephson . . . 1917. . . .

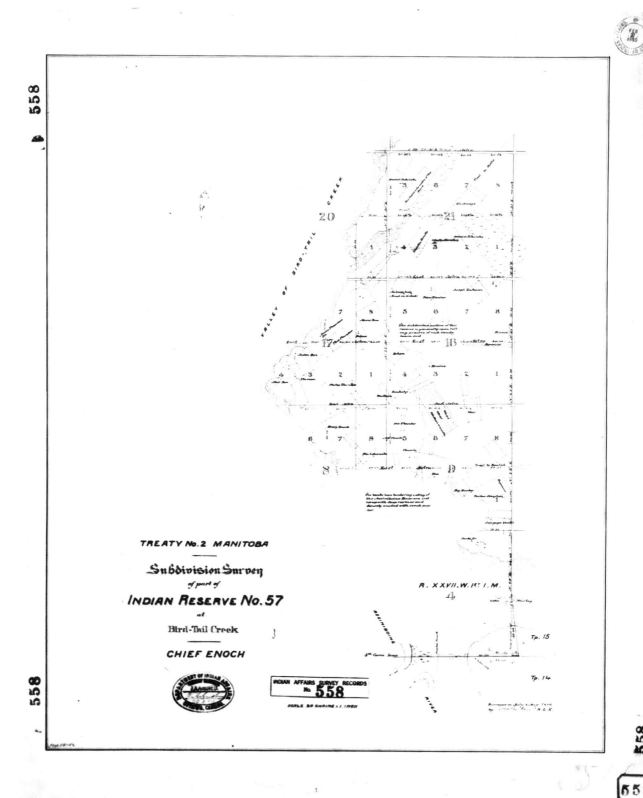

TREATY No. 2 MANITOBA

Subdivision Survey
of part of
INDIAN RESERVE No. 57
at
Bird-Tail Creek

CHIEF ENOCH

R. XXVII. W. 1ST I. M.

Birdtail Creek No. 57 1886 (C 107321).

Brandon Industrial School

[1891]   Brandon. Methodist Industrial School. (E. 1/2 Sec. 28, Tp. 10, Ra. 19, W. P.M.). John C. Nelson, D.L.S., Brandon, Man., Sept. 26th. . . .

1892   Plan of E. 1/2 Sec. 28, Tp. 10, R. 19, W. of P.M. for the Brandon Industrial School under the auspices of the Methodist Church. . . . John C. Nelson, D.L.S., 21/4/92.

Brokenhead No. 1

Refer to/Consulter: **Brokenhead No. 4**

Brokenhead No. 4

1876   Province of Manitoba. Plan shewing enlargement of Brokenhead Indian Reserve, and subdivision of a part thereof. Surveyed by Duncan Sinclair, D.L.S., September 1876.

1920 (1937)   Treaty 1. Plan of Brokenhead I.R. No. 4. Compiled from surveys . . . 1910 . . . [to/jusqu'à] 1920. . . . Drawn by H.W.F. [Additions 1937/Additions en 1937.]

1928   Plan of Brokenhead Reserve. H.J. Bury, July 1928.

Buffalo Point No. 36

1884   Plan of survey of Indian Reserve No. 36, Lake of the Woods, as surveyed under instructions from . . . the Supdt. General of Indian Affairs, dated June 8th, 1881, by A.H. Vaughan, D.L.S. . . . Selkirk, 18th Feb., 1884. . . .

1912   See/Voir: **Shoal Lake No. 40**

1935   Buffalo Point I.R. 36, Lake of the Woods, Manitoba. Surveyed by E.G. Waller, M.L.S., Sept. 1935. Plotted by G.R. . . .

Chemahawin No. 32A

1883 (1930)*   Plan of the Chimawawin Indian Reserve at the head of Cedar Lake, Great Saskatchewan River. Gloucester, March 1883. W.A. Austin, C.E., D.L.Sur. Treaty 5, 1882. [Additions 1930/Additions en 1930.]

1885   Treaty No. 5. Plan of 50 acres addition to Indian Reserve at Chimawawin [corrected to/corrigé pour] Chemahawin, Saskatchewan District. This plan is correct and is prepared under instructions from the . . . Supt. General of Indian Affairs. Ottawa, Feby. 1885. T.D. Green, D.L.S. S.B.

Chemahawin No. 32B

1883 (1930)   See/Voir: **Chemahawin No. 32A**

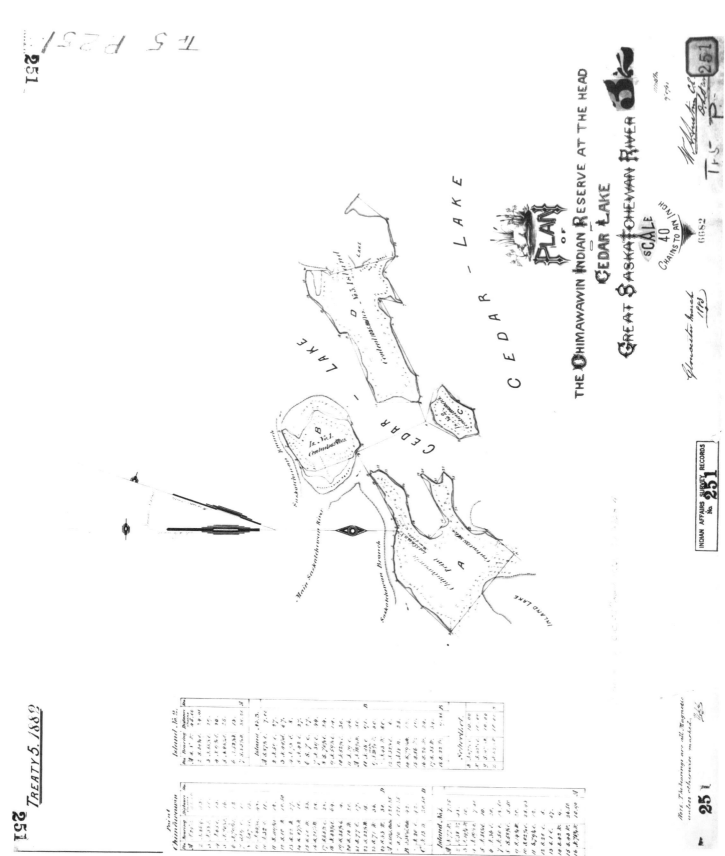

Chemahawin No. 32A 1883 (1930) (C 107329).

Chemahawin No. 32C

1883 (1930)   See/Voir: **Chemahawin No. 32A**

Chemahawin No. 32D

1883 (1930)   See/Voir: **Chemahawin No. 32A**

Chimewawin No. 32A

Refer to/Consulter: **Chemahawin No. 32A**

Chimewawin No. 32B

Refer to/Consulter: **Chemahawin No. 32B**

Chimewawin No. 32C

Refer to/Consulter: **Chemahawin No. 32C**

Chimewawin No. 32D

Refer to/Consulter: **Chemahawin No. 32D**

Clear Lake No. 61A

1908 (1935)   Tr. 2. Plan of Clear Lake I.R. No. 61A in Tp. 20, R. 19, W. of 1st M., Manitoba. Ottawa, Canada, 16 Mar., 1908. Certified correct, J.K. McLean. [Additions to 1935/Additions jusqu'en 1935.]

Clearwater Lake No. 61A

Refer to/Consulter: **Clear Lake No. 61A**

Crane River No. 6A

Refer to/Consulter: **Crane River No. 51**

Crane River No. 51

1888   Treaty No. 2, Manitoba. Indian Reserve No. 6a [i.e. 51] at Crane River, Lake Manitoba. Headman Ah yah peet oh pee tung. Surveyed in August 1888 by A.W. Ponton, D.L.S.

1888 (1913)   Treaty No. 2, Manitoba. Survey of Indian Reserve No. 6a [corrected to/corrigé pour] 51 at Crane River, Lake Manitoba. Headman Ah-yah-peet-oh-pee-tung. Surveyed in August 1888 by A.W. Ponton, D.L.S. [Additions 1913/Additions en 1913.]

Crane River No. 52

Refer to/Consulter: **Ebb and Flow No. 52**

MANITOBA

Cross Island No. 19

Refer to/Consulter: **Cross Lake No. 19**

Cross Lake No. 19

1913   Tr. 5. Plan of surrendered portion, I.R. No. 19 at Cross Lake, Donald F. Robertson, D.L.S., June 1913.

1913 (1926)   See/Voir: **Cross Lake No. 19A**

Cross Lake No. 19A

1913 (1926)   Plan of Blocks 19A, 19B, 19C, Cross Lake Indian Reserve. Treaty 5, Province of Manitoba. Surveyed by Donald F. Robertson, D.L.S., Sept. 23rd, 1913. . . . [Additions 1926/Additions en 1926.]

Cross Lake No. 19B

1913 (1926)   See/Voir: **Cross Lake No. 19A**

Cross Lake No. 19C

1913 (1926)   See/Voir: **Cross Lake No. 19A**

Dakota Plain No. 6A

[1894]   See/Voir: **Swan Lake No. 7**

Dauphin River No. 48A

1912 (1921)   Treaty No. 2. Dauphin Indian Reserve No. 48-A, Lake St. Martin. Plan showing the additions to the Lake St. Martin Indian Reserve No. 48 surveyed at the mouth of the Dauphin River at Sturgeon Bay, Lake Winnipeg, Manitoba. Certified correct and surveyed by H.B Proudfoot, D.L. Surveyor, Toronto, June 1st, 1912. . . . [Additions 1921/Additions en 1921.]

Dawson Bay No. 65A

1889   Treaty No. 4, Province of Manitoba. Sketch of Indian Reserve No. 65A, Fishing Station at Dawson's Bay, Lake Winnipegosis, for Indians of Pelly Agency. . . . Surveyed in September 1889 by John C. Nelson, D.L.S. in charge of Ind. Res. Surveys.

1889 (1953)   Treaty No. 4, Province of Manitoba. Survey of Indian Reserve No. 65a (Fishing Station) at Dawson's Bay, Lake Winnipegosis, for Indians of Pelly Agency. . . . Surveyed in September 1889 by John C. Nelson, in charge of Indian Reserve Surveys. [Additions to 1953/Additions jusqu'en 1953.]

[1889] [Plan showing the location of a proposed reserve for the Fort Pelly Indians, on Lake Winnipegosis/Plan indiquant l'emplacement de la réserve qu'on se propose de constituer à l'intention des Indiens de Fort Pelly, sur le lac Winnipegosis.]

[1889] [Plan showing a proposed reserve for the Fort Pelly Indians on Lake Winnipegosis, and other reserves in the area/Levé indiquant la réserve qu'on se propose de constituer à l'intention des Indiens de Fort Pelly sur le lac Winnipegosis, ainsi que d'autres réserves de la région.]

1894 (1924) Treaty No. 4, Province of Manitoba. Survey of Indian Reserves No. 65A & 65E at Dawson's Bay, Lake Winnipegosis. Band of Chief "The Key". Surveyed in October 1893 by John C. Nelson, D.L.S. in charge Indian Reserve Surveys, Ottawa, April 1894.... [Additions to 1924/Additions jusqu'en 1924.]

1926 (1930) Treaty 4. Plan of addition to Indian Reserve No. 65A at Dawson's Bay, Lake Winnipegosis, Manitoba. Surveyed by G.H. Herriot, D.L.S., 1926.... [Additions 1930/Additions en 1930.]

Dawson Bay No. 65B

1893 Treaty No. 4, Province of Manitoba. Survey of Indian Reserve No. 65b at Steep Rock Point, Dawson's Bay, Lake Winnipegosis, band of Chief "The Key". Surveyed in September 1893 by John C. Nelson, D.L.S. in charge of Indian Reserve Surveys....

1926 (1930) See/Voir: **Dawson Bay No. 65F**

Dawson Bay No. 65C

Refer to/Consulter: **Swan Lake No. 65C**

Dawson Bay No. 65D

Refer to/Consulter: **Dog Island No. 65D**

Dawson Bay No. 65E

1894 (1924) See/Voir: **Dawson Bay No. 65A**

Dawson Bay No. 65F

1926 (1930) Treaty 4. Plan of Indian Reserve No. 65F and addition to I.R. No. 65B at Dawson Bay, Lake Winnipegosis, Manitoba. Surveyed by G.H. Herriot, D.L.S., 1926. [Additions 1930/Additions en 1930.]

Dog Creek No. 7

Refer to/Consulter: **Dog Creek No. 46**

MANITOBA

Dog Creek No. 46

1877
Tracing of the lakes and lands claimed by Sousons'e [sic] band as made by the Chief and his Councillors on the 21st day of September, 1877.

1888
Treaty No. 2, Manitoba. Indian Reserve No. 7 [i.e. 46] at Dog Creek, Lake Manitoba. Chief Mway tway ahswing. Surveyed in 1878 by H. Martin, D.L.S. Alterations made in boundaries July 1888 by A.W. Ponton, D.L.S.

1888 (1919)
Treaty No. 2, Manitoba. Survey of Indian Reserve No. 7 [corrected to/corrigé pour] 46 at Dog Creek, Lake Manitoba. Chief Mway-tway-ah-swing. Showing changes made in 1888. Surveyed by H. Martin, D.L.S. in 1878. Changes in boundaries surveyed in July 1888 by A.W. Ponton, D.L.S. . . . [Additions to 1919/Additions jusqu'en 1919.]

[1889]*
[Dog Creek Reserve No. 46/Réserve Dog Creek N° 46.] H. Martineau, Indian Agent.

1912
Plan of Rock Island in Lake Manitoba, situated in Sec. 2, Township 22, Range 9, West of Pr. Meridian, to be added to Dog Creek Indian Reserve No. 46. Surveyed by Donald F. Robertson, D.L.S., October 1912. 46 A, Treaty 2. . . .

Dog Island No. 65D

1893
See/Voir: **Dawson Bay No. 65B**

1894 (1895)
Treaty No. 4, Province of Manitoba. Survey of Indian Reserve No. 65d at Dog Island, Dawson's Bay, Lake Winnipegosis, for the band of Chief "The Key". . . . Surveyed in October 1893 by John C. Nelson, D.L.S. in charge of Indian Reserve Surveys, Ottawa, April 1894. . . . [Additions 1895/Additions en 1895.]

Dog Lake

Refer to/Consulter: **Dog Creek No. 46**

Ebb and Flow No. 52

1874 (1924)
Plan of the Crane River Indian Reserve, west of Ebb and Flow Lake, part of Lake Manitoba. Surveyed by William Wagner, D.L.S., February 1874. Note — This reserve is now called Ebb and Flow I.R. No. 52 . . . 23/1/24.

1881
Crane River Indians Reserve, west of Ebb and Flow Lake, extension southwards. Winnipeg, Oct. 1881. W.A. Austin, C.E., D.L. Surveyor. . . . [2 copies]

1913 (1916)
Tr. 2. Plan of Ebb & Flow Indian Reserve No. 52. Resurveyed by Donald F. Robertson, D.L.S., 1913. . . . [Additions 1916/Additions en 1916.]

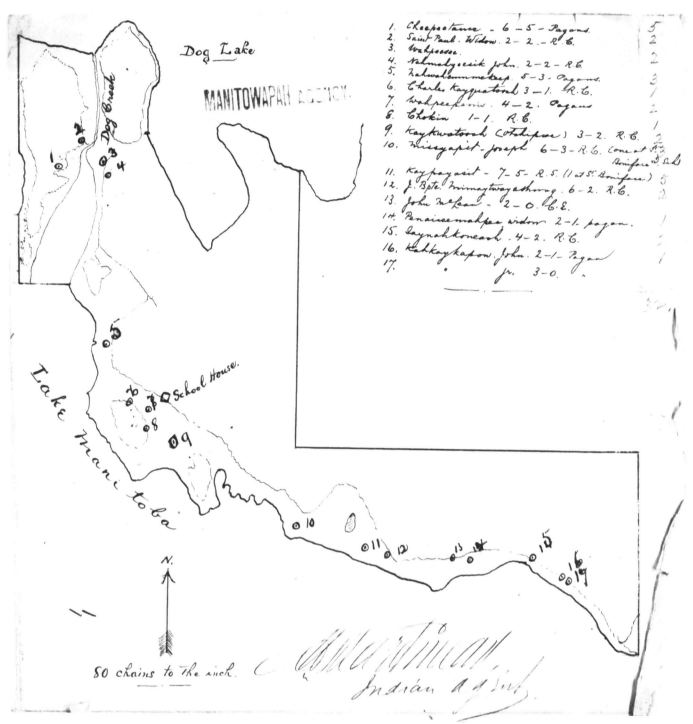

Dog Creek No. 46 [1889] (NMC 10746).

MANITOBA

Elkhorn

1886 (1912)   Plan of addition to Elkhorn, being subdivision of portions of N.W. 1/4 Sec. 34 and S.E. 1/4 Sec. 4, Tp. 11, R. 28; Tp. 12, R. 28 . . . Manitoba. Winnipeg, April 16, 1886. . . . true copy . . . 1912. . . .

Fairford No. 50

1881   Fairford band Reserve showing an equal portion cut off the south & added to the north; also the claim of Charles Wood. Ottawa, Dec. 1881. W.A. Austin, C.E., D.L. Surveyor. . . . [3 copies]

1904   Plan of settlement at the Fairford Mission Indian Reserve, Province of Manitoba. Department of the Interior, Ottawa, 27th October, 1904. . . . Compiled from official surveys by: A.F. Martin, D.L.S., 1877; W.A. Austin, D.L.S., 1881. Treaty 2.

1912   Indian Reserve No. 50. Fairford. Plan showing north and south Fisher Islands, Lake St. Martin, Manitoba. An addition to above reserve, also tie-line to Tp. 30: R. 9: W. Certified correct and surveyed by H.B. Proudfoot, D.L. Surveyor. Toronto, June 1st, 1912.

1912   Tr. 2. Fairford (Manitoba). Plan of the subdivision of part of the surrendered portion of Indian Reserve No. 50, "Fairford". Certified correct and surveyed by H.B. Proudfoot, D.L. Surveyor. Ottawa, May 1st, 1912.

1912 (1913)   Tr. 2. Indian Reserve No. 50, Fairford. Plan showing Blocks 1, 2 & 3, additions to Indian Reserve No. 50 in lieu of the land expropriated, across the reserve, by the Canadian Northern Railway — also the location of the Fairford town-plot, the Hudson's Bay Company reserve and the Anglican mission lot on the south side of the Fairford River. Certified correct and surveyed by H.B. Proudfood, D.L. Surveyor, Toronto, June 1st, 1912. [Additions 1913/Additions en 1913.]

1912 (1913)   Plan showing Block No. 4, an addition to Indian Reserve No. 50; Anglican mission lot on the north side of the Fairford River, I.R. 50; re-survey of part of Indian Reserve No. 48; an addition to Indian Reserve No. 48; disputed boundary between bands Nos. 48 and 50; Baptist mission lot. Indian Reserves No. 48, Lake St. Martin [corrected to/corrigé pour] Little Saskatchewan; No. 50, Fairford. Treaty 2. Certified correct and surveyed by H.B. Proudfoot, D.L. Surveyor. Toronto, June 1st, 1912. [Additions 1913/Additions en 1913.]

1930   Plan of Fairford Indian Reserve No. 50 in Township 30, Range 8, 9 and 10, West of Prin. Mer.; in Township 31, Range 8 and 9, West of Prin. Mer., Province of Manitoba. . . . Department of the Interior, Ottawa, 5th July, 1930. . . . Treaty 2.

Fisher Island No. 21F

Refer to/Consulter: **The Pas No. 21F**

Fisher River No. 44

1878 (1917)   Plan of Indian Reserve at Fisher River on the west side of Lake Winnipeg, District of Keewatin, according to the provisions of Treaty No. 5 and surveyed under instructions from the Surveyor General dated 18th June, 1877, by Duncan Sinclair, D.L.S. Reserve No. 86 [i.e. 44]. . . . Winnipeg, Ma., 2nd Mar., 1878. [Additions 1917/Additions en 1917.]

1896   Plan showing additions to the Fisher River Indian Reserve. Surveyed in Sep't. 1895 by the late J.C. Nelson, Esquire, D.L.S. Drawn, W.A. Austin, C.E., D.L.S., Ottawa, 29 April, 1896.

1911 (1917)   Treaty No. 2. Plan of Fisher River Indian Reserve No. 44 with additions & I.R. No. 44A in Townships 28 & 29, Ranges 1 W. & 1 & 2 E. P.M., Manitoba, as resurveyed by J.K. McLean, D.L.S. 1910. . . . Ottawa, Canada, 28th February, 1911. . . . [Additions to 1917/Additions jusqu'en 1917.]

Fisher River No. 44A

1911 (1917)   See/Voir: **Fisher River No. 44**

Fisher River No. 86

Refer to/Consulter: **Fisher River No. 44**

Fishing Station No. 1A

Refer to/Consulter: **St. Peters Fishing Station No. 1A**

Fishing Station No. 21

Refer to/Consulter: **Stony Point No. 21**

Fishing Station No. 32F

Refer to/Consulter: **Poplar Point No. 32F**

Fishing Station No. 65A

Refer to/Consulter: **Dawson Bay No. 65A**

Fort Alexander No. 3

1874   Plan. Shewing the settlement and Indian Reserve near the mouth of the Winnipeg River, N.W. Territory. Surveyed by (Sdg.) John W. Harris, Deputy Surveyor. Winnipeg, February 1874. Certified copy. . . .

MANITOBA

1891 (1957)   Tr. 1. Plan of settlers claims within the Indian Reserve at Fort Alexander, Manitoba. Winnipeg, July 2nd, 1891. Surveyed by R.C. McPhillips, D.L.S. [Additions to 1957/Additions jusqu'en 1957.]

[1901] (1953)   Plan of Indian Reserve at Fort Alexander, Manitoba. J. Lestock Reid, D.L.S. [Additions to 1953/Additions jusqu'en 1953.]

1904   Plan of Indian Reserve at Fort Alexander, Manitoba. Surveyed by J. Lestock Reid, D.L.S. 1904. . . . [2 copies]

1912   Winnipeg River Power Surveys. Fort Alexander. Topographic Sheet - No. 1 . . . from surveys by B.E. Norrish, M.Sc., Dec. 1910 - Jan. 1911. Department of the Interior, Canada . . . Water Power Branch . . . May 1912.

1921   [Plan of Fort Alexander Reserve No. 3/Plan de la réserve Fort Alexander n° 3.]

1928   Plan of Fort Alexander Reserve. H.J. Bury, June 1928.

Gambler No. 63

1884 (1900)   Treaty No. 2. Gambler's Reserve, Assiniboine River. . . . A.W. Ponton, D.L.S., Ottawa, February 29th, 1884. [Additions 1900/ Additions en 1900.]

1886   Treaty No. 2, Manitoba. Subdivision survey into 80 acre lots of part of Indian Reserve No. 63 at Silver Creek. Chief The Gambler. Surveyed in August & September 1886 by A.W. Ponton, D.L.S.

[1898] (1964)   Gambler's Indian Reserve No. 63, Manitoba [showing lands surrendered in 1892 and 1898/indiquant des terres cédées en 1892 et 1898]. [Additions to 1964/Additions jusqu'en 1964.]

1900   Subdivision survey, Gambler's Reserve No. 63 near Binscarth, Manitoba. Surveyed by J. Lestock Reid, D.L.S., May 1900. [2 copies]

1919   Plan of public road through part of Secs. 23, 26 & 27, Tp. 18, Rg. 29 W., Municipality of Ellice, Manitoba, Gambler I.R. # 63. . . . 3rd . . . January . . . 1919. [Surveyed by/relevé par] George A. Warrington, M.L.S. . . .

Grand Rapids No. 33

1895 (1928)   No. 33. Treaty No. 5, Saskatchewan, North West Territory. Plan shewing additions to the Grand Rapids Indian Reserve. . . . Surveyed August 1895 by J.C. Nelson, Esquire, D.L.S. Drawn, W.A. Austin, C.E., D.L.S. . . . [Additions 1928/Additions en 1928.]

Hamilton's Crossing No. 8

Refer to/Consulter: **Indian Gardens No. 8**

Hay

Refer to/Consulter: **Swan River Hay**

Hay Land No. 21C

Refer to/Consulter: **The Pas No. 21C**

Hay Land No. 21D

Refer to/Consulter: **The Pas No. 21D**

Hole or Hollow Water No. 10

1884 (1916)   Plan of Hole or Hollow Water Reserve, Province of Manitoba, Treaty No. 2 [corrected to/corrigé pour] 5. Surveyed by . . . T.D. Green, D.L.S. . . . 1884. [Additions 1916/Additions en 1916.]

1928   Plan of Hollow Water Reserve. H.J. Bury, July 1928.

Hollow Water No. 10

Refer to/Consulter: **Hole or Hollow Water No. 10**

Indian Gardens No. 8

[1894]   See/Voir: **Swan Lake No. 7**

Indian Pear Islands No. 21

Refer to/Consulter: **The Pas No. 21P**

Indian Pear Islands No. 21P

Refer to/Consulter: **The Pas No. 21P**

Island Lake No. 22

1925 (1929)   Treaty 5. Plan of Island Lake I.R. No. 22, Manitoba. Surveyed by Donald Robertson, D.L.S., 1925 [Additions 1929/Additions en 1929.]

Island Lake No. 22A

1925 (1929)   Treaty 5. Plan of Island Lake I.R. No. 22A, Manitoba. Surveyed by Donald Robertson, D.L.S., 1925. [Additions 1929/Additions en 1929.]

Jackhead No. 43

1884 (1930)   Treaty 2. Plan of the Jackhead No. 43 Indian Reserve at Jack Fish Head [corrected to/corrigé pour] Jack Head, Province of Manitoba. Treaty No. 2. Surveyed . . . 1884, T.D. Green, D.L.S. [Additions 1930/Additions en 1930.]

MANITOBA

Jackhead No. 43A

1926 (1930)   Treaty 2. Plan of Jackhead I.R. No. 43A, Manitoba. Surveyed by H.A. Bayne, M.L.S., 1926. [Additions 1930/Additions en 1930.]

Lake of the Woods No. 36

Refer to/Consulter: **Buffalo Point No. 36**

Lake St. Martin No. 48

Refer to/Consulter: **Little Saskatchewan No. 48**

Lake St. Martin No. 49

Refer to/Consulter: **The Narrows No. 49**

Lake St. Martin No. 49A

Refer to/Consulter: **The Narrows No. 49A**

Little Grand Rapids No. 14

1888   Treaty No. 5, Manitoba. Indian Reserve No. 48A [i.e. 14] at Little Grand Rapids, Beren's River. Headman Dick Green. . . . Surveyed in September 1888 by A.W. Ponton, D.L.S.

1888 (1930)   Treaty No. 5, Manitoba. Survey of Indian Reserve No. 48a [corrected to/corrigé pour] 14 at Little Grand Rapids, Beren's River. Headman Dick Green. Surveyed in September 1888 by A.W. Ponton, D.L.S. [Additions 1930/Additions en 1930.]

Little Grand Rapids No. 48A

Refer to/Consulter: **Little Grand Rapids No. 14**

Little Saskatchewan No. 48

1881   Little Saskatchewan band. Sandy Bay, Lake St. Marten. New reserve. Winnipeg, Nov. 1881. W.A. Austin, C.E., D.L. Surveyor. . . . [2 copies]

1912 (1913)   See/Voir: **Fairford No. 50**

Lizard Point No. 62

1884   Treaty No. 2. Way-way-see-capos' band, Bird-Tail Creek [corrected to/corrigé pour] Lizard Point No. 62. . . . A.W. Ponton, D.L.S., Ottawa, February 29th, 1884.

1908 (1953)   Treaty No. 2. Plan of subdivision of part of Waywayseecappo or Lizard Point Indian Reserve No. 62, Manitoba. Ottawa, Canada, 2nd March, 1908. Certified correct, J.K. McLean, D.L.S. [Additions to 1953/Additions jusqu'en 1953.]

Long Plain No. 6

1873 (1890) Plan of Township No. 9, Range 8, West of First Meridian [showing part of Long Plain Reserve No. 6/indiquant une partie de la réserve Long Plain n° 6]. . . . Dominion Lands Office, Ottawa, 1st June, 1873. . . . [Additions 1890/Additions en 1890.]

1874 Township No. 10, Range 8, W. of Principal Meridian [showing part of Long Plain Reserve No. 6/indiquant une partie de la réserve Long Plain n° 6]. . . . Dominion Lands Office, Ottawa, 1st March, 1874. . . .

1874 (1890) Plan of Township No. 10, Range 8, West of First Meridian [showing part of Long Plain Reserve No. 6/indiquant une partie de la réserve Long Plain n° 6]. . . . Dominion Lands Office, Ottawa, 1st March, 1874. . . . [Additions 1890/Additions en 1890.]

[1894] See/Voir: **Swan Lake No. 7**

1912 Plan of Long Plain Indian Reserve No. 6, Township 9 and No. 10, Range 8, West First Mer., Manitoba [showing proposed surrenders/indiquant les terrains qu'on se propose de céder]. Compiled from township plan. R.G. Orr, 1912.

1917 Plan of subdivision of part of Long Plain Indian Reserve No. 6, Tps. 9 and 10, Rg. 8, W. P.M., Manitoba. . . . [Surveyed by/Relevé par] John Francis, D. and M.L.S. . . . [3 copies]

[1918] Township diagram. Sketch of Township 10, R. 8, W. P.M. [showing part of Long Plain Reserve No. 6/indiquant une partie de la réserve Long Plain n° 6]. Plan by John Francis, D.L.S.

[1920] [Plan showing Sections 30 to 33, Township 10, Range 8, West of Principal Meridian, bordering Long Plain Reserve No. 6/Plan indiquant les sections n°ˢ 30 à 33, canton n° 10, rang n° 8, à l'ouest du premier méridien, en bordure de la réserve Long Plain n° 6.]

1921 Plan of special survey of Sec's 6, 7, 18, 19 & 30 to 36 (both inclusive) in Tp. 10, R. 8, W. P.M. Made under authority of the provisions of Chapter 182, M.C.S., 1913, Manitoba. . . . R.C. McPhillips, M.L.S. . . . 1921. . . .

Long Plain Sioux No. 6A

Refer to/Consulter: **Dakota Plain No. 6A**

Loon Creek No. 11

1885 Treaty No. 5. Plan of Indian Reserve at Loon Straits, Lake Winnipeg, Manitoba. This plan is correct and is prepared under instructions from the. . . Superintendent of Indian Affairs. Ottawa, 30th Jany., 1885. T.D. Green, D.L.S.

MANITOBA

Loon Straits No. 11

        Refer to/Consulter: **Loon Creek No. 11**

Lower Fairford No. 50

        Refer to/Consulter: **Fairford No. 50**

Moose Lake No. 31A

1894 (1922)   Saskatchewan [corrected to/corrigé pour] Man., Treaty No. 5. Moose Lake Reserves Nos. 31A, 31B, 31D, and 31E, situated near the Hudson's Bay Company's post on the south shore of Moose Lake. Surveyed by S. Bray, C.E., D.L.S., Asst. Chief Surveyor, Dept. of Indian Affairs, 28th Sept., 1894. [Additions to 1922/Additions jusqu'en 1922.]

1919   Plan shewing location of improvements on those portions of Sections 34 and 35, Township 54, Range 20, West of Pr. Mer., adjacent to the Hudson's Bay Company's Reserve on Moose Lake, also east boundaries of Indian Reserve No. 31A. Surveyed by E.S. Martindale, D.L.S., September 1919. . . . [4 copies]

Moose Lake No. 31B

1894 (1922)   See/Voir: **Moose Lake No. 31A**

1916 (1955)   See/Voir: **Moose Lake No. 31F**

Moose Lake No. 31C

1894 (1895)   Saskatchewan, Treaty No. 5. Big Island in Moose Lake, Reserve No. 31c of the Moose Lake band of Indians. Surveyed by S. Bray, C.E., D.L.S., Asst. Chief Surveyor, Dept. of Indian Affairs, 26th Sept., 1894. [Additions 1895/Additions en 1895.]

Moose Lake No. 31D

1894 (1922)   See/Voir: **Moose Lake No. 31A**

Moose Lake No. 31E

1894 (1922)   See/Voir: **Moose Lake No. 31A**

1916 (1955)   **See/Voir: Moose Lake No. 31F**

1919   See/Voir: **Moose Lake No. 31A**

Moose Lake No. 31F

1916 (1955)   Treaty No. 5. Moose Lake Indian Reserve No. 31F on Township 54, Ranges 19 and 20, West of Principal Meridian, Province of Manitoba. Surveyed by P.M.H. LeBlanc, D.L.S., 1916. [Additions to 1955/Additions jusqu'en 1955.]

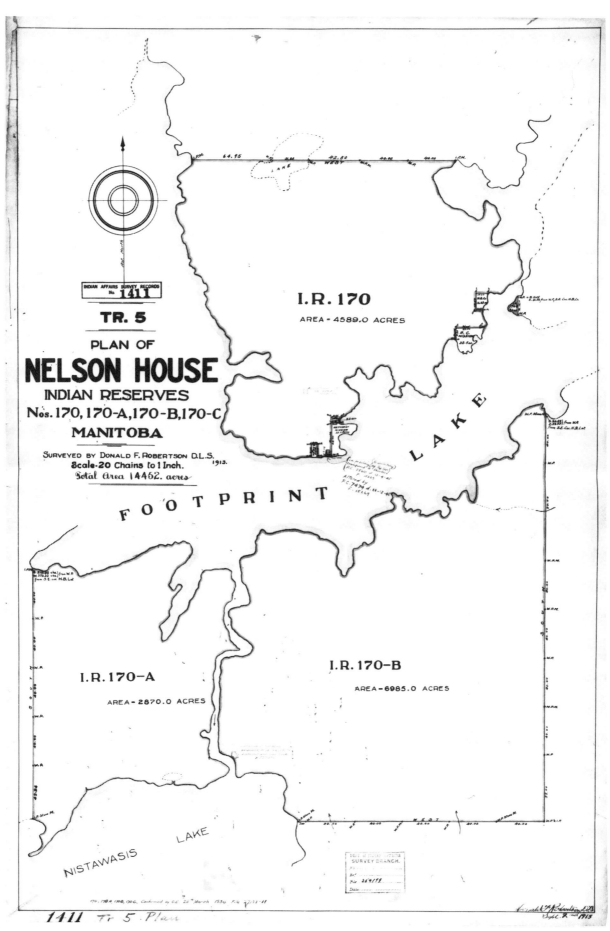

Nelson House No. 170 1913 (1945) (C 107326).

MANITOBA

Nelson House No. 170

1913 (1945)* Tr. 5. Plan of Nelson House Indian Reserves Nos. 170, 170-A, 170-B, 170-C, Manitoba. Surveyed by Donald F. Robertson, D.L.S., 1913. . . . [Additions to 1945/Additions jusqu'en 1945.]

Nelson House No. 170A

1913 (1945) See/Voir: **Nelson House No. 170**

Nelson House No. 170B

1913 (1945) See/Voir: **Nelson House No. 170**

Nelson House No. 170C

1913 (1945) See/Voir: **Nelson House No. 170**

Northwest Angle No. 34C

1912 See/Voir: **Shoal Lake No. 40**

Northwest Angle No. 37C

1912 See/Voir: **Shoal Lake No. 40**

Norway House No. 17

1910 (1923) Treaty No. 5. Plan of Norway House Indian Reserve No. 17, with addition and exchange, N.W.T. Surveyed by J.K. McLean, D.L.S., 1910. [Additions 1923/Additions en 1923.]

1910 (1940) Tr. 5, N.W.T. Plan of land belonging to Methodist mission & H.B. Co. at Rossville, Norway House Indian Reserve. Surveyed by J.K. McLean, D.L.S., 1910. . . . [Additions to 1940/Additions jusqu'en 1940.]

1925 Plan of a parcel of land in Norway House Indian Reserve No. 17, Manitoba, for the use of the Methodist Boarding School. Surveyed by H.W. Fairchild, 1924. G.P., 20th May, 1925.

Oak Lake No. 59

1901 Treaty No. 2, N.W.T. Plan of Oak Lake Sioux Reserve No. 59. . . . Surveyed by J. Lestock Reid, D.L.S., 1901.

Oak River No. 58

Refer to/Consulter: **Sioux Valley No. 58**

Oxford House No. 24

1884 (1895)   . . . Plan of part, Indian Reserve for band at Pas Mission. Treay [sic] No. 5, Saskatchewan District. Surveyed by T.D. Green, D.L.S. . . . 1884. . . . [Additions 1895/Additions en 1895.]

Pear Island No. 21A

Refer to/Consulter: **The Pas No. 21P**

Peguis No. 1B

1909 (1953)   Treaty No. 1. Plan of the Prince [corrected to/corrigé pour] Peguis Indian Reserve No. 1B for the St. Peters band of Indians on Fisher River, Manitoba. Surveyed Sept. & Oct.—1908. Ottawa, Canada, 11th January, 1909. Certified correct, J.K. McLean, D.L.S. [Additions to 1953/Additions jusqu'en 1953.]

1912   Treaty No. 1. Plan of the Peguis Indian Reserve No. 1B for the St. Peters band of Indians on Fisher River, Manitoba [showing river lots/indiquant les lots riverains]. Surveyed by J.K. McLean, D.L.S. in 1912. . . .

[1912] (1956)   Plan of river lots in Peguis Indian Reserve No. 1-B, Manitoba, being a subdivision of Secs. 19, 20, 29, 30, 31 and 32, Tp. 26, Rge. 1, Secs. 7, 8, 9, 16, 17, 21, 22, 27, 28, 34 and 35, Tp. 27, Rge. 1, Secs. 2, 3, 11 and 12, Tp. 28, Rge. 1, West of the Principal Meridian. [Additions 1956/Additions en 1956.]

[1915]   [Plan of part of the Peguis Reserve showing the land required by the Church of England on lot 24/Plan d'une partie de la réserve Peguis indiquant les terrains demandés par l'Église anglicane sur le lot 24.] [2 copies]

1921   Treaty 1. Plan of part of Township 27, Range 2, W. P.M., in Peguis Indian Reserve No. 1-B, Manitoba. Compiled from surveys of J.W. Tyrrell, D.L.S., 4th September, 1908. G.P., 16th Sept., 1921.

Pigeon River No. 13A

1911 (1930)   Treaty No. 5. Plan of Indian Reserve No. 13A on Pigeon River, being an addition to I.R. No. 13, Berens River, Manitoba. Surveyed by J.K. McLean, D.L.S., 1910. Ottawa, 28th January, 1911. Certified correct, J.K. McLean, D.L.S. . . . [Additions 1930/Additions en 1930.]

Pine Creek No. 66A

1887 (1917)   Treaty No. 2, N.W.T. Survey of Indian Reserve No. 66a (Band of Chief Kesikoose) on Pine Creek, Lake Winnipegosis. . . . Surveyed in August 1887 by A.W. Ponton, D.L.S. [Additions to 1917/Additions jusqu'en 1917.]

MANITOBA

1901	Plan of Township No. 34, Range 20, West of Principal Meridian [near Pine Creek Reserve No. 66A/proche de la réserve Pine Creek n° 66A]. . . . Department of the Interior, Topographical Surveys Branch, Ottawa, 9th August, 1901. . . .
[1901]	[Sketch showing the actual situation and the lands to be acquired for the boarding school at Pine Creek/Croquis indiquant la situation actuelle et les terrains devant être acquis pour la pension à Pine Creek.]
[1909]	Sketch of fractional Township Nos. 35, 36 and 37, Range 19, W. P.M. [showing/indiquant] the portions added to the Pine Creek [Reserve/réserve]. . . .

Pipestone No. 59

Refer to/Consulter: **Oak Lake No. 59**

Poplar Point No. 32F

1894 (1895)	No. 32F. Saskatchewan [corrected to/corrigé pour] Manitoba, Treaty No. 5. Poplar Point. A fishing station for the Chimawawin Indians. Situated on the mainland on a small channel south of the main channel of the Saskatchewan River and about ten miles west of Chimawawin. Surveyed by S. Bray, C.E., D.L.S., Asst. Chief Surveyor, Dept. of Indians Affairs, Sept. 10th, 1894. [Additions 1895/Additions en 1895.]
1919 (1946)	Manitoba, Treaty 5. Plan of addition to Poplar Point I.R. No. 32F and resurvey of I.R. No. 32F by W.R. White, D.L.S., Oct. 1919. . . . [Additions to 1946/Additions jusqu'en 1946.]

Portage La Prairie No. 8A

[1875]	[Two rough sketches of the reserve proposed to be allotted to Yellow Quill's band, containing 34,000 acres/Deux croquis préliminaires de la réserve qu'on se propose de donner à la bande Yellow Quill, d'une superficie de 34 000 acres.]

Potato Island No. 21G

Refer to/Consulter: **The Pas No. 21G**

Pow-was-an No. 37A

Refer to/Consulter: **Shoal Lake No. 37A**

Prince No. 1B

Refer to/Consulter: **Peguis No. 1B**

Red Rock River No. 24

Refer to/Consulter: **Oxford House No. 24**

Rock Island No. 46A

Refer to/Consulter: **Dog Creek No. 46**

Rocky Lake No. 21L

1919   Treaty 5, Man. Plan of Rocky Lake Indian Reserve No. 21-L in Tp. 59 - R. 28 - W. Pr. Mer. for The Pas band in part exchange for Birch River I.R. Surveyed by W.R. White, Sept. 1919. [2 copies]

Rolling River No. 67

[1882]   Plan of Township No. 17, Range 19 - Proposed reserve - South Quill. Dominion Lands Office. . . .

[1882]   Proposed "South Quill" Indian Reserve, at Rolling River. Plan of Township No. 17, Range 19. Dominion Lands Office. . . .

1890   Sketch of township outlines [showing Rolling River Reserve No. 67/indiquant la réserve Rolling River n° 67]. . . . Copy of plan accompanying letter . . . of 21st April, 1890. . . .

1890 (1893)   Treaty No. 4, Manitoba. Indian Reserve No. 67 at Rolling River for the band of Chief "South Quill" ("Shawenequanape"). . . . John C. Nelson, in charge Indn. Res. Surveys, 27/3/90. . . . [Additions 1893/ Additions en 1893.]

1897 (1906)   Treaty No. 2. Survey, Indian Reserve No. 67 for Chief South Quill's band on Rolling River, Province of Manitoba. . . . Surveyed in November 1894 by A.W. Ponton, D.L.S. Certified correct, A.W. Ponton, in charge of Indian Reserve Surveys, Man. & N.W.T., Regina, 19 February, 1897. [Additions to 1906/Additions jusqu'en 1906.]

Roseau River No. 2

1887   Treaty No. 1, Manitoba. Survey of Indian Reserve No. 2 on Roseau River for the bands of Wakowush, Keweetoyash & Manawanan. . . . Surveyed in Sept. & Oct. 1887 by A.W. Ponton, D.L.S.

1903   Plan of subdivided portion of Roseau River Indian Reserve No. 2, Man. Treaty No. 1. J. Lestock Reid, D.L.S., April 7th, 1903.

1903 (1960)   Plan of Roseau River Indian Reserve No. 2, Manitoba, showing the portion surrendered for sale. Subdivided under instructions from the Superintendent General of Indian Affairs dated 3rd March, 1903 by J. Lestock Reid, D.L.S. . . . [Additions to 1960/Additions jusqu'en 1960.]

MANITOBA

Rupert's Land Industrial School

[1897]   Lands of the Rupert's Land Industrial School. . . .

St. Boniface Industrial School

[1890]   [Plan showing proposed location of grounds for the St. Boniface Industrial School/Plan indiquant l'emplacement suggéré des terrains de l'école industrielle de Saint-Boniface.]

1903   Canadian Northern Railway. Plan of right of way of spur to Rat Portage Lumber Co. through Indian Industrial School property, St. Boniface, Manitoba. Engineer's Office, Winnipeg, July 3rd, 1903. . . .

St. Martin's Lake No. 48

                Refer to/Consulter: **Little Saskatchewan No. 48**

St. Martin's Lake No. 49

                Refer to/Consulter: **The Narrows No. 49**

St. Martin's Lake No. 49A

                Refer to/Consulter: **The Narrows No. 49A**

St. Peters No. 1

1875   Plan of river lots in the Parish of St. Peter, Province of Manitoba. Surveyed by A.W. Vaughan, Deputy Surveyor, Winnipeg, 1874. Dominion Lands Office, Ottawa, 1st January, 1875. . . . [3 copies]

[1877]   A. [Plan showing St. Peters Reserve No. 1/Plan indiquant la réserve St. Peters nº 1.] A.H.W.

1883   Plan of St. Peter's Indian Reserve, showing position of iron posts planted to mark boundaries. Selkirk, Aug. 31st, 1883. L.S. Vaughan, P.L.S.

1883   Plan shewing the ground set apart for the Roman Catholic mission, Indian Reserve, east side of Red River, St. Peters. Surveyed by C.J. Bouchette, D. & P.L.S. St. Peters Parish, 23rd Octbr., 1883.

1883   Plan of Roman Catholic school plot situate on the west bank of Nettlie Creek, Indian Reserve. Surveyed by C.J. Bouchette, D. & P.L. Surveyor, Winnipeg. St. Peters Parish, 24th Octbr., 1883.

[1884]   Sketch showing new main road [from south boundary of St. Peter's Reserve north of Lot. No. 15/partant de l'extrémité sud de la réserve St. Peters, au nord du lot nº 15], as approved by Provincial govt.

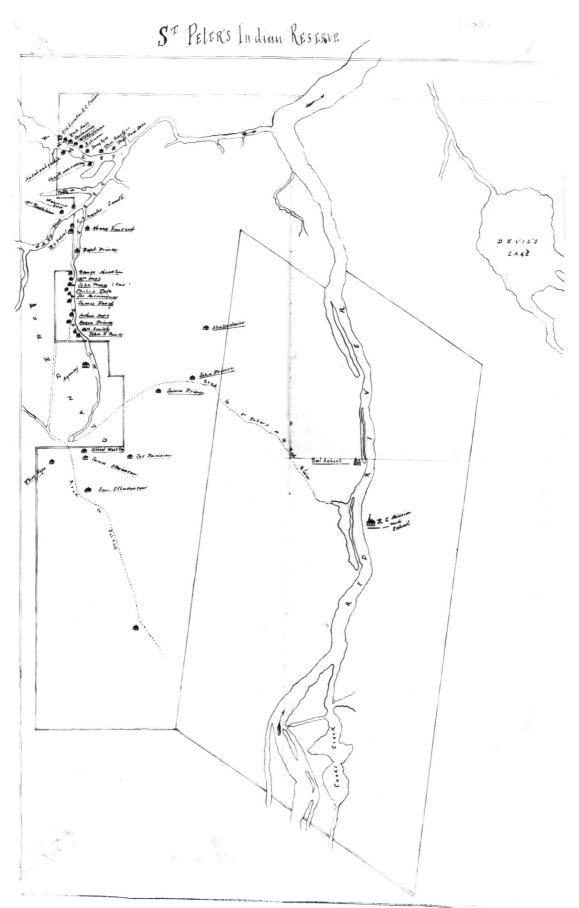

St. Peters No. 1 [1885] (NMC 12270).

MANITOBA

[1885]* St. Peter's Indian Reserve. [Plan showing old and new sites of school house, and Indian houses with names of occupants/Plan indiquant l'ancien et le nouveau site du bâtiment de l'école, ainsi que les habitations indiennes et le nom de leurs occupants.]

1888 Sketch showing claim of Edwd. Thomas in Parish of St. Peters, Man. L.T.G., 14/11/88.

[1897] Treaty No. 1, Manitoba. Resurvey & subdivision, St. Peters Indian Reserve No. 1. Surveyed by T.D. Green, D.L.S.

1899 Re-posting river lots in the Parish of St. Peter, Province of Manitoba. Surveyed by T.D. Green, D.L.S. Dept. of Indian Affairs, Ottawa, Ont., 23rd June, 1899. . . .

1903 River lots in the Parish of St. Peter, Province of Manitoba [showing claims to land held by white men and half-breeds on the St. Peter's Reserve/indiquant les terrains réclamés que détiennent des Blancs et des Métis dans la réserve St. Peters]. Surveyed by T.D. Green, D.L.S. Dept. of Indian Affairs . . . 23rd June, 1889. W.M. 17, 8, 03.

1904 Plan of subdivided portion, outer two miles east, St. Peters Indian Reserve. Treaty No. 1. Surveyed by J. Lestock Reid, D.L.S., November 1904.

1904 Plan of . . . part of Townships XIII & XIV, Ranges 5 & 6 E., St. Peters Indian Reserve. Surveyed by J. Lestock Reid, D.L.S., 1904. . . .

1904 (1946) Treaty No. 1, Manitoba. Plan 312. Resurvey & subdivision, St. Peters Indian Reserve No. 1. Surveyed by T.D. Green, D.L.S., 1897 and J.L. Reid, D.L.S., 1904. . . . [Additions 1946/Additions en 1946.]

1908 Plan of Townships 13 & 14, Ranges 5 & 6, E. P.M., St. Peters Indian Reserve. Surveyed by J.K. McLean, D.L.S., 1908 and J.L. Reid, D.L.S. in 1904. . . . [2 copies]

1908 Plan of parts of Township 14, Ranges 4, E. and 5, E. P.M., St. Peter's Indian Reserve. As surveyed by T.D. Green, D.L.S. in 1896 and resurveyed by J.K. McLean, D.L.S. in 1908. . . .

1908 (1946) Plan of Township 15, Ranges 5, E. and 6, E. P.M., St. Peters Indian Reserve. As surveyed by J.K. McLean, D.L.S. in 1908. . . . Selkirk, Man., 16th Sept., 1908. [Additions 1946/Additions en 1946.]

1908 (1949) Plan of Township 15, Range 4, E. and 5, E. P.M., St. Peter's Indian Reserve. As surveyed by T.D. Green, D.L.S. in 1896 and resurveyed by J.K. McLean, D.L.S. in 1908. . . . Selkirk, Man., 16th Sept., 1908. [Additions to 1949/Additions jusqu'en 1949.]

1908 (1964)   Plan of river lots in the Parish of St. Peter, St. Peters Indian Reserve, Province of Manitoba, showing the subdivisions surveyed by J.K. McLean, D.L.S. 1908. . . . [Additions 1964/Additions en 1964.]

1911   Plan of river lots in the Parish of St. Peter, St. Peters Indian Reserve, Province of Manitoba . . . Certified correct, J.K. McLean, D.L.S., Ottawa, Ont., 18th Decr., 1911.

1911   Plan of Township XIV, Ranges 5 & 6, E., St. Peters Indian Reserve. Certified correct, J.K. McLean, D.L.S., Ottawa, Ont., Dec. 18th, 1911. . . .

1912   Plan of part of Township 14, Ranges 4 and 5, E. P.M., St. Peters Indian Reserve. . . . Certified correct, J.K. McLean, D.L.S., Ottawa, Ont., 15th January, 1912. A.G.O., 1912.

1912   Plan of Township 15, Ranges 4, E. & 5, E. P.M., St. Peter's Indian Reserve. Certified correct, J.K. McLean, D.L.S., Ottawa, Ont., 15th January, 1912. . . .

1912   Plan of Township 15, Ranges 5 and 6, E. P.M., St. Peters Indian Reserve. Tr. 1. Certified correct, J.K. McLean, D.L.S., Ottawa, Ont., 15th January, 1912. . . .

1918   Plan showing hay lands in projected Sections 13 and 24, Tp. XV, R. IV, E. P.M. and projected Sections 7, 8, 9, 10, 13, 14, 15, 16, 17, 18, 19, 20, 21, 22, 23 & 24, Tp. XV, R. V, E. P.M. and projected Sections 18 & 19, Tp. XV, R. VI, E. P.M., St. Peters Indian Reserve, Province of Manitoba. Compiled by W.R. White, 21/3/18.

1935   Plan of part of Township 15, Ranges 4, 5 and 6, E. P.M. Selkirk, Man., 13th November, 1935, P.W. Mullins, M.L.S. [2 copies]

[1935]   Plan of part of Township 15, Ranges 4, 5 and 6, E. P.M. [showing the St. Peters hay land/indiquant les terres à foin de St. Peters]. [4 copies]

[1936]   [Part plan of Township 15, Ranges 5 and 6, E. P.M. showing hay land/Plan partiel du canton n° 15, rangs nos 5 et 6, à l'est du premier méridien, indiquant les terres à foin.] P.W. Mullins, Manitoba Land Surveyor and Civil Engineer. . . .

[1936]   [Three surveyor's diagrams of a portion of the St. Peters hay lands/Trois schémas d'arpentage d'une partie des terres à foin de St. Peters.]

St. Peters Fishing Station No. 1A

1895   Treaty No. 1. Lake Winnipeg. Plan of south-west quarter Section 31 of Township No. 16, Range 5, E. of 1st Meridian, small additional reserve for St. Peter's band. Surveyed August 1895 by the late J.C. Nelson, D.L.S. Drawn by W.A. Austin, C.E., D.L.S.

MANITOBA

Salt Channel No. 21D

1894 (1895)   Saskatchewan, Treaty No. 5. Indian Reserve at the Salt Channel. A timber limit for "The Pas" band situated near the Carrot River and about twenty miles west of "The Pas". Surveyed by S. Bray, C.E., D.L.S., Asst. Chief Surveyor, Dept. of Indian Affairs, 19th Nov., 1894. [Additions 1895/Additions en 1895.]

Sandy Bay No. 48

Refer to/Consulter: **Little Saskatchewan No. 48**

Shoal Lake No. 37A

[1890]   See/Voir: **Shoal Lake No. 39**

1898   See/Voir: **Shoal Lake No. 39**

[1898]   See/Voir: **Shoal Lake No. 39**

1912   See/Voir: **Shoal Lake No. 40**

1914   See/Voir: **Shoal Lake No. 40**

Shoal Lake No. 39

1890   Sketch showing survey in connection with islands in Shoal Lake on which the Indians of band 39 and 40 have or had gardens, referred to in instructions dated Ottawa, 16th June, 1890. Surveyed in Sept. 1890 by (Sd.) A.W. Ponton, D.L.S. . . .

[1890]   [Map showing location of the islands in Shoal Lake to which Chief She-she-gence's band is entitled, and other reserves in the area/ Carte indiquant l'emplacement des îles du lac Shoal qui reviennent de droit à la bande du chef She-she-gence, ainsi que d'autres réserves de la région.]

[1897]   [Sketch showing the location of the Shoal Lake Reserve No. 39/ Croquis indiquant l'emplacement de la réserve Shoal Lake n° 39.]

1898   Sketch showing approximately the mining locations applied for in Indian Reserve No. 39, Shoal Lake, Lake of the Woods, Ont. Compiled from plans and sketches of record in the Dept. of Indian Affairs . . . 25th Jany., 1898. S. Bray, O. & D.L.S.

1898   Plan of mining locations Nos. CR 36, CR 37, CR 38, CR 38A, CR 38B and CR 38C, Shoal Lake, Lake of the Woods, Ont. . . . [Surveyed by/ Relevé par] Cyrus Carroll, Dominion and Ontario Land Surveyor . . . 8th . . . January, 1898.

1898 — Plan of mining locations Nos. CR 38, CR 38A and CR 38B, Shoal Lake, Lake of the Woods. . . . [Surveyed by/Relevé par] Cyrus Carroll, Dominion and Ontario Land Surveyor . . . 8th . . . January, 1898.

1898 — Plan of mining location J.E.S. 78, Indian Reserve 39, west of Shoal Lake, District of Rainy River, Ontario. J.E. Schwitzer, Ontario Land Surveyor. Rat Portage, Jan. 3rd, 1898.

[1898] — [Plan showing location of reserves in the Shoal Lake area/Plan indiquant l'emplacement des réserves dans la région du lac Shoal.]

[1898] — [Three sketches showing the location of the Shoal Lake Reserves No. 39 and 37A/Trois croquis indiquant l'emplacement des réserves Shoal Lake nos 39 et 37A.]

[1898] — [Plan of the Shoal Lake Reserve No. 39 showing mining locations Nos. CR 36, CR 37 and CR 38/Plan de la réserve Shoal Lake n° 39, indiquant les concessions minières nos CR 36, CR 37 et CR 38.]

[1898] — [Plan of the Shoal Lake Reserve No. 39 showing mining locations Nos. CR 36, CR 37, CR 38, CR 38A, CR 38B and CR 38C/Plan de la réserve Shoal Lake n° 39, indiquant les concessions minières nos CR 36, CR 37, CR 38, CR 38A, CR 38B et CR 38C.]

[1898]* — Sketch shewing in red point of land applied for as a mining claim on Shoal Lake, L. of the Woods. . . .

[1898] — Part of Indian Reserve 39 [showing location applied for/indiquant la concession demandée].

Shoal Lake No. 39A

1912 — See/Voir: **Shoal Lake No. 40**

1914 — See/Voir: **Shoal Lake No. 40**

Shoal Lake No. 40

1890 — See/Voir: **Shoal Lake No. 39**

[1890] — See/Voir: **Shoal Lake No. 39**

1912 — Manitoba. Lake of the Woods sheet, East of Principal Meridian. Revised to the 7th March, 1912. [Verso: Sketch showing Snake Lake area/Croquis montrant la région de Snake Lake.]

1912 — Plan of Indian Reserves 39A and 40 and 34B2, Shoal Lake, Ontario and Manitoba. Resurveyed 1911. Surveyed by J.W. Fitzgerald, O.L.S., Peterboro, Jany. 10th, 1912.

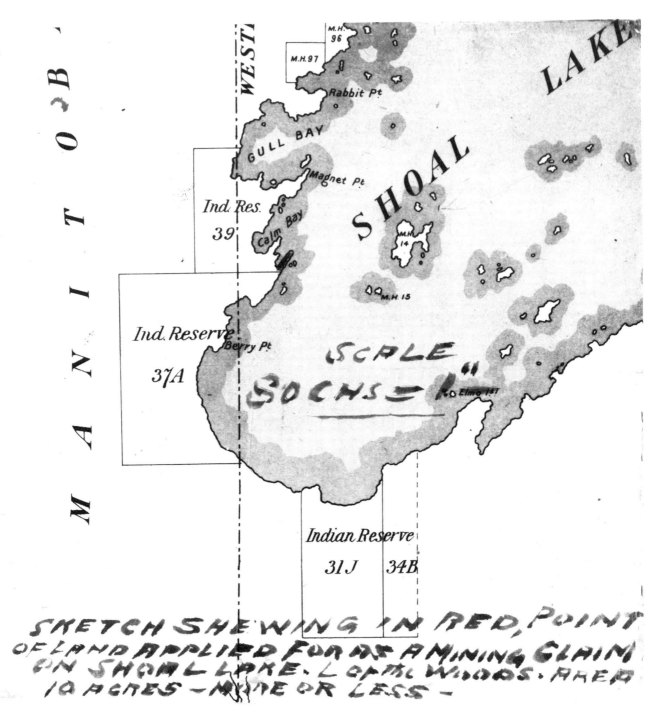

Shoal Lake No. 39 [1898] (NMC 12463).

1914   Greater Winnipeg Water District. Sketch map of portions of Indian Reserve No. 40 to accompany District's application for land required. 21st Feby., 1914. [2 copies]

1914   Greater Winnipeg Water District. Map, Winnipeg to Shoal Lake showing vicinity of line of proposed acqueduct. . . . Feb. 26th, 1914.

1919   Greater Winnipeg Water District. Plan of proposed additional land at Indian Bay. 26/6/19. [2 copies]

1920   Plan of Reserve No. 40, Shoal Lake, H.J. Bury, Dec. 1920.

Short Bears No. 6

Refer to/Consulter: **Long Plain No. 6**

Sioux Valley No. 58

1891 (1927)   Treaty No. 2, Manitoba. Re-survey of the boundaries of Sioux Indian Reserve No. 58 at Oak River for the band of Chief "Taninyahdinazin", alias "Jim". . . . Surveyed in Oct. & Nov. 1891, John C. Nelson, D.L.S. . . . [Additions to 1927/Additions jusqu'en 1927.]

1894 (1927)   Treaty No. 2, Manitoba. Subdivision survey of the Sioux Indian Reserve No. 58 at Oak River. Band of Chief Taninyahdinazin (alias James McKay). . . . Surveyed in Oct and Nov. 1891 by T.D. Green, D.L.S. Ottawa, Ont. 26th April, 1894. [Additions to 1927/Additions jusqu'en 1927.]

Sousonse

Refer to/Consulter: **Dog Creek No. 46**

South Quill No. 67

Refer to/Consulter: **Rolling River No. 67**

Split Lake No. 171

1913 (1923)   Tr. 5. Plan of Split Lake Indian Reserves Nos. 171, 171-A & 171-B, Manitoba. Surveyed by Donald F. Robertson, D.L.S., 1913. Donald F. Robertson, D.L.S., July 31st, 1913. [Additions to 1923/Additions jusqu'en 1923.]

Split Lake No. 171A

1913 (1923)   See/Voir: **Split Lake No. 171**

Split Lake No. 171B

1913 (1923)   See/Voir: **Split Lake No. 171**

MANITOBA

Stony Point No. 21

1894 (1917)   Saskatchewan [corrected to/corrigé pour] Manitoba, Treaty No. 5. Fishing station at Stony Point on the east shore of Clear Water Lake for The Pas band of Indians. Surveyed by S. Bray, C.E., D.L.S., Asst. Chief Surveyor, Dept. of Indian Affairs, 11th Oct., 1894. [Additions 1917/Additions en 1917.]

Swan Lake No. 7

1873   Plan of Township No. 5, Range 11, West of First Meridian [showing the Swan Lake Reserve No. 7/indiquant l'emplacement de la réserve Swan Lake nº 7]. . . . Dominion Lands Office, Ottawa, 1st April, 1873. [2 copies]

1876 [1888]   Proposed reserve, Yellow Quill band of Indians. Plan of Township No. 5, Range 11, West of 1st Meridian [showing the Swan Lake Reserve No. 7/indiquant l'emplacement de la réserve Swan Lake nº 7]. . . . (Sgd.) J. Lestock Reid, D.L.S. December 1876. . . .

[1894]   [Plan showing location of proposed choice of lands offered in compensation for the Swan Lake band/Plan indiquant l'emplacement des choix de terrains qu'on se propose de donner à la bande Swan Lake à titre de compensation.]

[1907]   Plan of Township No. 5, Range 11, West of First Meridian, showing the Swan Lake Indian Reserve . . . No. 7. Treaty No. 1. [2 copies]

1908 (1952)   Plan of part of Township No. 5, Range 11, West of First Meridian, Manitoba, showing the surrendered portion of Swan Lake I.R. No. 7. Surveyed by J.L. Reid, D.L.S., 1908. . . . [Additions to 1952/Additions jusqu'en 1952.]

1909 (1952)   Plan of Township No. 5, Range 11, West of First Meridian, showing the surrendered portion, Swan Lake Indian Reserve . . . No. 7. Treaty No. 1. J. Lestock Reid, D.L.S., February 6th, 1909. [Additions to 1952/ Additions jusqu'en 1952.]

Swan Lake No. 65C

1893 (1895)   Treaty No. 4, Province of Manitoba. Survey of Indian reserve No. 65C at Swan Lake. Band of Chief "The Key". . . . Surveyed in October 1893 by John C. Nelson, D.L.S. in charge Indian Reserve Surveys. [Additions 1895/Additions en 1895.]

Swan River Hay

[1889]   See/Voir: **Dawson Bay No. 65A**

1897 (1898)	Survey of Hay Reserve between Swan and Woody Rivers, Manitoba, for the Indians of the Swan River Agency. Treaty No. 4. Nos. 64, 65, 66. . . . Surveyed in October 1895 by A.W. Ponton, D.L.S. . . . in charge of Indian Reserve Surveys—Man. & N.W.T. Regina, 19th February, 1897. [Additions 1898/Additions en 1898.]

The Gambler No. 63

Refer to/Consulter: **Gambler No. 63**

The Narrows No. 49

1877 (1893)	Tr. 2. Plan of the survey of Saint Martins Lake Indian Reserve No. 49, Keewatin, contg. 4088 acres. Surveyed by H. Martin, Dom. Land Surveyor, Winnipeg, 21st May, 1877. . . . [Additions to 1893/Additions jusqu'en 1893.]
[1880]	Saint Martin's Lake [i.e. The Narrows] Reserve. [Sketch showing portion Indians propose being cut off and proposed addition/Croquis indiquant la partie que les Indiens proposent d'abandonner et celle qu'ils proposent d'ajouter.]

The Narrows No. 49A

[1880]	See/Voir: **The Narrows No. 49**

The Pas No. 21

Refer to/Consulter: **Stony Point No. 21**

The Pas No. 21A

N.D./S.D.	Townsite of The Pas, Manitoba. [2 copies]
N.D./S.D.	See/Voir: **The Pas No. 21B**
1883 (1940)	Treaty 5, 1882. Surveys of part of The Pas Indian Reserve, Saskatchewan River, including portions A . . . B . . . C . . . D . . . E . . . F . . . G. . . . Gloucester, Feby. 1883. W.A. Austin, C.E., D.L.S. [Additions to 1940/Additions jusqu'en 1940.]
1894	Plan of part of The Pas Indian Reserve, Saskatchewan River, including portions A . . . B . . . C . . . D . . . E . . . F . . . G . . . H . . . I . . . J . . . K. . . . Surveyed by W.A. Austin, D.L.S., Feby. 1883 and S. Bray, C.E. D.L.S., Oct. 1894. . . . [2 copies]
1907	Plan of the townplot of The Pas on Block A of The Pas Indian Reserves on the Saskatchewan River. J.K. McLean, D.L.S. in 1907. [3 copies]
1912	Plan of the townplot of The Pas on Block A of The Pas Indian Reserves on the Saskatchewan River, Manitoba. Surveyed by J.K. McLean, D.L.S., 1907 & H.B. Proudfoot, D.L.S., 1911. . . . Dept. of Indian Affairs . . . 1912. [4 copies]

1912 (1919)   Plan of sub-division of Blocks 30, 42 to 85, shown on the original plot of The Pas made by J.K. McLean, D.L.S., 1907. Surveyed by H.B. Proudfoot, 1911. Certified correct . . . by H.B. Proudfoot, D.L. Surveyor, Ottawa, April 1912. [Additions to 1919/Additions jusqu'en 1919.]

[1912]   Part of The Pas townplot [showing position of Block 85/indiquant l'emplacement du bloc 85.]

1913   Plan of cemetery road at The Pas, being part of Block "A", Indian Reserve No. 21, Manitoba. . . . R.A. McLellan, D.L.S. . . . 8th . . . October . . . 1913.

1917   Sketch plan of river lots in the vicinity of Pas, Province of Manitoba. Compiled from official surveys . . . 1906 . . . [to/jusqu'en] 1917. Department of the Interior, Ottawa. . . .

1917   Plan showing land to be transferred by the Department of Indian Affairs to the Department of Railways and Canals for the purposes of the Hudson Bay Railway, being a part of Block A of The Pas Indian Reserve No. 21. . . . Chief Engineer, 25th Oct., 1917. . . . [2 copies]

[1917]   . . . [Sketch showing/Croquis indiquant] lots 53, 45 and 46 [The Pas/Le Pas], as registered with the right of way eliminated.

1919 (1920)   Plan showing the posts renewed in The Pas townsite by W.R. White, 1919. . . . [Additions 1920/Additions en 1920.]

1920   Plan of the subdivision of Block 3, Town of The Pas. Surveyed by Chas. M. Teasdale, D.L.S., July 1920. . . . [2 copies]

1920 (1923)   Plan of the townplot of The Pas on Block A of The Pas Indian Reserves on the Saskatchewan River, N.W.T. Surveyed by J.K. McLean, D.L.S. in 1907. . . . Surveyed in 1911 by H.B. Proudfoot. . . . Approved 2nd October . . . 1920. . . . [Additions to 1923/Additions jusqu'en 1923.]

1928   Plan showing re-subdivision of part of the Townplot of The Pas, Manitoba, being part of Block A — Indian Reserve No. 21. . . . R.A. McLellan, M.L.S. . . . 17th . . . March . . . 1928. . . .

1931   Plan of special survey of part of Block "A" of The Pas Indian Reserve . . . The Pas, Manitoba. . . . (Sgd.) R.A. McLellan, Manitoba Land Surveyor . . . 6th . . . November . . . 1929. . . . Registered . . . 1931. . . .

The Pas No. 21B

N.D./S.D.   Manitoba. Plan of Township 56, Range 26, West of the Principal Meridian. . . . The Pas, Block B [and other reserves in the area/et d'autres réserves de la région].

1883 (1940)   See/Voir: **The Pas No. 21A**

1894   See/Voir: **The Pas No. 21A**

1917   See/Voir: **The Pas No. 21A**

The Pas No. 21C

N.D./S.D.   See/Voir: **The Pas No. 21B**

1883 (1940)   See/Voir: **The Pas No. 21A**

1894   See/Voir: **The Pas No. 21A**

1917   See/Voir: **The Pas No. 21A**

The Pas No. 21D

N.D./S.D.   See/Voir: **The Pas No. 21B**

1883 (1940)   See/Voir: **The Pas No. 21A**

1894   See/Voir: **The Pas No. 21A**

1917   See/Voir: **The Pas No. 21A**

The Pas No. 21E

N.D./S.D.   See/Voir: **The Pas No. 21B**

1883 (1940)   See/Voir: **The Pas No. 21A**

1894   See/Voir: **The Pas No. 21A**

1917   See/Voir: **The Pas No. 21A**

The Pas No. 21F

1883 (1940)   See/Voir: **The Pas No. 21A**

1894   See/Voir: **The Pas No. 21A**

The Pas No. 21G

1883 (1940)   See/Voir: **The Pas No. 21A**

1884 (1895)   See/Voir: **Oxford House No. 24**

1894   See/Voir: **The Pas No. 21A**

The Pas No. 21H

N.D./S.D.   See/Voir: **The Pas No. 21B**

MANITOBA

| 1894 | See/Voir: **The Pas No. 21A** |

1894 (1930) Saskatchewan, Treaty No. 5. Plan showing Blocks H, I, J and K of "The Pas" Indian Reserve. Surveyed by S. Bray, C.E., D.L.S., Asst. Chief Surveyor, Dept. of Indian Affairs, October 1894. [Additions to 1930/Additions jusqu'en 1930.]

The Pas No. 21I

N.D./S.D. See/Voir: **The Pas No. 21B**

1894 See/Voir: **The Pas No. 21A**

1894 (1930) See/Voir: **The Pas No. 21H**

The Pas No. 21J

N.D./S.D. See/Voir: **The Pas No. 21B**

1894 See/Voir: **The Pas No. 21A**

1894 (1930) See/Voir: **The Pas No. 21H**

The Pas No. 21K

1894 See/Voir: **The Pas No. 21A**

1894 (1930) See/Voir: **The Pas No. 21H**

The Pas No. 21P

1883 (1930)* 21P. The Pas Indian Reserve. Plan shewing islands in Indian Pear Island Lake as also their connection (approx.) with reserve north of river. Gloucester, February 1883. W.A. Austin, C.E., D.L. Surveyor. . . . Treaty 5, 1882. [Additions 1930/Additions en 1930.]

Turtle Mountain No. 60

1886 Treaty No. 2, Manitoba. Subdivision survey of Indian Reserve No. 60 at Turtle Mountain. Chief Hda-mani (Walking Bell). . . . Surveyed in July 1886 by A.W. Ponton, D.L.S.

1910 Plan of Sec. 31, Tp. 1, R. 22, W. of 1st M., being Indian Reserve No. 60 of Turtle Mountain. Surveyed by J. Lestock Reid, D.L.S., 1910. . . .

Valley River No. 63A

1894 (1938) Treaty No. 2. Survey of Indian Reserve No. 63a at Valley River, Province of Manitoba, for Indians of Gambler's band, in lieu of surrendered portion of Indian Reserve No. 63. . . . Surveyed in September 1894 by A.W. Ponton, D.L.S. . . . [Additions to 1938/Additions jusqu'en 1938.]

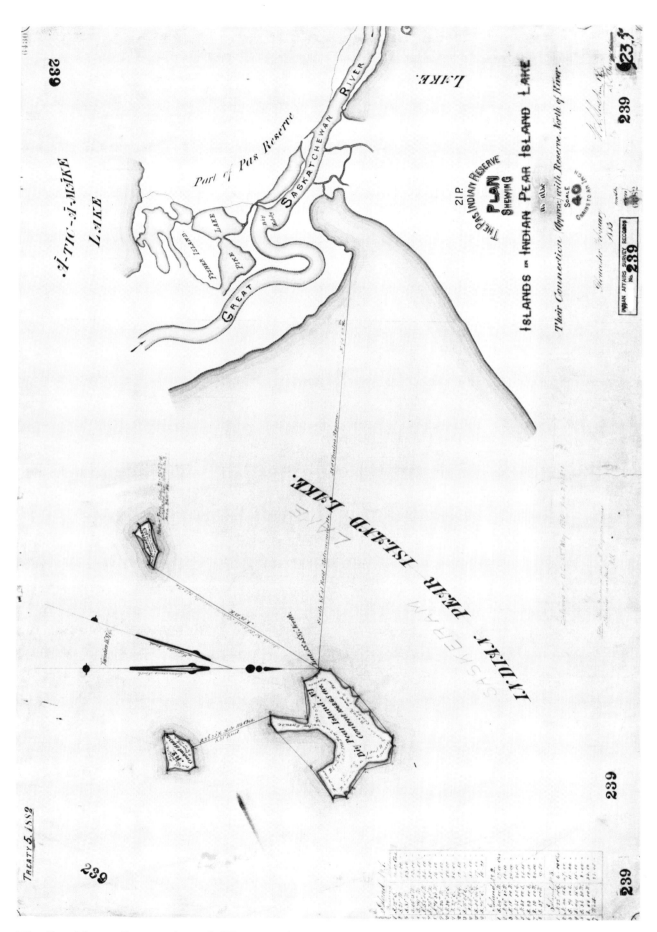

The Pas No. 21P 1883 (1930) (C 107319).

MANITOBA

Waterhen No. 45

1877 — Plan of the survey of Water Hen River Indian Reserve, Keewatin, containing 4616 acs. Surveyed by (sd.) H. Martin, Domn. Land Surveyor, Winnipeg, 21st May, 1877.

1881 — Water Hen River Reserve. Sketch shewing shore south of reserve. Survey of extension not made. Glo'ster, Dec. 1881. W.A. Austin, C.E., D.L. Surveyor. . . . [2 copies]

1916 (1918) — Tr. 2. Waterhen Indian Reserve No. 45, Manitoba [showing/in-diquant] lands to be added to reserve . . . [and/et] portion of reserve to be surrendered. . . . [Surveyed by/Relevé par] Charles Dudley Brown . . . D. & M.L.S. . . . Winnipeg . . . 14th . . . June, 1916. [Additions 1918/Additions en 1918.]

Waywayseecappo No. 62

Refer to/Consulter: **Lizard Point No. 62**

Yellow Quill No. 7

Refer to/Consulter: **Swan Lake No. 7**

Yellow Quill No. 8A

Refer to/Consulter: **Portage La Prairie No. 8A**

YUKON TERRITORY — GENERAL MAPS/
TERRITOIRE DU YUKON — CARTES GÉNÉRALES

1898   General map of the northwestern part of the Dominion of Canada. . . . Published by authority of the . . . Minister of the Interior, December 1898. . . .

YUKON TERRITORY — SETTLEMENTS/
TERRITOIRE DU YUKON — AGGLOMÉRATIONS

Carcross No. 4

1905   Cariboo Crossing No. 4. Plan of lots 15 & 16, Group 6, Yukon Territory. Surveyed by H.G. Dickson, D.L.S., May 1905. . . .

Carcross No. 9

1912   Plan of lot for Chooutla Indian School at Carcross, Yukon Territory. Surveyed by J.D. Craig, D.L.S., October 4th — 9th, 1912. . . . [2 copies]

Cariboo Crossing No. 4

        Refer to/Consulter: **Carcross No. 4**

Lake Laberge

1901   Plan of lots 1 and 2, Group 8, Yukon Territory. Surveyed by C.W. MacPherson, D.L.S., July 1900. Department of the Interior, Topographical Surveys Branch, Ottawa, 27th September, 1901. . . .

Little Salmon River

1916   Little Salmon River I.R. No. 10. Plan of survey of lot 3, Group 904, Yukon Territory, being an Indian reserve situated at the junction of Little Salmon and Lewes Rivers. Surveyed for the Department of Indian Affairs in July 1916 by J.H. Brownlee, D.L.S. . . .

Mayo No. 6

1915   Mayo No. 6. Plan of survey of lot 10, Group 12, Y.T., being an Indian reserve about one mile below Mayo on the Stewart River. Surveyed for the Department of Indian Affairs by J.H. Brownlee, D.L.S., July 1915. . . .

McQuesten No. 3

1904   No. 3. Plan of lots 4 and 5, Group 7, Y.T., the Indian Reserve at McQuesten. Surveyed by A.J. McPherson, D.L.S., September 21-24, 1903. . . . Department of the Interior, Topographical Surveys Branch, Ottawa . . . 1904. . . .

YUKON TERRITORY/TERRITOIRE DU YUKON

Moosehide Creek No. 2

1900 (1907)   Plan of lot 35, Group 2, Moosehide Creek Indian Reserve No. 2, Yukon Territory. Surveyed by Paul T.C. Dumais, D.L.S. . . . 14th . . . May, 1900. . . . Department of the Interior, Topographical Surveys Branch. . . . [Additions 1907/Additions en 1907.]

Moosehide Creek No. 2A

1907   No. 2A. Plan of survey of lot 387, Gr. 2, Y.T. Surveyed by C.W. MacPherson, D.L.S., Oct. 1907. . . .

Selkirk No. 7

1901 (1916)*   A block selected for an Indian reserve near Selkirk, No. 7, Yukon. Plan of lot 6, Group 4, Yukon Territory. Surveyed by C.W. MacPherson, D.L.S., Aug. 1900. Department of the Interior, Topographical Surveys Branch, Ottawa, 2nd July, 1901. . . . [Additions to 1916/Additions jusqu'en 1916.]

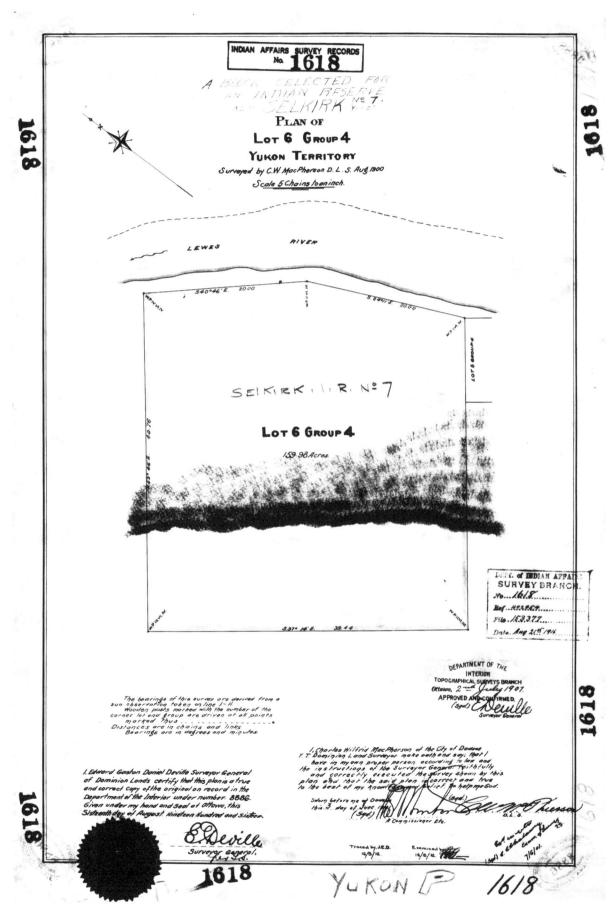

Selkirk No. 7 1901 (1916) (NMC 6166).

NORTHWEST TERRITORIES — GENERAL MAPS
TERRITOIRES DU NORD-OUEST — CARTES GÉNÉRALES

1875   Carte des expéditions chez les Dindjié et les Déné septentrionaux.
        Émile Petitot, prête missionnaire. Dressée par lui-même de 1862 à
        1873. Dessinée par J. Hansen. . . . Publiée en 1875. . . .

1875   Carte du bassin du Mackenzie, dressée de 1862 à 1873 par E. Petitot,
        missionnaire oblat de Marie I. Bulletin de la Société de géographie.
        Juillet 1875. Dessinée par J. Hansen. [2 copies]

NORTHWEST TERRITORIES — SETTLEMENTS/
TERRITOIRES DU NORD-OUEST — AGGLOMÉRATIONS

Fort Simpson

1944*   . . . Plan of Simpson Settlement, Northwest Territories. . . . Compiled
        from official surveys by S.D. Fawcett, D.L.S., 5th March, 1914.
        Department of Mines and Resources, Ottawa, 21st November,
        1944. . . . Compiled, drawn and printed at the Surveyor General's
        Office, Ottawa, Canada. [2 copies]

Fort Smith

[1914] Proposed reserve for wood bison, fur-bearers, etc. . . .

Resolution

1926 (1927)   Plan of part of lot 20, Resolution Settlement, N.W.T. . . . [Surveyed
              by/Relevé par] Richard Wm. Cautley . . . D.L.S. . . . 13th . . . January,
              1926. . . . [Additions 1927/Additions en 1927.]

Salt Plain No. 195

1923   See/Voir: **Salt River**

Salt River

1923   Plan of an Indian fishing reserve on the Salt River, Northwest
        Territories, 1922. (Signed) W.L. Cassels, B. Sc. G.P., 14 Sept., 1923.

Simpson

        Refer to/Consulter: **Fort Simpson**

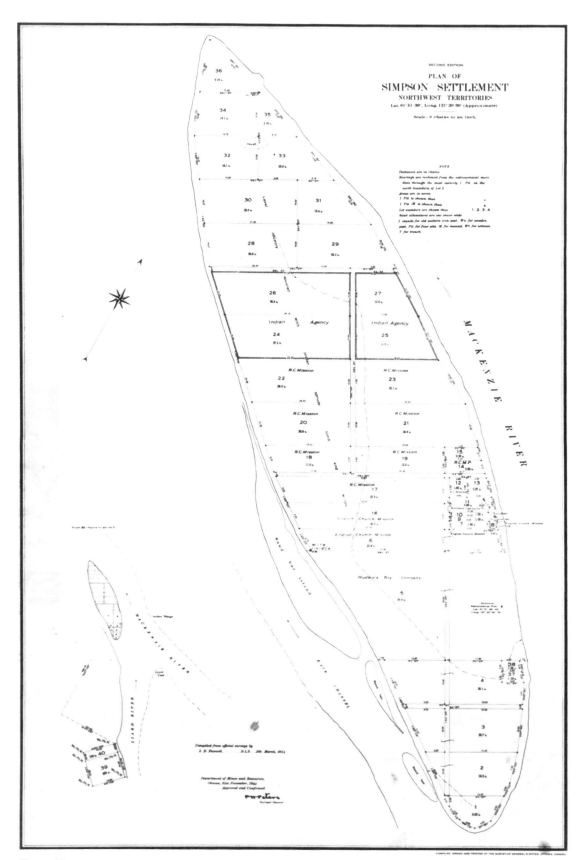

Fort Simpson 1944 (NMC 6167).

APPENDIX: LIST OF RESERVES AND SETTLEMENTS BY NUMBER (WESTERN CANADA)/APPENDICE: LISTE DES RÉSERVES ET AGGLOMÉRATIONS PAR NUMÉRO (L'OUEST CANADIEN)

N.B. All reserves and settlements listed here are situated in the areas of the numbered treaties of Western Canada. Reserves in the Treaty 3 area of Ontario, except those which are partially in Manitoba, are not included. Reserves listed are not necessarily in existence today.

Toutes les réserves et les agglomérations suivantes se trouvent dans les régions des traités numérotés de l'Ouest canadien. Les réserves de la région du traité nᵒ 3 de l'Ontario, sauf celles dont une partie se trouve au Manitoba, ne sont pas incluses. Les réserves inscrites sur cette liste n'existent pas nécessairement aujourd'hui.

No Nᵒ	Reserve or Settlement/ Réserve ou agglomération	Province or Territory/ Province ou territoire
1	St. Peters	Man.
1A	St. Peters Fishing Station	Man.
1B	Peguis	Man.
1C	Peguis Fishing	Man.
2	Roseau River	Man.
2A	Roseau Rapids	Man.
3	Fort Alexander	Man.
4	Brokenhead	Man.
5	Sandy Bay	Man.
6	Long Plain	Man.
6A	Long Plain Sioux	Man.
7	Swan Lake	Man.
7A	Swan Lake	Sask.
8	Indian Gardens	Man.
8A	Portage La Prairie	Man.
9	Black River	Man.
10	Hole or Hollow Water	Man.
11	Loon Creek	Man.
11A	Loon Straits	Man.
12	Bloodvein River	Man.
13	Berens River	Man.
13A	Pigeon River	Man.
14	Little Grand Rapids	Man.
15	Deer Lake	Man.
16	Poplar River	Man.
17	Norway House	Man.
18	Pine River	Man.
19	Cross Lake	Man.
19A	Cross Lake	Man.
19B	Cross Lake	Man.
19C	Cross Lake	Man.
20	Cumberland	Sask.
20A	Pine Bluff	Man.
20B	Pine Bluff	Man.
20C	Muskeg River	Man.
20D	Budd's Point	Man.

APPENDIX/APPENDICE

No / N°	Reserve or Settlement / Réserve ou agglomération	Province or Territory / Province ou territoire
21	Stony Point	Man.
21A	The Pas	Man.
21B	The Pas	Man.
21C	The Pas	Man.
21D	The Pas	Man.
21D	Salt Channel	Man.
21E	The Pas	Man.
21F	The Pas	Man.
21G	The Pas	Man.
21H	The Pas	Man.
21I	The Pas	Man.
21J	The Pas	Man.
21K	The Pas	Man.
21L	Rocky Lake	Man.
21M	Bignell	Man.
21N	The Pas	Man.
21P	The Pas	Man.
21R	The Pas	Man.
22	Island Lake	Man.
22A	Island Lake	Man.
23	God's Lake	Man.
24	Oxford House	Man.
25	York	Man.
26	Churchill	Man.
27	Birch River	Sask.
27A	Carrot River	Sask.
28	Shoal Lake	Sask.
28A	Shoal Lake	Sask.
29	Red Earth	Sask.
29A	Carrot River	Sask.
30	Pas Mountain	Sask.
31	Moose Lake	Man.
31A	Moose Lake	Man.
31B	Moose Lake	Man.
31C	Moose Lake	Man.
31D	Moose Lake	Man.
31E	Moose Lake	Man.
31F	Moose Lake	Man.
31G	Moose Lake	Man.
32	Chemahawin	Man.
32A	Chemahawin	Man.
32B	Chemahawin	Man.
32C	Chemahawin	Man.
32D	Chemahawin	Man.
32E	Chemahawin	Man.
32F	Poplar Point	Man.
32G	Chemahawin	Man.
33	Grand Rapids	Man.

No N°	Reserve or Settlement/ Réserve ou agglomération	Province or Territory/ Province ou territoire
34C	Northwest Angle	Man.
36	Buffalo Point	Man.
36A	Reed River	Man.
37A	Shoal Lake	Man./Ont.
37C	Northwest Angle	Man.
39	Shoal Lake	Man./Ont.
39A	Shoal Lake	Man./Ont.
40	Shoal Lake	Man./Ont.
43	Jackhead	Man.
43A	Jackhead	Man.
44	Fisher River	Man.
44A	Fisher River	Man.
45	Waterhen	Man.
46	Dog Creek	Man.
46A	Rock Island	Man.
48	Little Saskatchewan	Man.
48A	Dauphin River	Man.
48B	Little Saskatchewan	Man.
49	The Narrows	Man.
49A	The Narrows	Man.
50	Fairford	Man.
51	Crane River	Man.
52	Ebb and Flow	Man.
57	Birdtail Creek	Man.
57A	Birdtail Hay Lands	Man.
58	Sioux Valley	Man.
59	Oak Lake	Man.
59A	Oak Lake	Man.
60	Turtle Mountain	Man.
61	Keeseekoowenin	Man.
61A	Clear Lake	Man.
61B	Bottle Lake	Man.
62	Lizard Point	Man.
62A	Fishing Station	Man.
63	Gambler	Man.
63A	Valley River	Man.
64	Cote	Sask.
65	The Key	Sask.
65A	Dawson Bay	Man.
65B	Dawson Bay	Man.
65C	Swan Lake	Man.
65D	Dog Island	Man.
65E	Dawson Bay	Man.
65F	Dawson Bay	Man.
66	Keeseekoose	Sask.
66A	Keeseekoose	Sask.
66A	Pine Creek	Man.
67	Rolling River	Man.

APPENDIX/APPENDICE

No N°	Reserve or Settlement/ Réserve ou agglomération	Province or Territory/ Province ou territoire
68	Pheasant Rump	Sask.
69	Ocean Man	Sask.
70	White Bear	Sask.
71	Ochapowace	Sask.
72	Kahkewistahaw	Sask.
72A	Kahkewistahaw	Sask.
73	Cowessess	Sask.
73A	Leech Lake	Sask.
74	Sakimay	Sask.
74A	Shesheep	Sask.
75	Piapot	Sask.
75A	Hay Lands	Sask.
76	Assiniboine	Sask.
78	Standing Buffalo	Sask.
79	Pasqua	Sask.
80	Muscowpetung	Sask.
80A	Last Mountain Lake	Sask.
80B	Hay Lands	Sask.
81	Peepeekisis	Sask.
82	Okanese	Sask.
83	Star Blanket	Sask.
84	Little Black Bear	Sask.
85	Muskowekwan	Sask.
86	Gordon	Sask.
87	Day Star	Sask.
88	Poor Man	Sask.
89	Fishing Lake	Sask.
89A	Fishing Lake	Sask.
90	Nut Lake	Sask.
91	Kinistino	Sask.
91A	Kinistino	Sask.
94	White Cap	Sask.
94A	Wahpaton	Sask.
94B	Wahpaton	Sask.
95	One Arrow	Sask.
96	Okemasis	Sask.
97	Beardy	Sask.
98	Chacastapasin	Sask.
99	Muskoday	Sask.
100	James Smith	Sask.
100A	Cumberland	Sask.
101	Sturgeon Lake	Sask.
101A	Sturgeon Lake	Sask.
102	Muskeg Lake	Sask.
103	Mistawasis	Sask.
104	Atakakup	Sask.
105	Meadow Lake	Sask.
105A	Meadow Lake	Sask.

No N°	Reserve or Settlement/ Réserve ou agglomération	Province or Territory/ Province ou territoire
106	Montreal Lake	Sask.
106A	Little Red River	Sask.
106B	Montreal Lake	Sask.
106C	Little Red River	Sask.
106D	Little Red River	Sask.
107	Young Chipewyan	Sask.
108	Red Pheasant	Sask.
109	Mosquito	Sask.
110	Grizzly Bear's Head	Sask.
111	Lean Man	Sask.
112	Moosomin	Sask.
112A	Moosomin	Sask.
112B	Moosomin	Sask.
112C	New Moosomin	Sask.
112D	Thunderchild & Moosomin	Sask.
112E	Moosomin	Sask.
112F	Moosomin	Sask.
113	Sweet Grass	Sask.
113A	Sweet Grass	Sask.
113B	Sweet Grass	Sask.
114	Poundmaker	Sask.
115	Thunderchild	Sask.
115A	Thunderchild	Sask.
115B	New Thunderchild	Sask.
115C	New Thunderchild	Sask.
115D	Thunderchild	Sask.
116	Little Pine & Lucky Man	Sask.
117	Witchekan Lake	Sask.
118	Big River	Sask.
118A	Big River	Sask.
119	Seekaskootch	Sask.
120	Makaoo	Sask./Alta.
120A	Hay Lands	Alta.
121	Unipouheos	Alta.
122	Puskiakiwenin	Alta.
123	Kehiwin	Alta.
124	Big Head	Sask.
125	Saddle Lake	Alta.
125A	Cache Lake	Alta.
126	Bear's Ears	Alta.
127	Blue Quill	Alta.
128	White Fish Lake	Alta.
129	Makwa Lake	Sask.
129A	Makwa Lake	Sask.
129B	Makwa Lake	Sask.
129C	Makwa Lake	Sask.
130	Waterhen	Sask.
131	Beaver Lake	Alta.

APPENDIX/APPENDICE

No N°	Reserve or Settlement/ Réserve ou agglomération	Province or Territory/ Province ou territoire
132	Michel	Alta.
133	Alexis	Alta.
133A	Wabamun	Alta.
133B	Wabamun	Alta.
133C	Buck Lake	Alta.
134	Alexander	Alta.
135	Stony Plain	Alta.
136	Papaschase	Alta.
137	Samson	Alta.
137A	Samson	Alta.
138	Ermineskin	Alta.
138A	Pigeon Lake	Alta.
138B	Louis Bull	Alta.
139	Montana	Alta.
140	Montana	Alta.
141	Sharphead	Alta
142	Stony	Alta.
142A	Stony	Alta.
142B	Stony	Alta.
143	Stony	Alta.
144	Stony	Alta.
144A	Big Horn	Alta.
145	Sarcee	Alta.
146	Blackfoot	Alta.
146C	Blackfoot Timber Limit	Alta.
147	Peigan	Alta.
147B	Peigan (Timber Limit)	Alta.
148	Blood	Alta.
148A	Blood	Alta.
149	Cold Lake	Alta.
149A	Cold Lake	Alta.
149B	Cold Lake	Alta.
150	Drift Pile River	Alta.
150A	Sucker Creek	Alta.
150B	Freeman	Alta.
150C	Halcro	Alta.
150D	Pakashan	Alta.
150E	Swan River	Alta.
150F	Assineau River	Alta.
150G	Sawridge	Alta.
150H	Sawridge	Alta.
151	Peace River Crossing	Alta.
151A	Peace River Crossing	Alta.
151B	John Felix Tustawits	Alta.
151C	Taviah Moosewah	Alta.
151D	Alinckwoonay	Alta.
151E	Duncan Tustawits	Alta.
151F	David Tustawits	Alta.

150

No / N°	Reserve or Settlement/ Réserve ou agglomération	Province or Territory/ Province ou territoire
151G	Gillian Bell	Alta.
151H	Louison Cardinal	Alta.
151K	William McKenzie	Alta.
152	Beaver	Alta.
152A	Neepee Chief	Alta.
152B	Horse Lakes	Alta.
152C	Clear Hills	Alta.
154	Sturgeon Lake	Alta.
154A	Sturgeon Lake	Alta.
154B	Sturgeon Lake	Alta.
155	Utikoomak Lake	Alta.
155A	Utikoomak Lake	Alta.
155B	Utikoomak Lake	Alta.
156	Lac La Ronge	Sask.
156A	Potato River	Sask.
156B	Kitsakie	Sask.
156C	Sucker River	Sask.
157	Stanley	Sask.
157A	Stanley	Sask.
157B	Old Fort	Sask.
157C	Four Portages	Sask.
157D	Fox Point	Sask.
157E	Fox Point	Sask.
158	Little Hills	Sask.
158A	Little Hills	Sask.
158B	Little Hills	Sask.
159	Saulteaux	Sask.
159A	Saulteaux	Sask.
160	Wood Mountain	Sask.
160A	Maple Creek	Sask.
161	Ministikwan	Sask.
161A	Ministikwan	Sask.
162	Fox Lake	Alta.
163	Beaver Ranch	Alta.
164	Boyer	Alta.
164A	Child Lake	Alta.
165	Canoe Lake	Sask.
165A	Canoe Lake	Sask.
165B	Canoe Lake	Sask.
166	Wabasca	Alta.
166A	Wabasca	Alta.
166B	Wabasca	Alta.
166C	Wabasca	Alta.
166D	Wabasca	Alta.
167	Heart Lake	Alta.
168	Halfway River	B.C.
168A	West Moberly Lake	B.C.
169	East Moberly Lake	B.C.

APPENDIX/APPENDICE

No Nᵒ	Reserve or Settlement/ Réserve ou agglomération	Province or Territory/ Province ou territoire
170	Nelson House	Man.
170A	Nelson House	Man.
170B	Nelson House	Man.
170C	Nelson House	Man.
171	Split Lake	Man.
171A	Split Lake	Man.
171B	Split Lake	Man.
172	St. John	B.C.
173	Tall Cree	Alta.
173A	Tall Cree	Alta.
174	Fort McKay	Alta.
174A	Namur River	Alta.
174B	Namur Lake	Alta.
175	Clearwater	Alta.
176	Gregoire Lake	Alta.
176A	Gregoire Lake	Alta.
176B	Gregoire Lake	Alta.
178	House River Indian Cemetery	Alta.
179	Fort Smith	N.W.T.
181	Norman	N.W.T.
182	Simpson	N.W.T.
183	Jean Baptiste Gambler	Alta.
184	Amisk Lake	Sask.
184A	Birch Portage	Sask.
184B	Pelican Narrows	Sask.
184C	Sandy Narrows	Sask.
184D	Woody Lake	Sask.
184E	Mirond Lake	Sask.
184F	Sturgeon Weir	Sask.
185	Good Hope	N.W.T.
186	Resolution	N.W.T.
187	Carcajou	Alta.
188	Wrigley	N.W.T.
189	Hay River	N.W.T.
190	Providence	N.W.T.
191	Chitek Lake	Sask.
192	La Plonge	Sask.
192A	Elak Dase	Sask.
192B	Kneel Lake	Sask.
192C	Dipper Rapids	Sask.
192D	Wapachewunak	Sask.
192E	Ile a la Crosse	Sask.
193	Peter Pond Lake	Sask.
193A	Churchill Lake	Sask.
193B	Turnor Lake	Sask.
194	Janvier	Alta.
195	Salt Plain	N.W.T.
196	Fitzgerald	Alta.

APPENDIX/APPENDICE

No N°	Reserve or Settlement/ Réserve ou agglomération	Province or Territory/ Province ou territoire
197	Brochet	Man.
198	Pukatawagan	Man.
199	Highrock	Man.
200	Southend	Sask.
201	Chipewyan	Alta.
201A	Chipewyan	Alta.
201B	Chipewyan	Alta.
201C	Chipewyan	Alta.
201D	Chipewyan	Alta.
201E	Chipewyan	Alta.
201F	Chipewyan	Alta.
201G	Chipewyan	Alta.
202	Sunchild	Alta.
203	O'Chiese	Alta
203A	O'Chiese Cemetery	Alta.
207	Bushe River	Alta.
209	Hay Lake	Alta.
210	Zama Lake	Alta.
211	Amber River	Alta.
212	Upper Hay River	Alta.
213	Bistcho Lake	Alta.
214	Jackfish Point	Alta.
215	John D'Or Prairie	Alta.
216	Eden Valley	Alta.
217	Morin Lake	Sask.
218	Bittern Lake	Sask.
219	Grandmother's Bay	Sask.
220	Lac la Hache	Sask.
221	La Loche	Sask.
222	La Loche	Sask.
223	La Loche	Sask.
224	Chicken	Sask.
225	Chicken	Sask.
226	Chicken	Sask.
227	Fond du Lac	Sask.
228	Fond du Lac	Sask.
229	Fond du Lac	Sask.
230	Minoachchak	Sask.
231	Root Lake	Man.